THE RADICAL CENTER

Understanding the New Christian Re•Formation

D. PAUL BARNES

Chicago Spectrum Press
Louisville, KY 40245

Website addresses and Internet links recommended throughout this book are offered as a resource. These are not intended in any way as an endorsement by the author or the publisher of their content.

Chicago Spectrum Press
12305 Westport Rd.
Louisville, Kentucky 40245
502-899-1919

Printed in the U.S.A.

10 9 8 7 6 5 4 3 2 1

ISBN: 978-1-58374-265-5

Foreword

My name is Paul Barnes. For twenty-eight years I was the Senior Pastor of an evangelical church in Denver, Colorado. When my wife and I founded the church in 1979, it consisted of our six-week old daughter and us. We had 35 people at our first service, mostly some old friends and family members who came to support us. After that first Sunday, our attendance went downhill. When I left the church 28 years later we had over 1,200 active families (around 3,600 people), an annual budget of around five million dollars, property valued at around 20 million dollars, over 50 paid staff members, and a whole host of programs, activities, and ministries designed for the suburban, upwardly mobile, Christian family. By all accounts of church growth theories, I was a successful pastor, pastoring a thriving church: we had strong attendance, lots of acreage and buildings, and healthy contributions.

You would have thought after graduating from one of the premier seminaries in the country, having been in ministry for more than 28 years, spending my entire adult life in the Christian world and the environment of the church, I would have figured out this thing called Christianity.

Nothing could be further from the truth. I love the church. It was my life's work, passion, and calling, and yet, at the same time I hate the church. Generally, it is an incredibly dysfunctional organization, bound up by dogma and tradition that keep it chained to the past, and with each passing day it grows more irrelevant to the present.

But since I love the church, I wrote this book. When you love something, no matter how unlovely that thing may be—you want the best for it.

Being in ministry and having this kind of love/hate relationship with the very thing with which you are so intertwined can be unsettling, especially when as a minister, your flock expects you be the "answer man"—Carnac the Magnificent who knows all, who never questions or experiences doubt, the one they can turn to for help with their own uncertainties.

If you sit in the pew of a church and look at your ministers and think, "I wish I were like them…I wish I had everything figured out like they do," may I let you in on a little known and even less publicized ministerial secret? Ministers are filled with doubts. Lots of them. You would be shocked to realize how frequently a pastor will preach a sermon and say something with confidence, assurance, and authority in order to bolster a congregation's sagging faith, all the while thinking, "If only *I* believed this to be true." I realize I may sound like the innocent little boy shouting so that all in the Christian Kingdom can hear, "The emperor has no clothes!," but this is the truth, and rare is the congregation that allows its pastor the freedom to express that kind of uncertainty. That's tragic. Paul Tillich said, "Doubt is not the opposite of faith. It is one element of faith." A healthy faith, a strong faith *is* one that wrestles with the doubts and uncertainties that are naturally embedded within this mystery called Christianity.

The Radical Center is a book that wrestles with some of those challenges. It's also an exploration of my own journey over the last number of years as I have looked more intently at the underbelly of Christianity. I do think that my years in ministry have given me insight into the Christian world and that I have some worthwhile things to say for those who are willing to listen.

I'm not an armchair quarterback, observing from the comfort of my living room the deteriorating condition of the Christian Church, making pious platitudes about how things need to be different. No, I've been fighting in the trenches. For close to thirty years I've seen it up close and personal and as Pogo said, "I've seen the enemy and the enemy is us." The Church of Jesus Christ is going through a season of profound change. Many will choose to close their eyes and ignore what is happening, preferring instead to tenaciously hang on to the faith of their fathers. Others, the more daring among us, will be willing to explore these changes and ultimately embrace them. Regardless of where you land once you've finished reading this book, my prayer is that it will at least be something that challenges you to *think.*

And as you think, process, digest, and wrestle with some of the ideas presented here, I pray your faith will be the stronger for it. I pray that in confronting your own doubts you will find greater assurance and confidence for the faith you profess.

I pray for all of us, that as we continue our journey toward the Celestial City, our cry will continually be, "I do believe. Help me overcome my unbelief!" (Mark 9.24)

Contents

Preface

"If you have a new world, you need a new church. You have a new world."[1]

Prim-er
1. A small book for teaching children to read
2. A small introductory book on a subject
3. A short informative piece of writing
—Merriam-Webster Online Dictionary

This book falls into the second definition above: a small introductory book on a subject. There is no shortage today of volumes being written about the radical changes going on within Christianity. As I read many of these, I sometimes find them overwhelming—difficult to process and hard to understand. Numerous words are thrown around which often can be more confusing than helpful: "post-modern," "emerging," "missional," and "progressive." I wondered if it might be helpful for average Christian readers to have something in their possession that could introduce what is admittedly a very deep, complex, and far reaching subject.

As a primer, *The Radical Center* seeks to summarize a few of the key thoughts and ideas a handful of authors have been considering. The book is my attempt to synthesize some of the works that are being written about this period of transition the Christian church is experiencing. I prefer to call this time a Re•Formation, because we are living in a season of change where the church is in the process of re-forming itself. The church is being altered, taking a different shape and structure. The changes being birthed in the new Re•Formation are not just cosmetic—they are systemic, affecting some fundamental beliefs and premises that Christians have had for centuries.

While many Christian leaders, pastors, and academicians agree that something is happening, there remains a great deal of uncertainty as to exactly what *is* transpiring and what the church will ultimately look like once this re•forming process is complete. Actually, *complete* may not be an accurate way to describe it—perhaps *evolving* is a better term. While some in the Christian community have a strong visceral reaction to the term *evolution,* it really isn't something that should scare us. All evolution means is a gradual process of change or growth.

For 2,000 years the church has been in a process of evolution. Changing times, political and social upheaval, and different cultures all force the church to continually be re-evaluating how to best minister to the needs of the current generation. Sadly, change is hard and comes slowly for the behemoth known as the Christian church, yet eventually it does change.

But there is something about this period that seems fundamentally different. After talking about a new movement for the past few decades, it appears that as we move further into the 21st century, we are beginning to see its outlines more clearly. Just as the church was about to experience a massive upheaval when Martin Luther posted his 95 Theses to the door of the Castle Church, we are living with the same kind of smoldering change. Had someone from the *Medieval Catholic*

Times (an imagined church newspaper of his day) interviewed him, I'm sure Luther would have been hard pressed to foretell the end result of the Protestant Reformation. Likewise, those first few generations of Protestants probably had little idea how far reaching and transforming their movement would be.

Although many current writers acknowledge we are in a period as significant as Luther's Reformation, they also are the first to admit that they really aren't sure where this new Re•Formation will ultimately lead us. Like it or not, we're going to have to get comfortable with the uncertainty that comes with this season of transition. A new course is being charted for the church. It's exciting. It's scary. It's filled with a lot of reservations, but also with a tremendous amount of unlimited potential for positive influence.

Retired Episcopal Bishop John Spong wrote a book entitled, *Why the Church Must Change or Die.* While I don't embrace some of the content of his work, I do understand the title. The church, as we currently know it, has grown anemic and irrelevant, in that it has become ineffective in helping bring about real change in people's lives. It is irrelevant in that people in society generally feel the church has very little to offer which would help with the messiness of their lives.

Often, because of our behavior and actions, we have become marginalized—set off to the side of society with most people paying very little attention to our occasional outbursts.

The church is no longer a prophetic voice to society but sadly has become filled with navel-gazers—people who seem to be primarily interested in what the faith can do for them. It's the "Jesus and me" mentality. Christianity has become a watered down faith, highly individualistic, strongly independent, and structured in such a way that it continually feeds the self-centered (and dare I say narcissistic?) desires of the people sitting in the pews. It needs a transfusion of sorts to be revitalized and once again become a significant influence in society. Prayerfully, the new Re•Formation will accomplish that.

First, some disclaimers. The title of this book is taken from a chapter in Adam Hamilton's book, *Seeing Gray in a World of Black and White.* Adam is the Senior Minster of The Church of the Resurrection in Leawood, Kansas—the premier United Methodist Church in the United States. When I came across his chapter entitled "The Radical Center" I knew that was what the theme of this book needed to be. Thank you, Adam.

Second, much of the material for this book has been drawn from files of material that I have accumulated over a number of years. I will have to confess that while pondering the perceived changes within our faith, my focus these past many years has not been on the idea of writing another book. I've been otherwise preoccupied. I have attempted to acknowledge and document as many sources as possible. If I have overlooked someone's name or unintentionally used material from an author's work, not only do I apologize, but also I ask for your forgiveness. The thoughts you'll find here have been fermenting in my mind and heart for many years. Over time (especially as you get older) thoughts have a tendency to meld together into a hodge-podge of ideas so that sometimes it is not certain if a notion comes from your own brain or from that of someone else. If there is the need to acknowledge another's work, I will do everything I can to make it right and give credit where credit is due.

Third, in many ways, the thoughts presented in *The Radical Center* chronicle my own faith journey. A few years ago I developed a seminar based on my previous book.[2] Whenever I teach this class in various churches, I consistently get comments from people that I should write a follow up book which would address more in depth my own spiritual evolution and growth. Life is not static, or at least it shouldn't be. Growth and change are a normal, healthy part of human development. Gail Sheehy said, "If we don't change, we don't grow and if we don't grow, we aren't really living." Over the years I've noticed that a very small percentage of people actually seem to thrive on change while the vast majority of us would strongly prefer to never have to experience anything that upsets the apple cart of our life. For many our life's motto would be similar to the Duke of Cambridge who once said, "Any change at any time for any reason is to be deplored." I address some of the dynamics of change in the first chapter because I think it's important we look within ourselves before we begin to look at the issues *The Radical Center* explores. I have been on a deeply personal and life-transforming journey for the past many years...and it continues to this day. Much of what you read here reflects facets of that expedition.

Finally, you will notice I have numerous references to John Wesley and the movement he and his brother Charles began—Methodism. I confess that after spending a lifetime in the confines of Evangelicalism (a movement I address later on), there is much within Methodism that I find attractive. I'm not talking about the United Methodist Church and how the faith is currently being practiced by the particular denomination, but rather how Methodism was initially envisioned and why the movement resonated so powerfully in the hearts and lives of people. Are there similarities between our time and theirs? Are there things we can learn from Wesley and the evangelical movements of the 18th and 19th century that might help us understand this new Re•Formation? I believe there are.

In many ways, John Wesley was the first *contemporary* Christian leader and thinker. What I mean by that is, Wesley's world, though it was grounded in the 18th century, was very similar to ours today. We rightly feel that our time is undergoing rapid change. The era in which Wesley lived (1703-1791) and the century following his death were also times of dramatic change:

- The industrial revolution forever changed the human landscape and only exacerbated the social problems of income disparity, mistreatment of adult and children workers, slums and poverty, educational disadvantage, and a host of other social troubles.
- The seeds of dynamic change that blossomed in the 1700s began in the 1400s with the discovery of new lands and cultures (the American continent) and developed with the works and philosophical positions of Martin Luther, Copernicus, Galileo, Descartes, and, most of all, Newton.
- The world was growing smaller and the universe was getting bigger.
- Individuals began to realize there is an enormous world of humanity outside their own small village, hamlet, or circle of relations. As contact with others expanded, multi-culturalism and thoughts of what it means to live in that world community became more pressing.
- As the immensity of the universe began to be understood, the smallness of humankind became more pronounced and long held theological ideas began to be called into question.

- England had gone through great turmoil in the 1600s, including violent upheavals against monarchy and a civil war based partly on religious differences. This resulted in the breakdown of long-standing hierarchies and power structures that spawned a widespread belief that man is in control and is capable of building the perfect society without the need of God or divine guidance.

Out of this grew movements that are still with us today such as socialism, communism and deism. Most of our founding fathers were Deists who believed that God exists, but is no longer involved in the development of the universe God created. The impact of Deism and the French Enlightenment (also known as the Age of Reason) was very strong. At its core, the Enlightenment was a critical questioning of traditional institutions, customs, and morals combined with a strong belief in rationality and science. Many questioned whether Christianity would survive without the authority of the state—especially in the atmosphere of religious freedom and the separation of church and state in the newly founded United States. The French skeptic Voltaire (1694-1778) said, “Another century and there will not be a Bible on earth.”

Yet while Voltaire and his friends expected the demise of Christianity, a powerful revival was sweeping England, Scotland, and Ireland. Wesley and his Methodist movement had to wrestle with these philosophical, theological, social, and scientific paradigms. In so many ways, he was a man concurrent with our times and his insights on how Christians are to live in the tension of life with God and life in this world are relevant to us today. He found it necessary to develop new practices of ministry in order to effectively reach people in his day, invite them into a relationship with Christ, form them as disciples, and enable their participation in mission. Yet at the same time he desired his movement to be a faithful but contemporary expression of the heart of Scripture and tradition, what he termed "primitive Christianity."

Let me briefly highlight what I believe to be a few of the similarities:

1. Wesley's view on Christian discipleship aligns with the new Re•Formation's direction. For the past hundred years or so, our understanding of Christianity has been somewhat schizophrenic. One group has made the faith all about social justice issues—addressing the social inequities and ills in our society—while another group has made it all about making a decision to follow Christ (in contemporary terms, "asking Jesus into your heart or getting saved, having a personal relationship with Jesus, and having your sins forgiven") which then gets you a ticket to heaven. For Wesley, there never was this kind of separation. The gospel had a two-fold emphasis—personal salvation as well as social transformation. Thus his understanding of discipleship involved being committed to both of those gospel goals. Making a decision to follow Christ was merely the first step onto a road which one would then follow the rest of his or her life. In others words, salvation is not a point-in-time event but a lifelong journey of growth in God. In addition, salvation not only entailed the forgiveness of sins, but it was also the living of a new life that resulted in individual commitments to personal holiness and social transformation. In Wesley's time this emphasis on social holiness was done through ministries to the poor, working to abolish slavery, ministering to prisoners, addressing the rights of women and children, and focusing on education.

In our current Christian structure, this two-fold emphasis has been split asunder between the two groups, generally known as the liberals and conservatives. The new Re•Formation is a movement that is seeking to once again bring these two aspects of genuine Christianity back together.

2. Wesley's understanding of the role of the church in society parallels the path of the new Re•Formation. There is a growing commitment to the idea that the church is not to be separate from the world in order to avoid contamination; rather it is to actively participate in the mission of God in the world. For many, this seems obvious; however for the past number of decades there has been a large contingent of the church that has emphasized a doctrine of separation. That is changing. No longer is there giving lip service to "go into all the world and make disciples"[3] while practicing the opposite—"come out from among them and be ye separate."[4] The focus of the church becomes inviting others to join in this mission of reaching out to the world, rather than simply gaining more members. Wesley believed that God had raised the "people called Methodists…to reform the nation, particularly the church, and to spread scriptural holiness over the land."[5] One of the emphases of the new Re•Formation is that it is looking for ways to aggressively help bring about the Kingdom of God on this Earth.
3. Then there is the idea that all of life is sacred and there is no division between "secular" and "sacred." This view, held by both individuals within the new Re•Formation and by Wesley, is that all of life is potentially sacred; all of culture is subject to transformation and renewal by the Kingdom of God. There is a rejection of these

unbiblical dualisms: sacred/secular, public/private, mind/body, faith/reason that are all so essential to Enlightenment thought. "For emerging churches, there are no longer any bad places, bad people, or bad times. All can be made holy. All can be given to God in worship. All modern dualisms can be overcome."[6] What has resulted in this dualism has been the compartmentalization of our lives that enables people to be "spiritual" while "leaving their secular lives untouched."[7] In the new Re•Formation there will be a commitment to the idea that there is no facet of our lives or our world that is to remain untouched by God. Wesley sought to reframe nature and history within the larger context of God's redeeming and renewing purpose and activity. He had a deep sense of God's universal transforming reality. He also saw the saving power of God at work in every human being through "prevenient" grace. There were not two categories of people, the elect and the dammed, but only one category—sinners who are loved by God and have worth and dignity by virtue of that love. Finally, his classes and bands (addressed in the chapter "A Rope of Sand") were occasions where people regularly gathered to ask what it means to live as a Christian in everyday life. They had a spirituality that touched every aspect of their lives and world.

4. Wesley had a perceptive belief that community was the key to personal transformation (again addressed in "A Rope of Sand"). There is today a growing conviction that the risen Christ is present in the *community* of believers through the power of Holy Spirit. The Spirit then leads and empowers that community into mission. The church is people—not a building. Church is not something we go to, it is who we are. The lifestyles of members and the practices of the

community must be radically transformed in light of the coming kingdom and the mission of God. To facilitate this, groups that are moving into the new Re•Formation are often networks of small fellowships in which a central practice is mutual accountability. They also seek to discover what it means to be a genuine community, a group of people together in relationship ministering to the world, rather than simply a gathering of individuals.

5. Wesley believed in what he called "catholic spirit" or what one contemporary called "generous orthodoxy"[8] for the new Re•Formation movement. It is the growing idea that Christians need to emphasize our common points of similarity rather than continually accentuating our theological differences. Wesley distinguished essential doctrines from opinions and in regard to opinions, his opinion was, "...we think and let think." I address his somewhat short list of essentials in the chapter, "What about the Bible?" For Wesley, a catholic spirit didn't mean finding the lowest common denominator among various Christian groups, but rather it meant Christianity in which, though diverse and at times contradictory in beliefs and practices, there was a commitment to love one another in Jesus Christ, and be open to learning from one another. This idea is especially prevalent in the new Re•Formation. No longer is there the arrogant assertion that one group has all the answers—and in a move that is sure to be disturbing to many—not even within one religion. But rather in Brian McLaren's words, it "is not to claim to have the truth captured, stuffed, and mounted on the wall. It is rather to be in a loving...community of people who are seeking the truth...on the road of mission...and who have

> been launched on the quest by Jesus, who, with us, guides us still."[9]

After all that, it may seem as if I'm getting paid to do a commercial for the United Methodist Church. That's not the case. However, my comments do reflect my own spiritual journey over many years. I readily admit that I find much within Methodism very appealing. That doesn't mean there are not worthy ideas found within other denominations also, but *if* there is a denomination today that has inherent within it some of the necessary tools needed to help the church move through this time of change into the new Re•Formation, I believe Methodism could be it. I realize a statement like that might seem absurd for those who understand how anemic and weak the denomination known as the United Methodist Church is today. Wesley himself was concerned about the Methodist movement faltering. Here are his words:

> "I am not afraid that the people called Methodists should ever cease to exist either in Europe or America. But I am afraid lest they should only exist as a dead sect, having the form of religion without the power. And this undoubtedly will be the case unless they hold fast the doctrine, spirit, and discipline with which they first set out."[10]

As with many other denominations, the United Methodist Church is in decline. Some are even predicting that within another 30 years, it will have become extinct in America. It remains to be seen if, as a denomination it will be able to pull itself out of its free-fall, but as mentioned earlier, if we can give attention to how the movement was originally envisioned, not how it is currently practiced, I believe there is much to learn. My prediction is that once the new Re•Formation is in full swing, we will find many of Wesley's principles (reframed and reworked) helping form the foundation of the movement. If nothing else, the thoughts and comments surrounding the Methodist movement might be helpful in stimulating deeper discussion among those who are sincerely seeking a different form of their faith than what they're currently experiencing.

In many ways, the new Re•Formation is about both stepping back into our rich Christian history as well as moving forward into a bold new world. Rather than speaking of this Re•Formation as a "new" versus "old" phenomena, consider that it's more of an ancient/future approach. Or as one book subtitle rendered it, it is "Vintage Christianity for New Generations."[11] The new Re•Formation will be a unique blending of traditional Christian spirituality and practices combined with a very forward-looking, progressive movement that effectively interact with a post-modern culture. How these two seemingly polar ideas will coalesce is now coming into sharper focus.

Every author brings his or her unique perspective to a topic. In my conversations with others, I'm finding that many individuals sitting in the pews of churches are unsettled. They intuitively sense that something is happening in the Christian world, but they don't know what. Growing increasingly dissatisfied with "church" as they've known it, some have started searching for different ways of expressing and living out their faith, while others have simply given up and dropped out. The dropouts find themselves joining a growing group of once faithful and committed churchgoers who now find that for them, the church has become irrelevant. The recent buzz about the "emerging church" has left many others confused, uncertain as to what it means and how it will affect them.

My belief is that if people can begin to understand a little about what is happening, perhaps they will once again become excited about what God is doing in this world and how they can be vital part of God's work. If people can begin to understand, maybe the dropouts will drop back in and the dissatisfied will be encouraged to rethink their dissatisfaction.

> "Behold, I am about to do something new.
> See, I have already begun! Do you not see it?
> I will make a pathway through the wilderness.
> I will create rivers in the dry wasteland."
>
> –Isaiah 43.19 (NLT)

God *is* doing a new thing. Let's begin exploring what it is.

Endnotes

[1] Brian D. McLaren, *The Church on the Other Side: Doing Ministry in the Postmodern Matrix* (Grand Rapids: Zondervan, ©2000), 11.

[2] D. Paul Barnes, *Skipping Stones: A Journey of Faith in the Messiness of Life* (Chicago Spectrum Press, ©2009). While *Skipping Stones* dealt with my own very personal journey through a dark period of life, *The Radical Center* focuses on broad themes and seeks to explore the current church scene and where we may be headed as a Christian community.

[3] Matthew 28.19

[4] II Corinthians 6.17 (KJV)

[5] John Wesley, "Minutes of Several Conversations" Q.3, in *The Works of John Wesley*, ed. Thomas Jackson (Grand Rapids: Baker, ©1978), Vol. 8, p. 299.

[6] Eddie Gibbs and Ryan K. Bolger, *Emerging Churches: Creating Christian Community in Postmodern Cultures* (Grand Rapids: Baker, ©2005), p. 67.

[7] Ibid, p. 77.

[8] Hans Frei, "Response to 'Narrative Theology: An Evangelical Appraisal,'" *Trinity Journal* 8:1 (Spring, 1987), p. 24.

[9] Brian D. McLaren, *A Generous Orthodoxy* (Grand Rapids: Zondervan, ©2004), p. 293. Brian is a key leader in the Emerging Church movement among Evangelicals. The author of close to twenty books, his focus has been on attempting to help people wrestle with Christianity in the context of the cultural shift towards postmodernism.

[10] *The Works of John Wesley,* Vol. 9. *The Methodist Societies: History, Nature, and Design*, ed. Rupert E. Davies, *Thoughts upon Methodism* (Nashville: Abingdon Press, ©1989), p. 527.

[11] Dan Kimball, *The Emerging Churches: Vintage Christianity for New Generations* (Grand Rapids: Zondervan, ©2003).

Part One

Where Have We Come From
and
Where Are We Now?

1

Change Is Good: You Go First!

"Your life is a journey you must travel with a deep consciousness of God."

— I Peter 1.18 (The Message)

Before proceeding any further it might be helpful to address the subject of change—primarily because the issues the church is facing today as it begins this process of Re•Forming will force many of us to experience change—both personal and ecclesiastical. If we are intent upon being thoughtful and committed followers of Christ, we will be challenged to examine these issues and respond. And change, especially as it relates to our faith, frequently does not come easy.

This verse from I Peter resonates with me. For one thing, it reflects something that I believe very deeply and that is we are all on a journey through life. One of the goals of living is to discover where God is and how God is guiding us in our particular expedition. As we do that, we come to discover the incredible value our individual life has and we are able to see God working in the unique situations of our lives.

A second reason that verse speaks to me is because I strongly believe God *is* constantly working in our lives both in big and small ways, but most of the time we aren't aware of it. Often, because of the busyness of our lives, the pressures, the stresses, the schedules we keep, and the multiplicity of distractions that we have, we don't have our spiritual antenna up high enough to recognize God's involvement with us. That's why we need to travel with a deep consciousness of God as we journey through life.

Nowhere is that more clearly seen than when it comes to change in our lives. I believe change is one of those places where God knocks on our door and says, "Pay careful attention now, because we're going to be doing something new, and we're going to be doing it together." The problem is—change is very hard for most of us. A friend of mine gave a sermon once on change and one of the lines he had in his message was: "Change is good: You go first!"

It was Benjamin Franklin who said only two things are certain in life, death and taxes. I believe we can add a third certainty—change. As Peter Drucker said, "Everybody has accepted by now that change is unavoidable. But that still implies that change is like death and taxes—it should be postponed as long as possible and no change would be vastly preferable."[1]

As mentioned earlier, change is a very difficult thing for many to accept. There is something in human nature that seems to take comfort in the known, security in the familiar. As Laurence Peter pointed out, "A rut is nothing more than a grave with the ends knocked out." And while that may be the case, many might be thinking (myself included) that a rut isn't all that bad a place to be.

A clever piece of writing shows how change and progress can be hard for some. Someone with a great imagination wrote a fictional letter supposedly from Martin Van Buren to President Andrew Jackson. Here's what the letter said:

> *To: President Jackson.*
> *The canal system of this country is being threatened by the spread of a new form of transportation known as "railroads." The federal government must preserve the canals for the following reasons:*
> *1. If canal boats are supplanted by "railroads," serious unemployment will result. Captains, cooks, drivers, repairmen and lock tenders will be left without means of livelihood, not to mention the numerous farmers now employed in growing hay for the horses.*
> *2. Boat builders would suffer and towline, whip and harness makers would be left destitute.*
> *3. Canal boats are absolutely essential to the defense of the United States. In the event of the expected trouble with England, the Erie Canal would be the only means by which we could ever move the supplies so vital to waging modern war.*
> *As you may well know, Mr. President "railroad" carriages are pulled at the enormous speed of 15 miles per hour by "engines" which in addition to endangering life and limb of passengers, roar and snort their way through the countryside, setting fire to crops, scaring the livestock and frightening women and children. The Almighty certainly never intended that people should travel at such breakneck speed.*

While it may bring a smile, this story reveals an insight about human nature: people can foolishly oppose change and ignore its potential benefits merely because it upsets their comfortable status quo. Whether it's moving from the horse and buggy to the car, from the typewriter to the computer, from the record player to the I-Pod, or from a laptop to the cell phone, we are constantly being confronted with change.

On a spiritual level, the new Re•Formation represents a change of cataclysmic proportions. There are a number of ways in which we can respond:

1. Ignore it and pretend it isn't happening (like an Ostrich putting its head in the sand);
2. Fight it because we think it's an assault on everything we hold dear;
3. Learn from it because we recognize that some things within the church and within us do need to change;
4. Embrace it because we sincerely desire to be a part of what God is doing and we earnestly want to be included in this new journey—even if it is frightening and we don't know where it will ultimately lead.

Someone once said, "A ship in harbor is safe, but that's not what ships are built for." As difficult as it might be for us, we are like ships as we journey through life. Staying in the harbor is definitely safe, but that's not how God has designed us. Life is best lived when we are out in the open ocean, being tossed by the winds and waves. As André Gide commented, "One doesn't discover new lands without consenting to lose sight of the shore for a very long time." This is where the new Re•Formation is going to take us—away from the shore, the security of the known and out into the dark, foreboding, possibly treacherous, and uncertain waters of the unknown.

Security is highly overrated however. Helen Keller remarked, "Security is mostly a superstition. It does not exist in nature, nor do the children of men as a whole experience it. Avoiding danger is no safer in the long run that outright exposure. Life is either a daring adventure or nothing." Douglas

MacArthur commented, "There is no security on this earth. Only opportunity." The new Re•Formation will be nothing less than a daring adventure full of exciting opportunities for those willing to embark on it. But what might keep us from this quest?

Some will not take the journey because they like staying in the harbor. This is more of an emotional response to potential change. As previously mentioned, there is security and comfort in our habit patterns, and our way of life as we've built it. Nowhere is this seen more clearly than in our comfort level with spiritual things. We go to a particular church because that church reinforces our basic convictions and beliefs. When we walk through the doors, we know what to expect, what the service will be like, how the message will confirm our convictions and that is comforting. By very definition, the change that is coming with the new Re•Formation implies that we're going to have to let go of that comfortable position and begin thinking differently about what life in God is really like. For many, this will be an emotional change they are just not ready to make.

Peter Senge made the comment that, "People don't resist change. They resist being changed." Frequently, it's not change itself that people resist; it is the fact that intuitively, inside us, we know that change is going to cause *us* to have to change, to have to adjust, to have to chart a new course. That's what we don't like.

A second reason why this journey will be difficult is because we think we're better off where we are. In 1994 James Belasco and Ralph Stayer wrote a book entitled, *Flight of the Buffalo* and here's what they wrote: "Change is hard because people overestimate the value of what they have and underestimate the value of what they may gain by giving that up."

In other words we tend to think that where we are right now is perhaps the best place we can be. That's not necessarily true. This is more of a mental response to change. Thinking that we have the best of all worlds right now can keep us from exploring the possibility that there might be a better world "out there." Sadly, even if we know that sometimes where we are right now isn't necessarily the best place to be, frequently we would still prefer to stay right where we are rather than go through the agony of changing.

I think of this in relation to women who are in abusive relationships. What causes a woman to stay with an abusive mate? There is a thought process that occurs. She begins to think, "I can't leave him. I don't have the education I need to get a good job. I have no skills. I have the kids to think about, and how I would provide for them. Where would I live? How would I survive?" By the time she's processed these questions, she concludes it's better to stay in her intolerable situation than to change it for one that might be even more intolerable.

As this idea relates to the new Re•Formation here's how it plays out: there are millions of frustrated Christians sitting in churches all across America today. They find themselves growing increasingly disenchanted with church as they've known it. There is a boring predictability to the services; the message is not relevant to their lives; they have questions about life and God that simplistic answers no longer satisfy; they find their own spiritual life dying on the vine. With no power or enthusiasm in their faith, they see no perceptible difference between themselves, their Christian friends, and the people around them who have no connection with God or a church. In short, their church and the faith as they've known and experienced it all their life are just not working for them anymore.

Yet the thought of changing, of having the foundation of their spiritual life shaken to its core, is more than they can accept. Whereupon a thought process occurs: "I'm not that happy with my church. I'm bored with my spiritual life. I'm tired of simplistic answers to difficult questions, but I don't know of anything better. I don't want to drop out of church and besides my friends are here. I guess it's just better that I stay where I am and see if I can't make the best of it."

Remember, there is a fundamental principle of change. People generally do not change until the pain of *staying* where they are becomes greater than the pain involved in *changing* where they are. Or as Anais Nin said, "There came a time when the risk to remain tight in the bud was more painful than the risk it took to blossom."

Here is a third thought: many years ago I realized that the older we get, the less willing we become to take chances. Instead, what we try to do is preserve our gains. We begin to live our lives and focus our attention on how to retain what we have accumulated, achieved and accomplished over the years. We start playing it safe. For many people the mantra of their life is, "Come weal come woe, my status is quo." In many ways, this is a very natural part of getting older. It's one thing to be brave, daring, and adventurous about the future when you're twenty-five. It's another thing entirely when you are sixty-five and you are much more aware of your own mortality.

It is because of this reason that the new Re•Formation will, in many ways, be spearheaded by the younger generation, the twenty and thirty-something young adults who are disillusioned with the way their parents "did" church and lived the Christian life. These individuals will be on the front lines of exploring the new dimensions of this Re•Formation and as they do so they will challenge the comfort zone of those who have gone before them. But just because a person is older does not mean that they could not, and should not be open to the coming changes.

One caveat needs to be given. Just as ballasts give ships stability when being rocked by the waves, I think it's a good thing to have people within the Christian community who say, "Wait a minute. Let's not go so fast. I know things aren't what they should be, but let's proceed cautiously." Christians who *react* to the changes and ideas being put forth will be the ballast for the new Re•Formation. Admittedly, these individuals can be annoying, but they do become a steadying influence that will help keep the boat afloat while going through this period of turbulence and unsettledness.

One final thought as to why we resist change—we fear a loss of control. If truth were told, most human beings are control freaks. We like to be in the driver's seat, or as Ernest Henley famously said, "I'm the master of my fate. I'm the captain of my soul." In my opinion, this is one of the primary reasons why it is so difficult for people to become followers of Jesus Christ. At a fundamental spiritual level, salvation, or becoming a disciple of Jesus, is all about giving up control, letting go of the steering wheel, slipping over into the passenger seat, and letting Jesus drive the car. Salvation equals surrender. It means giving up our rights, the right to control our life and destiny and submit to the controlling influence of God.

The new Re•Formation is going to challenge that desire to control. By its very nature there is an uncertainty about what we are going through and where it will all lead. People will feel a loss of control and that will be tremendously unsettling. For that reason many will become resistant and even begin to forcefully challenge the thoughts and ideas that the new Re•Formation brings.

About five years ago, I experienced an earth shattering, life altering change. It's not necessary to go into detail here, but suffice it to say that my world and the world of all those around me was shaken to the core. As I've dealt with the massive turmoil this change caused, I've been given a sense of clarity by a book written by William Bridges.[2]

Bridges says there are three stages that we all go through when we experience change. These changes are true for all of us, regardless of whether we choose to make a change in our life or some change is forced upon us.

- **Endings.** Every transition begins with this step. Some part of our life, as we've known it, comes to an end. Too often however, we misunderstand this stage of a transition. Because we are emotionally reeling from something that has happened, we confuse the ending with finality. We begin to think, "That's it. My life is over." The reality is yes, some *part* of our life might be over, but that ending *needs* to take place in order to get to the next stage of the transition process. While going through this stage, we must give ourselves the freedom to experience all the natural emotions that come with it: grief, sadness, disappointment, hurt, fear, loss, anger, bitterness, resentment, and whatever else surfaces.
- **Neutral Zone.** This is the second phase of a transition. It is a seemingly unproductive time and we are most anxious to get through it as quickly as possible. During the Neutral Zone we feel like we are in limbo, hanging

between heaven and earth. We feel disconnected from people and things in the past and yet we are emotionally unconnected to the present. We feel directionless, unsure of what to do next and where we need to go. It is an extremely uncomfortable place to be and for that reason we wish to get through it as soon as possible.

However, it is here that most of our personal growth takes place. By rushing through this step, we frequently short-circuit the lessons we need to learn. Often what happens then is we jump out of the frying pan and into the fire. By not allowing this season of the change process to accomplish its work in us, we end up in our new situation not that much different than where we were. That's not good. This part of the transition process is described well by Marilyn Ferguson who said, "It's not so much that we're afraid of change or so in love with the old ways, but it's that place in between that we fear…it's like being between trapezes. It's Linus when his blanket is in the dryer. There's nothing to hold on to."

- **The New Beginning.** This final step is when we begin to get our bearings again, our feet on solid ground, and we launch into new activities. This does not happen simply by "gutting it out" and getting through the Neutral Zone. There is an internal compass and some external signs that give us the indications that we are ready for the New Beginning and are starting to fully live life once again.

These stages of transition are all part of the process that people will go through as they come to grips with the new Re•Formation. There will be an incredible sense of loss for some, with all the emotions that accompany that loss. There will be a period of extended uncertainty as one moves out into uncharted waters. But finally there will come a time of renewed excitement and exhilaration as the new direction becomes clear and new doors of opportunity for growth and change open up.

Before we continue, this might be a good spot for a prayer.

My Lord God,
I have no idea where I am going.
I do not see the road ahead of me.
I cannot know for certain where it will end.
Nor do I really know myself,
and the fact that I think that I am following
your will does not mean that I am actually doing so.
But I believe that the desire to please you does in fact please you.
And I hope I have that desire in all that I am doing.
I hope that I will never do anything apart from that desire.
And I know that if I do this, you will lead me by the right road though I may know nothing about it. Amen.
—Thomas Merton
"The Road Ahead"

Endnotes

[1] Peter Drucker, *Management Challenges for the 21st Century* (Harper Paperbacks, ©2001)

[2] William Bridges, *Transitions: Making Sense of Life's Changes* (DeCapo Press, ©1980)

2

Where Have We Come From?

"No one puts new wine into old wineskins. For the wine would burst the wineskins, and the wine and the skins would both be lost. New wine calls for new wineskins."
–Mark 2.22 (NLT)

To better understand what is happening in the current Christian environment, it is important that we take a look back to see what has happened over the last 2,000 years of Christian history. This is no small task, but it will be a helpful perspective.

In her profound book, *The Great Emergence: How Christianity is Changing and Why,*[1] Phyllis Tickle takes us on a fascinating journey through that history. Her basic premise is that about every 500 years the church holds what she calls a "giant rummage sale." These rummage sales are times when the church cleans out the basement and attic and discards established form, practice, and theology in order to make way for something new and radically transforming.

Up to now, there have been three Re•Formations that the church has experienced. Tickle explores these in depth in her book. For our purposes, I'll simply highlight them.

1. The one that occurred in 590 under Gregory the Great. The fall of the Roman Empire and the coming of the Dark Ages led to immense changes in the ecclesiastical world.
2. The Great Schism that occurred around 1054. At this time, the church was split into two warring factions: Eastern Orthodox (with its headquarters in Constantinople) and Roman Catholic (with its headquarters in Rome). At that time the church had two different popes, who ultimately ended up excommunicating each other. Sadly, some of the Crusades were actually waged by the Roman Catholic Church against Greek Orthodox Christians.
3. The Great Protestant Reformation of 1517. We'll look at this one a bit more in depth in just a moment.

From my personal perspective, I would add a fourth to this list, the very first one to have occurred: the Jerusalem Council held in approximately 50 CE. The church was almost split apart within about 20 years of its founding over the issue of Gentiles being part of the Christian movement. The decision of Jerusalem Council put Jewish converts to "the Way" and Gentile converts on equal footing, thus opening the doors of Christianity to the vast majority of the human race. Had that event turned out differently, there would be no Christianity as we know it today.

Tickle maintains that when each rummage sale is over there have been three consistent results:

1. A new, more vital form of Christianity emerges,
2. The organized, current expression of the faith is reconstituted into a more pure expression of its former self,

3. When the old is broken open, the faith spreads dramatically and exponentially increases the range and depth of Christianity's reach.[2]

The rummage sale that we are most familiar with would be the one that occurred around 500 years ago in 1517, when Martin Luther nailed his 95 Theses to the doors of the Castle Church in Wittenberg, Germany. This event is widely regarded as the catalyst for what has become known as the Protestant Reformation.

The 95 Theses were Luther's attempt to speak out against abuses he observed in the Roman Catholic Church, particularly the selling of indulgences. When a priest granted an indulgence, it promised remission of punishment for a sin that had already been forgiven. The Roman Church sold indulgences primarily for the purpose of building cathedrals, like St. Paul's. That practice (in addition to others, like Papal authority) deeply disturbed Luther.

According to Tickle, a very important question that is always present when the Church goes through its rummage sale and begins to re•form is: "Where now is the authority?" In other words, whom or what do Christians look to as the basis for their final authority in determining matters of faith and practice? Before the Protestant Reformation, that authority had been vested in the Pope. He determined what was right or wrong, biblical or non-biblical, heresy or orthodoxy.

As the Protestant Reformation grew in popularity the authority began to migrate from the Pope to something else. Along with the concept of the priesthood of believers (the idea that every Christian could approach God personally without the need of an intercessor, like a priest), a battle cry developed: *Sola Scriptura, Scriptura Sola*—Only Scripture, Scripture Only. Rejecting the authority of the Pope, Protestants began to place the ultimate authority for spiritual matters in the Good Book—the Bible. From that point forward and for the last 500 years, the newly re•formed church would be built on the principle that the Bible is the supreme and definitive guide which would shape both Christian thought and practice.

Today, 500 years later, as we begin clearing out the garage for another rummage sale, many of even the most diehard Protestants have grown suspicious of *Scripture Only*. We question what that concept means. Are we to understand it literally or metaphorically? Are there other ways that we should interpret it? In addition to the Bible, are there other components in how we live life and process decisions that might serve us well as we wrestle with some of the complex issues of our 21st century world? With all of the advances and discoveries in science, biology, anthropology, archeology, paleontology, geology, and astronomy, many thoughtful Christian are wondering how can we continue to maintain a simplistic view of life by falling back on the well worn mantra, "The B-I-B-L-E, yes, that's the Book for me!"

We will look at this issue more in depth in a later chapter, but for now, perhaps *the* most important concept that comes from Tickle's book is this: as the Protestant Reformation picked up steam, Luther's battle cry of *Sola Scriptura* produced an unintended consequence: *the creation of a paper pope which replaced a literal flesh and blood one*. According to some within the Protestant movement, the Bible has become nothing less than the fourth member of the Trinity. It has taken on the role of the ultimate authority for the Christian. Today, in the current Re•Formation that idea is being challenged and once again the ultimate question is hovering over us—once this new Re•Formation has been established, where *then* will the authority lie? Just as the Protestant Reformation dealt a staggering blow to the concept of papal infallibility, once the new Re•Formation is established, a similar blow will have been leveled against the concept of biblical infallibility.

Questioning how we are to understand the Bible creates anguish, confusion, and anger for many Christians today. In fact in some circles, it will be called heresy. That is to be expected and it is understandable. Remember what I said earlier in regards to the first stage of any transition—the Ending? There are a wide variety of emotions that we experience, including grief, sadness, disappointment, hurt, fear, loss, anger, bitterness, and resentment. All of those will come into play as a Christian thinks through the ramifications of questioning the ultimate authority of our most holy book.

What we must realize however is that this type of distress has been part of each of the preceding Re•Formations the church has experienced. We just weren't around to see it and experience it. But since *we* are living through this one—it's up close and personal. The challenge for us is will we be able to discuss with objective passion our own angst and anger as we see something being challenged that we've held so sacred?

Endnotes

[1] Phyllis Tickle, *The Great Emergence: How Christianity is Changing and Why* (Baker Publishing, © 2008).
[2] Ibid, p. 13ff.

3

The Issues

If we are in the beginning stages of a new Re•Formation, what issues will this new form of Christianity address? Obviously there will be other concerns that surface over the next few decades and beyond, but currently there are six topics coming into sharper focus:

1. A new understanding of Scripture

Without doubt this will be the most monumental change that will take place and it will not come without a great deal of angst and conflict. The ultimate result however, will be an approach that takes the Bible seriously and authoritatively, but not literally. This is addressed in the chapter, "What about the Bible?"

2. A new perspective on homosexuality

The battle over Scripture will be a very long and drawn out struggle. The subject of homosexuality however is one of the most pressing issues before us and it will be the first to be resolved. Because of my own personal connection with this subject, I have chosen to take a more in-depth look at the issue. Ultimately, in the new Re•Formation, there will be an affirmation that *all* people are welcome in the family of God and that *all* people, regardless of sexual orientation are capable of serving God based upon their gifts, abilities, and calling. The chapters that explore this issue are "The 800 Pound Gorilla," "The Old Testament Passages on Homosexuality," and "The New Testament Passages on Homosexuality."

3. A greater openness to inter-faith dialogue

The current Christian system of Christ being the only way to God will be moderated by an approach that seeks to understand the similarities between world religions rather than focusing on the differences. Rather than taking a provincial view of what is involved in having a relationship with God—a view by the way, which condemns the vast majority of the human race to hell—there will be a greater understanding that God is bigger than any one denomination. Indeed, God is bigger than any one religion, the implications of which will have to be thoroughly fleshed out. "Does it make sense that the Creator of the universe would be known in only one religious tradition?"[1] This will be addressed in the chapter, "Is Jesus the Only Way?"

4. A clearly articulated theology of creation

Concern for the creation has traditionally been pretty far down on the list of priorities for many Christians. The reasons for this are intriguing. Over the last number of decades, there has been attention placed on eschatological Christianity—the idea that Jesus is coming back soon. Without consciously identifying it, I think this has left many Christians with a *laissez faire* attitude regarding environmental issues. If Jesus is coming back soon, there's no need to be too concerned about those problems. After all, we're here to play, not stay. I'm also alarmed at how many Christians seem to associate environmental concerns with what they consider to be secular humanism. This has resulted in an almost condescending dismissal of any suggestions that our world is facing tremendous ecological and environmental threats. In the new

Re•Formation, Christians will be more focused on our role as righteous stewards of the earth and its ecosystems. I will briefly touch on this in the chapter, "For the Beauty of the Earth."

5. A renewed focus and energy directed at social justice

The concept of Christians helping usher in the Kingdom of God by reaching out to the marginalized and downtrodden in whatever way God may direct will become a primary issue. Working to help alleviate social problems has always been an emphasis within certain segments of the Christian community. However over the last 100 years or so, this has been minimized by the three major expressions of Christianity: Fundamentalism, Evangelicalism, and Pentecostalism. The principal emphasis of these movements has been focused on getting people saved and having a personal relationship with God. Only recently have some within these groups begun to see the need to once again re-enter the world with the aim of trying to address the glaring social problems within our own society as well as around the world. This is explored in the chapter, "Jesus Loses His Hands."

6. A revived commitment to genuine community

In our highly individualistic age, isolation and independence have become the norm—even for Christians. Individualism is a core cultural value in the United States. The result of this has been a fracturing of relationships, resulting in people having a variety of interpersonal contacts but very few genuine, significant friendships. The concept of authentic Christian community and the benefits that brings will be rediscovered. This will radically reshape what the church looks like and how it functions but it will be one of the most positive benefits coming out of the new Re•Formation. This will be briefly explored in the chapter, "A Rope of Sand."

To varying degrees, each of these issues will dominate new Re•Formation thought and dialogue. All of these subjects will be met with a certain amount of skepticism and in some cases, outright hostility. It is to be expected that there will be pushback and resistance from some segments of the Christian community. That tension is a normal part of the continuing evolution of the church as it seeks to remain a viable presence of God on earth. It is through this healthy conflict of the new clashing with the old, that new forms of Christian vitality and ministry will be formed. We need to be reminded of what Phyllis Tickle said—that after each rummage sale is over there are three consistent results:

1. A new, more vital form of Christianity emerges,
2. The organized, current expression of the faith is reconstituted into a more pure expression of its former self,
3. When the old is broken open, the faith spreads dramatically and exponentially increases the range and depth of Christianity's reach.[2]

I have chosen to focus on these six issues in varying degrees. Every one of the topics are worthy of an extended look and there are many fine authors who are addressing them. Again, the intent of *The Radical Center* is to serve as a primer. I desire to give some brief thoughts and observations on the state of the church, where we are, where we seem to be heading and the issues before us. My hope is that it will stimulate the reader to a more in-depth exploration of the subjects that interest them.

Although it has not always been the case, Christians in every generation should have one primary passion: striving to insure that Christianity is adequately and accurately reflecting Jesus. To the degree that it is, we celebrate that victory. To the degree that it is not, we seek to improve. Prayerfully as these current issues come into sharper focus, our wrestling with them will help the continually changing face of Christianity to more closely resemble the Christ we seek to follow.

Endnotes

[1] Marcus Borg, *Reading the Bible Again for the First Time,* (HarperOne, ©2001) p. 14.

[2] Tickle, *The Great Emergence,* p. 13ff.

4

The Blind Men and the Elephant Church

There is a very familiar story found in multiple traditions (Jain, Buddhist, Sufi Muslin, Hindu) known as *The Blind Men and the Elephant.*

One version of the story states that six blind men were asked to determine what an elephant looked like by feeling different parts of the elephant's body. The blind man who feels a leg says the elephant is like a pillar; the one who feels the tail says the elephant is like a rope; the one who feels the trunk says the elephant is like a tree branch; the one who feels the ear says the elephant is like a hand fan; the one who feels the belly says the elephant is like a wall; and the one who feels the tusk says the elephant is like a solid pipe. A king explains to them: "All of you are right. The reason every one of you is describing it differently is because each one of you touched a different part of the elephant. So, actually the elephant has all the features you mentioned."

Another version of the story is put in poetic form:

And so these men of Hindustan
Disputed loud and long,
Each in his own opinion
Exceeding stiff and strong,
Though each was partly in the right
And all were in the wrong

In the Buddhist version, the men cannot agree with one another and come to blows over the question of what the elephant is like and their dispute delights the king. The Buddha ends the story by comparing the six blind men to preachers and scholars who are blind and ignorant and hold to their own views: *"Just so are these preachers and scholars holding various views blind and unseeing...In their ignorance they are by nature quarrelsome, wrangling, and disputatious, each maintaining reality is thus and thus."*

The Buddha then speaks the following verse:

O how they cling and wrangle, some who claim
For preacher and monk the honored name!
For, quarreling, each to his view they cling.
Such folk see only one side of a thing.

The story has been seen as a metaphor in many disciplines to point out the incomplete nature of human understanding. We know some things. We don't know everything. Or as the Apostle Paul said, "Now all we can see of God is like a cloudy picture in a mirror. Later we will see God face to face. We don't know everything, but then we will..." (I Corinthians 13.12, CEV)

The story has also been used to illustrate the principle of living in harmony with people who have different belief systems; to convey the idea that truth can be stated in different ways; and that different belief systems can have part of the truth, but not all of it.

I reflect on this story when I think about the condition of the present day church in America. I believe that over the last 100 years, the Church of Jesus Christ has been held hostage by two extremes. At one extreme you have a group that is holding on to the tail of the elephant. At the other extreme you have a group grasping the trunk. Both are holding on to the same elephant but they have remarkably different understandings of just what it is they actually are hanging on to.

These two extremes are commonly known as liberalism and conservatism. It must first be said that even though I will use these terms, I do not believe they serve us very well any more. The complexity of the Christian Church scene is such that two simple, imprecise nouns, which seek to describe the environment in which we now find ourselves, are no longer adequate and should have a respectful funeral.

However, for our purposes here, let me define them because they are the terms I will use. At one extreme you have liberalism. To put some definition around the liberals—they would be the mainline denominations (Episcopal, Methodist, Presbyterian, Lutheran, and others),[1] characterized by a strong emphasis on the social gospel, approaching the Bible through the method of Higher Criticism, and experiencing a massive decline in membership over the last fifty to sixty years. All of these characteristics will be explored in further detail in the chapter, "The Rise and Fall of Evangelicalism."

At the other end you have conservatism. This would be the conservative denominations and churches primarily expressed in three different movements: Fundamentalism, Evangelicalism, and Pentecostalism—what I call the holy

Trinity of current Christianity. These groups to some degree or another place high value on Lower Criticism (the basis of literal interpretation of the Bible), minimal social involvement, a strong emphasis on an individual and personal relationship with God, and some rather remarkable numerical growth over the last forty to fifty years. Again, this will be further dealt with in the chapter, "The Rise and Fall of Evangelicalism."

Can we get a little more precise?

I would strongly recommend reading Chapter 6 of Phyllis Tickle's book, *The Great Emergence.* Her explanation of what she calls the *Quadrilateral*[2] is that as Christianity has continued its evolution, it has divided up into four categories.

Rather than having only two designations within the faith (Liberal and Conservative), there are now four. The LITURGICALS would include Roman Catholics, Anglicans, a few Lutheran congregations with a more liturgical bent, and Eastern Orthodox. The SOCIAL JUSTICE CHRISTIANS would have earlier been the mainline, non-Catholic denominations. Primarily the Social Justice Christians would have comprised the old group called, "Liberals."

The RENEWALISTS would include both Charismatic and Pentecostal Christians, while the last box, the CONSERVATIVES would be a bit more difficult to define, but within this group you would find the Fundamentalists and the Evangelicals. The reason Tickle uses the term Conservatives, is to try and give this group a more inclusive and neutral label. Taken together, the Renewalists and the Conservatives would have comprised the old group called, "Conservatives." Now, there are enough differences between the "holy Trinity"

The Quadrilateral

Liturgicals	Social Justice Christians
Renewalists	Conservatives

of Fundamentalism, Evangelicalism, and Pentecostalism to separate those groups.

The Gathering Center

Tickle uses the phrase, *The Gathering Center,*[3] to describe what is currently taking place. Again, her visual might be helpful (see page 50).

Because of cultural and sociological changes that we experienced in the 20th century, Christians in America began rubbing shoulders in a much deeper and more pronounced way with Christians from other groups. Religious observers in the 1980s began to refer to this as water cooler theology. No longer were people isolated and separated from one another as had been the case throughout much of history. In times

The Gathering Center

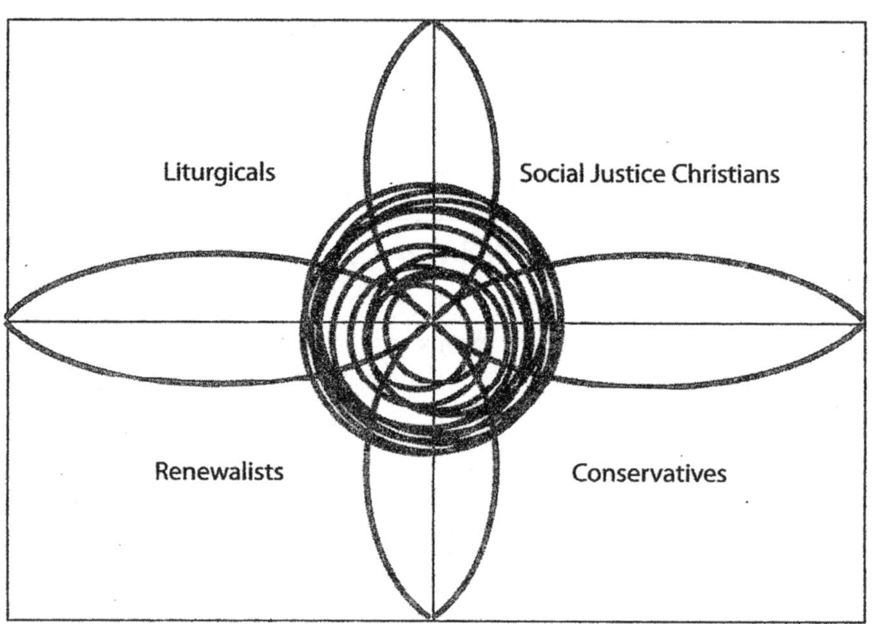

past, it was rare for a person to travel outside their clan, tribe, group, town, state, or country. Contact with people who had other ideas, philosophies, and religions would have been a limited experience for the vast majority of the human race. Meeting others who were "Christian," but who believed differently, would have also been a rarity. People tended to stay in their cultural and religious cocoons. The 20th century blew that isolationism to smithereens. Now, worldwide awareness was possible even for the individual living in the smallest of rural hamlets. Not only was this awareness now possible, it also became almost instantaneous. People began interacting and sharing ideas that would forever begin to alter individual perceptions and beliefs.

"Now the good Roman Catholic had to hear—or at least listen to—the spin an evangelical put on euthanasia; and the dyed-in-the wool Presbyterian had to consider tales of miraculous healing from Church of God in Christ folk who had seen the thing itself actually happen. Evangelicals, by default and unintentionally, began to hear things about, and observe lives governed by, liturgical seasons and unfathomable popish practices like observing fixed-hour prayer. Staid American Baptists heard about Taizé and found themselves buying into the whole thing, but so too did their Southern Baptist cousins to whom they hadn't spoken in over a century. And so it went. The center was beginning to form. The old, natal divisions were beginning to melt away, especially where their four corners met.

It was a slow process at first; and it certainly was an unintentional and unselfconscious one. It was just people—people swapping stories and habits, people admiring the ways of some other people whom they liked, people curious and able now to ask without offense. And more than anything else, it was people finding deep within themselves an empty spot or some niggling hunger or a restive, questioning impatience they had not experienced before, or at least had not been empowered to acknowledge before. So the swapping back and forth in public conversation and socializing went on."[4]

This new center that is now forming will become the heart of the new Re•Formation. Just as the rose became the chosen symbol of the Protestant Reformation, the means by which early protestors could safely signal their allegiances… so too will the new Re•Formation eventually find a symbol that will emphasize the unity that will now exist among people who have a broad diversity of theological perspectives and practices, but who are joined together by a mutually supportive and synergistic approach

to the faith—one that incorporates various aspects of all four quadrants of our current faith expressions, while at the same time ventures into new uncharted territory of belief and practice.

Let me conclude with some observations:

- Because of the entrenched nature of all four faith traditions, there will be very few churches within the four quadrants that will be able to transition into the gathering center.
- A handful of current churches that are beginning to address these issues might be able to make the move, but more likely what will happen is that individuals from the quadrants will leave their current churches and begin to search for groups that are already moving within the radical center.
- I would expect to see a continuing decline in all four quadrants as the new Re•Formation gathers momentum. This is because most local congregations and denominations are too immobile—restrained by their history, and paralyzed by their bureaucracy.[5] This will prohibit them from being able to make the underlying, systemic changes necessary to become part of the new Re•Formation movement.
- The mega church movement will eventually implode on itself, unable to be sustainable for a variety of reasons. That doesn't mean that mega churches will cease to exist, nor does it mean that an occasional entrepreneurial pastor will not be able to build a new mega church. It just won't be nearly as frequent as we currently see happening.

- This will also have significant implications for new churches that are started by various denominations within the four quadrants.
- The vast majority of new churches will fail within the first five years–unsustainable because the post-modern mindset will preclude people from attending "typical" churches.
- If a new church within one of the existing quadrants does succeed it will, no doubt remain small, as again, most people will not be satisfied with church as it was.
- Finally, if a new church is started with some radically different premises and values,[6] it stands a good chance of being in the forefront of the new Re•Formation movement and being an effective presence in society as we move forward.

Endnotes

[1] This is an overgeneralization for the purpose of simplifying this issue. In both the liberal and conservative denominations you have splinter groups that evidence greater or lesser degrees of liberal or conservative theology. For example, the Presbyterian Church USA is considered liberal, while the Presbyterian Church in America is considered conservative. The Southern Baptist Denomination is considered conservative while American Baptists are considered liberal. Again, my purpose here is to try and simplify very complex and convoluted denominational histories in order to explain my basic premise, that the church has been held hostage to two groups who have differing theological positions.

[2] The Quadrilateral diagram, Tickle, *The Great Emergence,* (Baker Books, a division of Baker Publishing Group, ©2008) p. 126. Used by permission.

[3] The Gathering Center diagram, Ibid, p. 128. Used by permission.

[4] Tickle, p. 133. Used with permission. All rights reserved.

[5] I had personal experience with this situation. In the church I pastored, I began to grow increasingly dissatisfied with where the church was heading and the general attitudes I sensed among many of our members. Consequently, I began to try and implement some significant changes that I felt would enable us to be a more effective presence in our community. The analogy I frequently used to describe this process was that we were attempting to take a cruise ship that was out in the middle of the ocean and trying to retrofit it to become a battleship without taking it in to dry dock. Logic and common sense would dictate that attempting something like that would be next to impossible. It was impossible and it didn't work. The push back we received, the exodus of people who didn't like the changes or understand them, the loss in revenue, all became contributing factors which helped me realize that even in a non-denominational church with a relatively short history (25 years), trying to make significant changes in how to "do" church was like trying to roll a two ton boulder uphill.

[6] It would seem that to be effective, a new church will need to have very clear positions on the current issues the new Re•Formation is dealing with: how they view and understand Scripture, homosexuality, inter-faith dialogue, a new creation theology, a renewed commitment to social justice issues in the context of personal transformation, and a passion for vital, genuine community.

A Checkered Past

"No man ever believes that the Bible means what it says: he is always convinced that it says what he means."

–George Bernard Shaw

"We do not read the Bible the way it is; we read it the way we are."

–Evelyn Uyemura

"Too often we see the Bible through whatever lens we get from our culture."

–Brian McLaren

"Both read the Bible day and night; but you read black where I read white."

–William Blake

As we begin this chapter, I have some exercises for you. Look at the diagrams on the next page and figure out how many **squares** there are in each illustration. If you're a competitive person, time yourself. Allow no more than 60 seconds on each diagram. The answers are at the end of the chapter…but don't peek![1]

How many squares do you see?

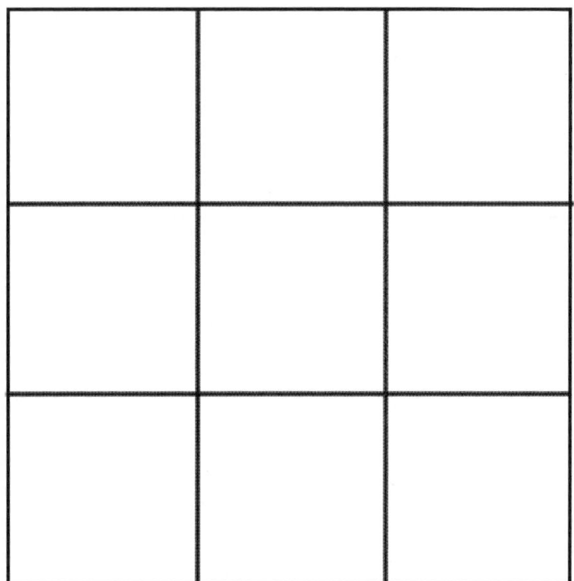

Figure 1

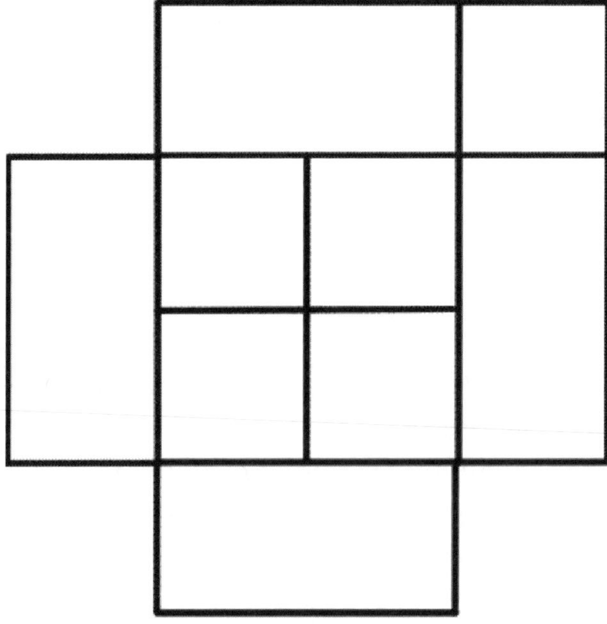

Figure 2

Typically, for most people, the first one is relatively easy, and the second diagram a little bit harder. However, both point out a fundamental principle of how people perceive things: **usually we cannot see what we have been conditioned not to see.** For example, in each diagram there are three different sizes of squares: small, medium, and large. Many people have no difficulty seeing the smaller squares in each illustration, and in the second diagram the medium size squares are relatively easy to spot. But did you find the larger square in the second diagram? How about the largest square in Figure 1, which is the entire box?

Usually we cannot see what we have been conditioned not to see. In different ways, the quotes from Shaw, Uyemura, McLaren, and Blake all speak to this truth. In approaching the Bible we all read it through rose-colored glasses that have been tainted by our culture, family, church environment, and a host of other outside forces. Sadly, many of us are not aware of just how deeply these factors play in to our approach, interpretation, and understanding of Scripture. Frequently, we assume a default position and think that our perception of the Bible is the only one *and* the correct one.

One of the great old hymns of the church is *Onward Christian Soldiers.* There is a line in the hymn that says, "Like a mighty army moves the church of God." I suggest that line needs to be changed to, "Like a mighty glacier moves the church of God." Jesus said he would build his church and the gates of hell were not going to prevail against it. With all of its shortcomings and imperfections, it would appear that the church is here to stay. Sadly however, rarely has the church been *proactive*–out in front of society, leading the charge on pressing issues that need to be addressed. Instead, the church is typically *reactive*–following behind, dragging its heels, trying to preserve the status quo, attempting to hold on to the traditional, seeking to protect its own interests, and insure its own self-preservation rather than trying to help take the lead in society.

A study of church history leads me to the following observation: because the church has been reactive rather than proactive, frequently it has had to change its position on a challenging issue—but only after much kicking and screaming, struggle, and resistance. Understanding some of these issues and the challenges the church faced as it tried to deal with these concerns will help us become more aware of how the church is dealing with current issues and why there is such strong opposition to some of the growing trends of the new Re•Formation. I want to look at a handful of issues that have presented the church an opportunity for growth. The challenge has been to work through preconceived ideas (even ones supposedly based in the Bible), stereotypes, personal, and group prejudices in order to come to a fuller, more complete, and ultimately correct understanding of a particular issue.

The Jew/Gentile Controversy

Initially the first converts to Christianity were Jews. "The Way" as it was known, was nothing more than a sect of Judaism. The adherents were Jewish men and women who had no thought or intention of forsaking their Jewish roots and heritage. They simply were following a Jewish teacher and unofficial rabbi named Jesus. One of the distinguishing marks of being a Jew was the fact that there was a definite line of demarcation between Jew and Gentile. The Jews were the chosen people, Gentiles were anything but.

Early on in the Christian movement, however, God began to reveal the fact that the message of Jesus was for a broader audience than *just* the Jews. It was a message for everyone. Even at Jesus' birth, this was the message that was proclaimed, though it seemed to be missed: "The angel said to them [the shepherds], 'Do not be afraid; for see—I am bringing you good news of great joy for *all* the people.'" (Luke 2.10, NRSV italics mine)

Before proceeding, let me ask a question: In the book of Acts, do you remember who was the very first non-Jewish convert to the Christian faith? Many people will say, Cornelius. The story of Cornelius is found in Acts 10 and we'll come back to that in a moment. But actually, there was someone before Cornelius who became the first Gentile convert.

In Acts 8 we have our answer. The Apostle Philip had an encounter with a man identified as an Ethiopian eunuch. This man was riding along in his chariot reading from the book of Isaiah when Philip encountered him. Philip asked him if he understood what he was reading, and the man said, "no." So Phillip explained to him the significance of the passage he was reading. The Eunuch responded, "Why shouldn't I be baptized?" And Philip's response was, "There is absolutely no reason for you not to be." They found some water, Philip baptized him, and we have the first Gentile convert to Christianity. This story is supremely important, so we'll spend a little time exploring it.

Here is where this gets interesting. In the Old Testament there is a fascinating verse. Deuteronomy 23.1 says, "No one who has been emasculated by crushing or cutting may enter the assembly of the Lord." What that meant was that any man, whose testicles were non-functional—either due to being crushed, cut off, or whatever—could not enter the assembly of the Lord. In other words they had to remain outside the tabernacle (or later on, the temple), somewhat separated, and never able to draw near to God.

It might be helpful to give an idea of what that meant.

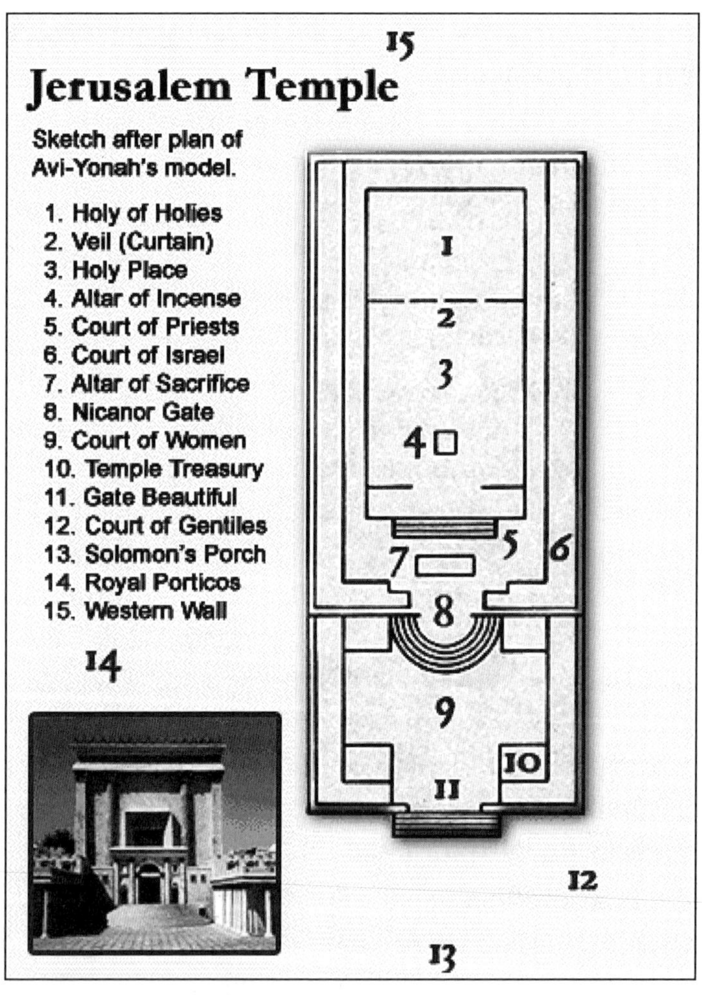

Solomon's Temple was arranged in the following way:

#1 was the Holy of Holies. This was the most sacred space within the Temple. It held the Ark of the Covenant that contained the stone tablets upon which the Ten Commandments had been written, and, according to some interpretations of Exodus 16.33-34 and Numbers 17.25-26, it also contained Aaron's rod that had budded and a jar of manna. This was the Ark made famous in the action packed movie, *Raiders of the Lost Ark.*

from Wikipedia, The Ark of the Covenant

Once a year, on the Day of Atonement, the High Priest would enter the Holy of Holies and sprinkle blood over the Ark. On that day the High Priest wore a special robe with bells sewn into the hem of the garment. Although it cannot be verified biblically, later tradition said that he would also have a rope tied to his ankle, which would allow the other priests to pull him out of the Holy of Holies in case God struck him dead. As long as they could hear the bells clanging, they knew he was still alive.

This Holy of Holies was separated from the rest of the Temple by a large curtain (#2). It was this curtain that was torn in two when Jesus died (Mark 15.38) symbolically indicating that intimate access to God was now available to everyone, not just the High Priest.

Numbers 3, 4, 5, and 7 were the locations where the priests would minister. Here the priests would daily go about their business of representing the people before God: offering sacrifices, burning incense, and saying prayers.

Number 6 was known as the Court of Israel. Israel, being no different than other nations of the time, was a patriarchal society, so the men had special privileges. The Court of Israel was the Court of Men—this was where the Jewish men could congregate and watch the proceedings as the sacrificial animals they brought were killed, cleansed, and offered up on the Altar of Sacrifice.

Further back from the proceedings was #9—The Court of the Women. This is where Jewish women would gather and it was as far as they could venture into the temple grounds. They were not allowed to proceed past the Gate of Nicanor (#8)

Finally, #12-15 was the Court of the Gentiles. This section of the Temple grounds was cordoned off by a three-foot high wall, and placed very conspicuously and at regular intervals were signs, which warned that no uncircumcised person (a Gentile) was to go past that wall under penalty of death. Gentiles who had any interest in the God of Israel (known as God-fearers) were allowed into the temple grounds but they were kept a distance away. It was a form of inclusive isolation.

In a very real sense, this Ethiopian Eunuch—this castrated Gentile—would have been in the back of the back group, since the Old Testament said no emasculated man could even enter the assembly of the Lord. Symbolically, this man would represent those who would try and experience God, although from a great distance. And remember, in addition to being castrated, he was also an Ethiopian. In other words he was black.

So here you have a black, castrated Gentile being the very first non-Jewish convert to Christianity. I don't know how that strikes you, but it gives me goose bumps. You talk about God demonstrating how *all-inclusive* the message of the Gospel really is—WOW! That is quite powerful. The fact that God would demonstrate how all-encompassing God's message of love and acceptance is by honoring a man who undoubtedly experienced a great deal of isolation, marginalization, and loneliness should be a humbling realization for all of us. As Paul says in Galatians 3.28 with God, "…there is no longer Jew or Gentile, slave or free, man or woman, (and may I add--black or white, gay or straight, young or old, rich or poor, educated or uneducated)—*all* are one in Christ." God made that truth perfectly clear by having a black, castrated Gentile become the first non-Jewish convert to the faith.

How sad it is that down through the centuries, the church has consistently tried to marginalize various groups and classes of people based on their skin color, their gender, their education, their financial status, and today, their sexual orientation, and say they either can't be part of the family or they can, but they'll be looked upon as second class citizens in the family of God. Inclusive isolation was not just a first century phenomena.

Moving ahead a few chapters in the book of Acts we come to the more familiar story of the Roman Centurion, Cornelius. The Apostle Peter has a vision of a sheet being let down in front of him with all kinds of animals that were unclean for a Jew. A voice told Peter to kill and eat whereupon Peter refused. This happened three times and each time, like the good Jew that he was, Peter refused to eat anything unclean. At that point in time he hears a knock at the door and servants of Cornelius have come to ask Peter if he would accompany them back to their master's house. Once there, Peter shares the story of Jesus at which point Cornelius and members of his household all become followers of the risen Christ. It is during this interaction that Peter has a profound insight: "I truly understand that God shows no partiality, but in every nation anyone who fears him and does what is right is acceptable to him." (Acts 10.34, NRSV)

The vision Peter had from God prepared him to accept a group of unclean Gentiles responding to the message of Christ. Thus the door was opened for non-Jews sharing in the blessings of God. But that's when the trouble began. As more and more Gentiles responded to the teachings of Jesus, the Jewish followers of Christ got into an uproar, because their theology did not allow for the fact that a Gentile could share in the same blessings that they had received. That idea was completely outside their frame of reference. It didn't fit their centuries old theology and belief system.

The controversy became so bad, that the Jerusalem Council was convened (Acts 15). A very lengthy and heated debate ensued as the early Christians argued over whether non-Jews could be saved. Some argued that if Gentiles did become followers of Jesus they should abide by the Jewish custom of being circumcised. The end result of the Council was to send a group of men to the cities where Gentiles had become Christians and instruct them that they could be part of the family of God, but with some restrictions: they were not to eat food that had been sacrificed to idols, or eat animals that had been strangled, and they were to abstain from fornication. Their concluding remarks were, "If you keep yourselves from these, you will do well." (Acts 15.29, NRSV). Again we see a sort of inclusive isolation: yes, Gentiles can be part of God's family, but with conditions.

At this point, it's important to emphasize what a huge issue this was in the first century church—one that almost split the church apart just about 20 years after it had been established. It was at the Jerusalem Council that it was finally acknowledged—"Yes, I guess we have to admit that God is bigger and more inclusive than our narrow Jewish theology has allowed for. So, I guess we'll accept the fact that Gentiles can become part of God's family."

We must not underestimate the emotion and angst, the conflict and controversy that went along with this debate. It was a transformative, reforming moment in the history of the early church. We read about these events 2,000 years later with a bit of unemotional detachment and think, "Oh, no big deal. I'm sure glad they got that squared away." But it must be emphasized that as we embark on the new Re•Formation *that* issue was every bit as big, controversial, and divisive as are the concerns the church is dealing with today.

I spent a significant amount of time on this first issue because it is foundational. It shows that from the beginning of the church, God was intentional in showing that all people—even the most marginalized in society are part of the family of God. It also shows that even from the very beginning, there was a tendency for people to be reluctant in considering something new, or more specifically, in considering a certain new group of people as being acceptable for the kingdom. But what we see in this situation is the church changing its position on a challenging issue.

Though each of the following issues are worthy of just as much an extended discussion, they will be summarized more concisely.

Mental Illness Being Attributed to Demon Possession

Until very recent times human beings have not understood the cause of mental illness. We now know that mental illness is caused by chemical imbalances in the brain. These include bipolar disorder, depression, schizophrenic disorders, panic disorder, and many others. Thankfully a host of medications have been developed that enable people who suffer with such issues to live more normal, wholesome, and productive lives rather than being debilitated by them.

In biblical times, and even for the last many centuries, because these illnesses were not understood, they were attributed to demon possession, or a spiritual illness, or malady of some kind. My purpose isn't to get into a debate about demon possession as it is to have us focus on the way people who have had legitimate mental illnesses have been treated down through the centuries. People have been shunned and feared, treated with misunderstanding and prejudice—with much of that treatment stemming from ignorance. I don't think we totally understand how detrimental and destructive that has been to the mentally ill. But up until the last century or so, that's how people were viewed...even by those within the Christian community.

We see this incomplete thinking occasionally reflected in Scriptural passages that highlight the generally accepted ideas of the day. One of the key beliefs was that afflictions of the brain and illnesses in the body were signs of disfavor from God. At the time of Jesus those who were lepers, who were troubled with other physical problems, or who had afflictions of the mind were outcast and were thought to be deserving of their pain because they must have done something wrong and were being punished by God. A classic example of this is the story of the man born blind. In John 9 Jesus walks by a man who had been blind from birth and his disciples asked him the question, "Who sinned, this man or his parents that he was born blind?" (John 9.2, NRSV) It was a very common, but misguided assumption of the day. Jesus' response put the issue in a proper context when he said, "Neither this man nor his parents sinned; he was born blind so that God's works might be revealed in him." (John 9.3, NRSV) As a result of his encounter with Jesus, the man was given his sight.

There is something to note in regard to the healing ministry of Jesus. Obviously he didn't heal everyone who was sick and afflicted, yet during his public ministry there were many who were healed. Those healings were designed to point people's attention to the uniqueness of this person called Jesus. Those works testified to the fact that in Jesus there was the full manifestation of God.

However, from the perspective of the person who was healed, I think we see something much more human and pregnant with intense emotion. When Jesus healed people, he did far more for them than just restore their sight, heal their leprosy, or bring peace to a troubled mind—he lifted those men and women out of their isolation. He took away from them the scorn and ridicule, rejection and shame, the stigma they had lived with for so many years. No longer were they feared, ignored, or isolated, instead they were brought back into the embrace of the human community. They were made whole people once again, being able to experience the love and acceptance of others.

"...for Christian thinkers from Dante to Luther and the Puritans, the body's discomfort was a sign of the soul's distemper...bodily health depended on overcoming sin."[2] Down through the centuries, until very recently the church has had an improper attitude toward people who were struggling with illnesses of various kinds—physical or mental. That attitude was reinforced by a peculiar (but peculiarly wrong) theology that did much more damage than good to those who were suffering. But again, over time the church had to change its position on an issue once thought to be understood.

The Earth as the Center of the Universe (Science vs. Scripture)

In the late 15th and early 16th century a priest by the name of Nicolaus Copernicus formulated a heliocentric theory of the universe. The idea put forth was contrary to popular belief and the teaching of the church. He stated that the Earth was not the center of the universe, but in fact, the Sun was. Copernicus is widely credited with the honor of being the man who started modern astronomy. When he built his telescope and viewed the heavens further than anyone had ever been able to see with just their eyes, he opened a whole new world of thought, possibilities, and scientific exploration.

When Galileo picked up this new idea and also began postulating that indeed, the Sun was the stationary body and the Earth revolved around it, a huge controversy and crisis was created for the church. Up until that time the teaching of the church was that the Earth was the center of everything. How could it not be? God's attention was focused on the Earth. God's highest creation (humankind) was on the Earth.

This dogma was firmly established because of verses plucked here and there from the Bible. Sadly for Galileo, he was called before a couple of inquisitions, declared a heretic, and placed under house arrest. He was threatened with death and forced to recant. It was then that he said, "I retract, but the Earth does move around the Sun just the same." In public he renounced his ideas, but in private continued to write and talk about them. Eventually, as science proved the truthfulness of Copernicus' and Galileo's claim, the church was forced to change its position.

There was a cardinal in the church at the time who was part of the inquisition held against Galileo. He made a statement I believe probably put him at odds with his fellow cardinals: "The Scriptures tell us how to go to heaven, not how the heavens go." That comment reflected the thoughtfulness of a man who was willing to not blindly accept church teaching, but allow for the possibility that a position the church had held for centuries might actually be in error.

It wasn't until 1992—359 years after Galileo's conviction as a heretic—that The Vatican Commission of Historic, Scientific and Theological Inquiry delivered a "not guilty" verdict. Galileo was declared innocent and his judges were excused and forgiven because they were unable at that time to understand or comprehend a nonliteral reading of Scripture.

Usually we can't see what we've been conditioned not to see. People back then had some presuppositions about things and they brought those presuppositions to bear on Scripture and thus made the claims that they did. That's a dangerous thing to do and yet we all do it. All of us bring presuppositions to our reading of Scripture and that strongly determines how we interpret and understand it. As Evelyn Uyemura said, "We do not read the Bible the way it is; we read it the way we are."

The Slavery Issue

Moving closer to our time, we must address the issue of slavery. Without doubt this has been one of the biggest blights on the Christian church. For centuries not only did the church not speak out against this horrible evil, it actually encouraged it. As the French political theorist Montesquieu wryly observed in 1748: "It is impossible for us to suppose these creatures [enslaved Africans] to be men; because allowing them to be men, a suspicion would follow that we ourselves are not Christians." In different forms, slavery existed within Christianity for over 18 centuries. In the early years of Christian history, slavery was a normal feature of the economy and society in the Roman Empire and this remained well into the Middle Ages and beyond. Most early Christian leaders supported slavery—including St. Augustine of Hippo—a man who did more to mold current theological thought than just about any other early Christian apologist.

In one sense, it's easy to see how this happened. The Old Testament sanctioned the use of regulated slavery, and whether or not the New Testament sanctioned or condemned slavery has been strongly disputed. For me, this is just another example of how we need to be so very careful in our perceived interpretation of the Bible—an issue I'll address in a later chapter.

A few centuries ago, as the abolition movement took shape across the globe, groups who advocated slavery's abolition worked hard to harness Christian teachings in support of their positions, using the "spirit of Christianity" argument, biblical verses, and textual considerations. These brave men and women faced a Christian majority who were biblically convinced that slavery was fine. People like Elizabeth Heyrick, Baroness Cox, David Livingstone, Granville Sharp,

Harriet Beecher Stowe, Harriet Tubman, William Wilberforce, and others dared to take on the entrenched Christian establishment and speak out against an evil that had been tolerated and biblically supported far too long.

At the height of the struggle in America over this issue, during the Civil War, preachers gave sermons from their pulpits in support of slavery. Using verses of Scripture, they confidently (and probably with a mixture of arrogance and ignorance) proclaimed slavery to be in complete harmony with God's will for humanity. Their attitudes support the comment made by Brian McLaren, "Too often we see the Bible through whatever lens we get from our culture."

We now know that enslaving another human being, treating them as one would a bag of flour, or a pet dog is totally unconscionable. Yet for 1800 years in the 2000-year history of Christianity, it was condoned. This issue has been particularly divisive among Christians. At the time of the Civil War, it was the reason for the split between northern Baptists and southern Baptists, as well as numerous other disputes among people of faith.

But slowly and surely the mighty glacier, known as the church finally, acknowledged the error of her ways and began developing a theology and practice that emphasized the dignity, worth, and inherent freedom all people should have—regardless of the color of their skin.

The Rights of Women

August 18, 1920, was a very significant day in the history of our nation. It was on that day the 19th Amendment to our constitution was ratified. This was the amendment giving women the right to vote. Today, looking back on it, it seems ludicrous that less than 100 years ago one half of the adult population in America was not allowed to express their opinion in the voting booth.

One of the first documents of the emerging feminist movement in the United States came out of the *Seneca Falls Declaration of Sentiments and Resolutions* of 1848:

> "The history of mankind is a history of repeated injuries and usurpations on the part of man toward woman...He allows her in Church, as well as State, but a subordinate position, claiming Apostolic authority for her exclusion from the ministry, and, with some exceptions, from any public participation in the affairs of the Church...He has created...a different code of morals for men and women...we insist that women have immediate admission to all the rights and privileges which belong to them as citizens of the Unites States...woman is man's equal—was intended to be so by the Creator...woman has too long rested satisfied in the circumscribed limits which corrupt customs and a perverted application of the Scriptures have marked out for her, and that it is time she should move in the enlarged sphere which her great Creator has assigned her."

Subjecting women to second-class status has deep, deep historical roots. Most cultures have been patriarchal—male dominated and controlled. In these environments, women have been reduced to being nothing more than the child bearer and in many ancient cultures considered to be the property of the man. Even today in many Middle Eastern cultures we see the remnants of this kind of oppression.

In America, using the Bible as primary ammunition continually encouraged the subordination of women. A literal, biblical interpretation has been fundamental to keeping women in their place and supporting this kind of inequality.

An excerpt from a sermon given by the Reverend R.L. Dabney in response to the idea of having women in the pulpit (1879) says, "The women is not designed by God, nor entitled to all the franchises in society to which the male is entitled...God has disqualified her for any such exercise of them as would benefit herself or society, by the endowments of body, mind, and heart he has given her, and the share he has assigned her in the tasks of social existence."

Fortunately, some segments of the church were much more responsive and open to the role of women:

- A fundamental belief of the Society of Friends (Quakers) has always been the existence of an element of God's spirit in every human soul. Thus all persons are considered to have inherent and equal worth, independent of their gender. In contrast with almost every other organized religion, Quakers have allowed women to serve as ministers since the early 1800s.
- 1853: the first women was ordained by the Congregationalist Church, later merging with other groups to become the United Church of Christ.
- 1865: The Salvation Army was founded and has always ordained both men and women.
- 1866: Helenor Alter Davisson was a circuit rider for the Methodist Protestant Church. She was the first woman to be ordained a minister in any Methodist denomination.
- 1889: The Cumberland Presbyterian Church ordained Louisa Woosley.
- 1892: Anna Hanscombe is believed to have been the first women ordained by the group which became Church of the Nazarene.

- 1909: The Church of God began ordaining women.
- 1911: Ann Allenbach was the first Mennonite woman to be ordained.
- 1914: Assemblies of God was founded and ordained its first woman clergy.

To this day however, many conservative faith groups still refuse to consider women for ordination, or key leadership positions, irrespective of their talents, training, and ability. Many teach that women have very specific roles, both in the family and in religious organizations, where positions of authority and power are reserved for males. This is especially prevalent in the fundamental and evangelical traditions that believe that it is unbiblical for a woman to have authority over a man. After all, I Timothy 2.12 (NASB) states, "I do not allow a woman to teach or exercise authority over a man, but to remain quiet."

Sadly and with much regret, I confess that this was my position while I was pastor of an evangelical church. Having graduated from a seminary that supported this view, I adopted it as a pastor. My own conviction regarding the issue changed many years ago, but I would never have been able to foster that kind of change in the church I was serving because of the conservative nature of most of its members. I remember quite vividly that in almost every new member class we would offer (a class which helped people who were interested in our church understand our positions, doctrine, and opportunities for ministry) someone would ask about this issue. When I gave them our official position, frequently they would choose not to become part of our church. Inside, I couldn't blame them and I also felt our church was the poorer for encouraging this kind of exclusion. Over the years, we lost the benefit of many qualified, bright, energetic, and talented women because of our position on this topic.

While there are still some holdouts regarding the rights and privileges women have within the Christian community, this is another one of those issues that has changed and is changing, albeit after centuries of unabashed sexism.[3]

The Segregation Issue

Being an adolescent during the turbulent 1960s was an unsettling experience. Our country was being torn apart at the seams, wracked with violence and turmoil both from within and without. The Vietnam War was raging and more and more Americans began violently protesting our involvement in Southeast Asia. One President had been assassinated and his brother had been killed while running for the office. We had a corrupt White House mired in scandal. The Civil Rights movement was in full swing, with race riots quite common in our major cities. Then the leader of the movement was murdered. It was a dark period in our country's history.

It was as if decades of pent up anger and frustration finally simmered over into a massive cathartic experience for our nation. Though it was a depressing time, it was necessary, if for no other reason than to lance a national boil that had festered far too long: segregation. Though slavery had officially been outlawed a century earlier, the consequences of that immorality continued to ripple through our nation. The Jim Crow laws were state and local laws that mandated a supposedly "equal but separate" status for black Americans. In essence all those laws did was to systematize a number of social, economic, and educational disadvantages. Black men and women were continually being reminded of their second-class citizenship in America. They were not allowed to vote. They were prohibited from buying homes in certain neighborhoods, and from shopping or working in certain stores. They had to go around to the alley and get a meal at the kitchen door of a restaurant or eat in a "Negros Only" restaurant. They had to drink from separate water fountains, use separate bathrooms, have separate waiting rooms in bus stations, sleep in separate motels, wash their clothes in separate Laundromats, ride in the back of a bus, go to separate schools, and attend separate churches.

What made the issue unconscionable was the fact that the Bible was used to support this un-Christian behavior. Dating back over hundreds of years, the "sin of Ham" or the "curse of Canaan" became a proof text that enabled whites to put other human beings into a "sub-human" category. In Genesis 9, Noah is sleeping naked, in a drunken stupor. His son Ham comes upon him and rather than covering him, runs and tells his brothers, Shem and Japheth. The "good" sons promptly cover their father's nakedness. In reaction to Ham's sinful act of looking upon the "nakedness of the father," Noah puts a curse on his grandson—Ham's son, Canaan: "Cursed be Canaan, slave of slaves shall he be to his brothers."

This curse gradually came to be interpreted to mean that Ham was literally turned black, and that his descendants would be similarly cursed, a color-coding that would in turn label them as the subservient race. While some Christian ministers attempted to speak out against such a flagrant twisting of a passage of Scripture, the majority won the argument and segregation remained a national blight until the Civil Rights movement of the 1960s. In fact, Jim Crow laws were still being enacted as late as 1965. Reverend Martin Luther King, Jr. said, "The greatest blasphemy of the whole ugly process was that the white man ended up making God his partner in the exploitation of the Negro."

Today, it is almost impossible to comprehend the Bible being used in this manner. Yet for hundreds of years it was. In the United States, racism was a legalized institution. Racism permeated popular American culture, from plays and motion pictures to television and advertising—which frequently featured insulting images of blacks. In a self-described "Christian" nation, acknowledging the rights and humanity of nonwhites became, for many, an unprecedented, un-Christian concept. But up until the Civil Rights Movement, there was strong Christian support for the attitude expressed by W.A. Plecker given in a 1924 speech on racial purity and white superiority, "Let us turn a deaf ear to those who would interpret Christian brotherhood to mean racial equality."

The Divorce Issue

With considerable justification, many people feel that the current high rates of marital breakdown, separation, and divorce are one of the most serious social problems in North America today. Many Christians have a keen interest to know what the Bible says about divorce. For some, the significance is intensely personal. They feel trapped in a toxic relationship, and are wondering what their religiously acceptable options are. When they speak to their spiritual counselor, they will usually obtain only one point of view. Within society generally, and among religious leaders, there is little consensus about divorce and remarriage. Even within the conservative wing of Christianity—Fundamentalism, Evangelicalism and Pentecostalism—there is great diversity of belief. A helpful book for those interested in pursuing this further would be H.W. House, Ed., *Divorce and Remarriage: Four Christian*

Views, InterVarsity Press, (1990). This book, while not for the casual reader, is helpful in understanding the different positions among Christians.

Some faith groups have taken and continue to take, a very dim view of divorce. They have responded to divorced individuals by excommunicating or "shunning" them, withholding giving of the Eucharist, denying a divorced individual the ability to get remarried, demanding lifetime celibacy for a divorced person, and refusing leadership opportunities within the church.

It wasn't that long ago that the Assemblies of God position paper on divorce stated in part:

> "...divorce is treachery (deceitful unfaithfulness) against your companion...Jesus forbade divorce as contrary to God's will and word...Paul forbade a Christian couple getting a divorce...Jesus permitted a Christian to initiate a divorce when fornication was involved...Jesus in His basic teaching forbade the remarriage of divorced persons...[Church] membership is open to all born-again believers...The offices of elder and deacon are not open to those who are remarried...We positively disapprove of Christians getting divorces for any cause except fornication and adultery."

Fortunately this position was tempered to reflect a more compassionate and humane view by a revision that was conducted in 2008.[4]

I think the United Methodist Church has one of the more grace-oriented statements:

> "God's plan is for lifelong, faithful marriage. However, when a married couple is estranged beyond reconciliation, even after thoughtful consideration and

> counsel, divorce is a regrettable alternative in the midst of brokenness. We grieve over the devastating emotional, spiritual, and economic consequences of divorce for all involved, understanding that women and especially children are disproportionately impacted by such burdens. It is recommended that methods of mediation be used to minimize the adversarial nature and faultfinding that are often part of our current judicial processes. Divorce does not preclude a new marriage. We encourage an intentional commitment of the Church and society to minister compassionately to those in the process of divorce, as well as members of divorced and remarried families, in a community of faith where God's grace is shared by all."[5]

As mentioned earlier there is very little consensus among faith groups regarding their understanding and application of Scripture in regards to divorce. This issue becomes especially important however, in the conservative wing of Christianity. Believing that divorce is acceptable only in the case of desertion or adultery, many churches have continued to use the Bible to encourage people stay in very unhealthy marriages as well as treat divorced people as second-class citizens in the family of God. Leadership opportunities have also been prohibited for a divorced person.

The church I pastored would have sadly been numbered among this group for the first years of its existence. Although there was never an intentional shunning of an individual who precipitated a divorce within our congregation (the "sinning" brother or sister), I know from later conversations that those individuals definitely felt rejected, shunned, ignored, and hurt—by their friends and church leadership. In addition, it was church policy to not allow a divorced person to serve as an elder or deacon within our congregation. As the years went by, it became increasingly apparent that this issue was not as black and white as we had tried to maintain and that the church was losing out on the wisdom, experience, and leadership of very competent individuals solely because of a broken marriage in their past. Taking a more holistic approach to the Scriptures as well as to the individuals involved enabled the church to modify this position and open the door to full participation in the life of the church to someone who had experienced a divorce.

Saying this will no doubt cause some to say that we had given in to the trends of society and abandoned our firm commitment to Scripture. From my perspective it was simply one of the positions that could no longer be supported by reason and experience, and needed to be more deeply explored. My personal opinion is that divorce is still a blight on our society, creating all kinds of issues and problems. The church should do as much as possible to try and encourage couples to stay together by providing counseling, classes, sermon series, mentoring, retreats, and whatever other avenues might be beneficial. However, the church has to face reality and acknowledge this is an ongoing problem of contemporary culture. To hold to a very narrow view of divorce as understood by a literal interpretation of the Bible is only going to continue to isolate the church from being an effective presence in society. In addition this approach will alienate more and more folks who have experienced divorce and found only judgment and condemnation when they turned to the church for help.

This brief overview of some of the issues the church has had to deal with down through the centuries has been written to show that the church is not a static institution, even though it is a slowly changing one. Just as all of life changes, the church has been forced to reevaluate long held positions, undergirded by the Bible, and reframe its views based on new discoveries, insights, common-sense wisdom, broader understandings of issues and culturally changing mores. In doing so, this does not mean the church is compromising—it means it is evolving, just as any living thing evolves.

As mentioned in the Preface, all evolution means is a gradual process of change or growth. It's not something that should scare us. It should challenge us to look to our present day and discover what issues the current church world is facing and begin digging deeper to discover and acknowledge the error of our ways. In the new Re•Formation, those present day concerns are ones surrounding our understanding of the Bible, homosexuality, the importance of inter-faith dialogue, our responsibility as stewards of creation, a reenergized commitment to social justice issues, and in addition to a revived commitment to genuine community, the question of what role local Christian communities will have in determining what is authoritative and what is not.

Essentially, we need to recognize that the church has had a very poor track record in terms of repeatedly marginalizing individuals and groups of people for a wide variety of reasons. The church of Jesus Christ should never again be guilty of sidelining *anyone*—regardless of the color of their skin, gender, physical or mental ability, education, sexual orientation, nationality, looks, economic status, social status, or faith history.

Every person has been created in the image of God and has value in God's eyes. As such, the church should affirm that all people are of sacred worth and there are no second-class citizens in God's family. Part of spiritual maturity and healthy spiritual living is learning to value the things God values. Prayerfully, this will be one of the major accomplishments of the new Re•Formation.

Endnotes

[1] In the first diagram there are a total of 14 squares. In the second diagram there are a total of 11 squares. If you can't find them all, get with someone and work on it together.

[2] Jackson Lears, professor of History, Rutgers University.

[3] Sexism: Discrimination against a person based on their gender rather than their individual merits.

[4] Assemblies of God position paper on Divorce and Remarriage, www.ag.org.

[5] *The Book of Discipline of the United Methodist Church,* (United Methodist Publishing House, Nashville, Tennessee © 2008) Paragraph 161 C, "Divorce," p.102. Used with permission. All rights reserved.

An Image Problem

"I love Jesus. It's his fan club that really creeps me out."
–Online Blogger

"Why is it that the word Christian, which should stand for people of extravagant grace and generosity, who are abundantly loving, who are associated with acts of courage, justice, and compassion, has become synonymous with butthead?"[1]

Christianity needs a makeover. It is suffering from a major image problem. In a recent survey that was conducted by the Barna Group (one of the best sources of reliable social research about Christians, Christianity, and the Church), one in four Americans said they couldn't think of a single positive societal contribution made by Christians in recent years. The researchers asked two open-ended questions: What were Christians' recent positive contributions and what were the negative ones? "Overall," researchers noted, "there was a more extensive and diverse list of complaints about Christians and their churches than there was of examples of the benefits they have provided to society."[2] The contributions, both good and bad shook out as follows:

POSITIVE CONTRIBUTIONS

- Helped poor or underprivileged people have a better life (19%)
- Helped advance belief in God or Jesus Christ or promote becoming an adherent of the Christian faith (16%)
- Helped shape or protect the values and morals of the nation (14%)
- Made positive contributions related to marriage (6%)
- Favorable actions related to abortion (5%)
- **Could not think of a positive contribution (25%)**

NEGATIVE CONTRIBUTIONS

- Violence or hatred incited in the name of Jesus Christ (20%)
- Opposition of Christians to gay marriage (13%)
- Churches too involved in politics (12%)
- Intolerance or bigotry from Christians (2%)
- Failure of believers to reflect genuine Christian values in their lifestyle (2%)
- **Could not think of a negative contribution (12%)**

When you have a quarter of the nation's population not being able to think of anything good about Christianity, alarm bells should be ringing in the Christian kingdom rather than church bells. Anyone familiar with history knows that over the centuries there have been many positive contributions made by Christians. Hospitals and orphanages were started. The Salvation Army and Red Cross both have Christian roots. Early on in America's history our major colleges were begun as Christian institutions because education was considered vital (Harvard, Yale, and Princeton). Christians were at the forefront of prison reform in England (The Society of Friends or Quakers), worked to establish child labor laws, and called for the abolition of slavery. The suffragette movement in both England and America had Christians involved. In 1844, the YMCA (Young Men's Christian Association) was established as a Christian organization. Many institutions that help children, the poor, the homeless, prisoners, the uneducated, the sick, the elderly, and the disenfranchised of society have been started by thoughtful, compassionate Christian people desiring to help ease the suffering of their fellow human beings.

Individually, there is an incredible amount of good that is done unsung, and unnoticed by the press—people who quietly and with no need to blow their own horn give of their time and resources to causes they find important. Statistically, Americans are a very generous people. According to the "Giving USA" report by the Center on Philanthropy at Indiana University, individual Americans donated more than 227 billion dollars in 2009. That figure was down only 0.4 percent from the previous year despite the U.S. recession. That is a staggering amount of money that went to a wide variety of various causes. But while Americans do exhibit a great deal of individual generosity, the Christian community apparently doesn't have a very good reputation among outsiders as doing much to help solve problems.

Tragically, while there has been much good done by Christians over the years, there has also been much evil done as well. It is this underbelly of the Christian movement that many in society are more familiar with—the Christian persecution of Jews, the Crusades, the silencing of Galileo, the Salem witch trials, the Inquisition, and the genocide of native peoples in the Americas. As Bishop Desmond Tutu remarked,

> "When the missionaries came to Africa, they had the Bible and we had the land. They said 'Let us pray.' We closed our eyes. When we opened them we had the Bible and they had the land."

The Barna survey highlights an interesting point: there doesn't seem to have been much good done of late by the Christian community (or at least that's the perception). It seems that within that last 60 or 70 years, working to help alleviate some of the social problems in our country has diminished. This is especially telling since this corresponds with the rise and domination of Fundamentalism, Evangelicalism, and Pentecostalism as the primary expressions of the Christian faith. Researchers noted that Evangelical Christians over the age of 25 and those who said they are "mostly conservative" on socio-political matters were least likely to list serving the poor as an important contribution.

I lay a great deal of the blame for the perception people now have of Christianity at the feet of these three movements. I don't believe it has been intentional, but because of the unique theologies these groups possess, they have fostered a number of unfortunate attitudes in their followers which has contributed to the negative opinion outsiders have of the faith:

- Hyper-individualism has struck a serious blow at the very foundation of Christianity. Rather than working together as a community of people who are seeking to extend the love and compassion of Christ to a needy world, the Christian faith has been reduced to a very self-focused, "Jesus and me" kind of mentality that basically views Christianity as nothing more than a faith that promises health, wealth, and prosperity for the individual.

- Legalism has produced a lack of grace and compassion towards the hurting people of the world and instead bred judgment and condemnation.
- I don't know how to talk about this unique group of people called televangelists other than to echo the words of the online blogger...they're just kind of creepy.
- Becoming identified with right-wing, Republican politics has produced the perception that unless people stand against the moral ills of our society (as defined by them) like abortion and gay rights, something is terribly wrong in their thinking.
- Many think it's absolutely impossible to be a true Christian and be a Democrat.
- Exhibiting an arrogant sense of "we have all the answers; we're right, you're wrong; it's our way or the highway."
- Proclaiming a self-righteous morality that causes outsiders to come away with the impression, "Christians think they're so much better than us."
- Possessing an attitude of "hate the sin but love the sinner" which ends up coming across as very disingenuous and judgmental. Or as one individual said, "Christians talk about hating sin and loving sinners, but the way they go about things, they might as well call it what it is. They hate the sin *and* the sinner."

The bottom line is Christians have become known for who we are standing up *against* rather than who we are standing up *for*. This perception makes it challenging for those Christians who are themselves unhappy and dissatisfied with how the faith has degenerated into an "us against them" mentality.

> "I'm tired of being a Christian butt," Jenny exclaimed with obvious exasperation.
>
> "What do you mean by that?" I asked.
>
> "I mean," she replied without hesitation, "I'm tired of having always to qualify the word *Christian* when I tell people I'm going to church. I might as well say I'm radioactive. They get a surprised look on their face and say, 'Not *you*, Jenny. You don't seem like the Christian type.' So I find myself throwing in more and more *buts* all the time. 'I'm a Christian, but…but…but…'"
>
> "Oh, I get it," I responded. "I thought you meant 'Christian butt'—b-u-t-t."
>
> She went right on. "Why should I have to explain to people 'I'm a Christian, but I don't think homosexuals are evil…I'm a Christian, but I believe women are equal to men…but I'm concerned about poverty…but I care about the Earth…but I don't think people who believe differently from me will fry in hell for eternity…?'"[3]

It was this dialogue with "a frustrated but searching for something better" Jenny, that led Eric Elnes to ask, how is it that the word Christian has become synonymous with *butthead?*

In his book *The Heart of Christianity,* Marcus Borg of Oregon State University describes how his university students have a uniformly negative image of Christianity. "When I ask them to write a short essay on their impression of Christianity," says Borg, "they consistently use five adjectives: Christians are literalistic, anti-intellectual, self-righteous, judgmental, and bigoted."[4]

Many within the Christian community might object rather defensively with this assessment, arguing that it is unfair to draw such sweeping generalizations. If you think that way, you'd be right in your logic but wrong in your conclusion. In his book, *UnChristian: What a New Generation Really Thinks about Christianity and Why it Matters,*[5] David Kinnaman, who is with the Barna Group, presents objective data that supports Borg's subjective anecdote. His three-year study documents how an overwhelming percentage of sixteen to twenty-nine year olds view Christians with hostility, resentment, and disdain.

According to Kinnaman's Barna study here are the percentages of people outside the church who think that the following words describe present-day Christianity:

- Anti-homosexual (91%)
- Judgmental (87%)
- Hypocritical (85%)
- Old-fashioned (78%)
- Too political (75%)
- Out of touch with reality (72%)
- Insensitive to others (70%)
- Boring (68%)

Kinnaman says it would be hard to overestimate, "...how firmly people reject—and feel rejected by—Christians."[6]

> "The nation's population is increasingly resistant to Christianity...the aversion and hostility are, for the first time, crystallizing in the attitudes of millions of young Americans. A huge chunk of a new generation has concluded they want nothing to do with us. As Christians, we are widely distrusted by a skeptical generation. We are at a turning point for Christianity

> in America. If we do not wake up to these realities and respond in appropriate ways, we risk being increasingly marginalized and losing further credibility with millions of people."[7]

Outsiders consider the Christian faith as it is practiced today to be unchristian, that is, "they think Christians no longer represent what Jesus had in mind, and that Christianity in our society is not what it was meant to be."[8]

The final assessment among outsiders? Something has gone terribly wrong with modern Christianity and they find it completely irrelevant.

Endnotes

[1] Eric Elnes, The Phoenix Affirmations, (Jossey-Bass Press, ©2006), xiv.

[2] *Denver Post* article, Oct. 26, 2010 p. 3, Section A.

[3] Elnes, xiv. Used with permission. All rights reserved.

[4] Marcus Borg, *The Heart of Christianity,* (Harper Press, ©2003), p. 21.

[5] David Kinnaman, *UnChristian: What a New Generation Really Thinks about Christianity and Why it Matters,* (Baker Books, ©2007) p.27.

[6] Ibid, p. 19.

[7] Ibid, p.39.

[8] Ibid, p. 15.

7

The Rise and Fall of Evangelicalism

This was a challenging chapter to write. In an attempt to chronicle some of the history of the Christian movement, I felt like I was walking on a tightrope. Let me say upfront that I'm not a church historian. There are many fine scholars who have devoted their lives to the study of church history. That being said, however, I'd like to share some thoughts.

There are two pitfalls to avoid. The history of Christianity is extremely complex and convoluted, so the first difficulty is to not get bogged down with too many details. I know history can be boring to some, but in this case having a general understanding of where we've come from as a Christian community is important. The second trap to be avoided is being so general that my treatment of recent events may be perceived as superficial or inadequate. What is important to me is that I convey, with accuracy, a few of the events that have shaped the current Christian scene in America.

I must have been about six or seven years old when I visited my grandparents one summer. I would stay with them every year for a couple of weeks and always had a great time. They lived in a very small town in the middle of Kansas. Grandpa owned one of the only two grocery stores in the hamlet and everyone knew him. Because of that, I would get special treatment and a lot of attention on my visits with them because I was "E. G.'s grandson."

On this particular occasion an event occurred that I still remember with great detail some 50 years later. We were going to have fried chicken for dinner so Grandpa went out to the hen house, grabbed a chicken, and brought it into the back yard. As a little boy I was fascinated with this whole process—up to a point. Once Grandpa got to the back yard he proceeded to wring the chicken's neck, breaking it very quickly and then with a hatchet chopped off its head.

It's what happened next that still remains as one of my greatest nightmares. The headless chicken began to chase me around the yard. If I went left, it went left. If I went right, it went right. If I zigzagged, it would zigzag, following me every step of the way (or so it seemed). With blood spurting out of it's now headless body and me screaming my head off in terror as it pursued me around the garden, it was a sight to behold. Grandma and Grandpa were both laughing hysterically at the spectacle. It wasn't that they were being mean or sadistic. I was a city boy. They were farm people and they were used to seeing a chicken flop around without its head. I wasn't.

I later learned that even though a chicken may be headless, there are still nerves that are reacting throughout the body causing it to move and fidget. This particular one must have had a lot of nerves because it was doing a whole lot more than fidgeting, as evidenced by my screaming like a maniac. I still remember how much I used to love my Grandma's fried chicken. I'll have to confess that after that day, it never had quite the same appeal.

Evangelicalism is somewhat like that decapitated chicken. The movement is dying, but in many ways one would not be able to discern that fact. It is still moving and shaking and touching some lives, but for all practical purposes, losing its impact. It's just that the obituary hasn't yet been written. Sadly, whenever that obituary *is* penned, I'm afraid one of the lines will have to be: "The movement died by suicide." We'll come back to that in a bit, but first some history.

History

There have been three primary movements that have defined conservative Christianity in the 20th and 21st Centuries—Fundamentalism, Evangelicalism, and Pentecostalism (Charismatics). While those within these groups like to regard themselves as the heirs of original Christianity, this is not an accurate view because these factions have emphasized certain doctrines and beliefs which were never very important within the Christian tradition and which do not appear to have played any particular role in the early church. Some of those doctrines would be dispensationalism, premillennialism, biblical inerrancy, and baptism of the Holy Spirit as evidenced by speaking in tongues.

How did these movements originate? All three of them began around the turn of the 20th Century. As such, it is important to note that they are all relative newcomers to the Christian scene. When compared to our 2,000-year history, any development within Christianity that is just a little over 100 years old would be considered a Johnny-come-lately. However, because these groups developed somewhat simultaneously with the advance of radio and television, these expressions of the Christian faith are the ones that most Americans are familiar with. The majority of airtime both on radio and Christian television is dominated by fundamentalist, evangelical, or charismatic programming. The second thing to note is that these three expressions of the faith are not the only representations of Christianity or the exclusive articulations of the faith, nor, as some might have us believe, are they the only *right* manifestations of Christianity. They are simply different forms of a faith that has taken on many different iterations in its 2000 years of development.

Towards the end of the 19th and into the 20th Century, there were a number of massive cultural shifts taking place that began to press in upon the traditional church in America. Tickle lists many of these (p. 76 ff.), including such factors as advances in science and psychology; Einstein's theory of Quantum physics; Albert Schweitzer's *The Quest of the Historical Jesus;* the invention of the car; and Karl Marx and a new political theory. Moving closer to our time she also talks about the Immigration and Nationality Services Act; the drug age of the 1960s through the 1970s; and moral shifts within our country, including the abortion decision Roe v. Wade, and the right-to-die activist, Jack Kevorkian.

For our purpose here I'd like to focus on three changes that early on became perceived threats to many thoughtful Christians. Two of the threats were external events that forced the church into a defensive posture with society. A third threat was an internal development that occurred within Christian theology which resulted in a split, initially known as the modernists versus the fundamentalists, later designated liberals and conservatives.

Charles Darwin and *Origin of the Species*

Without question Charles Darwin's theory of evolution rattled the very foundation of Christianity as it had been known. When *Origin of the Species* was published in 1859 the book produced a wide range of religious responses at a time of changing ideas and increasing secularization. The issues raised by the book were complex and there was a large middle ground of thought surrounding the ideas presented.

Even though the book barely hinted at the idea of human evolution, it quickly became central to the debate among Christian educators, pastors, and theologians. Some were open to the ideas presented within the book and felt they were compatible with Christian thought, while others perceived Darwin's theories as nothing less than an outright assault upon the sacred Scriptures and their teaching of humankind being created by God, in the image of God.

Sigmund Freud and the Theory of Human Psychosexual Development

Sigmund Freud was an Austrian born neurologist who founded the psychoanalytic school of psychiatry. His theories on human development and behavior were far-reaching and multi-faceted, but he seems to be best known among the general public as the man who developed the ideas of the *id, ego,* and *super-ego.* That, along with his theory of psychosexual development (the idea that much human behavior, development, and growth can be traced to sexual origins) was enough to again alarm the religious community of the early 1900s.

Having developed from strong Puritanical roots, American Christianity has long viewed sex in a negative light. It's been considered inappropriate to discuss; the covering of their private parts after Adam and Eve's sin proved the shamefulness of our naked bodies; and the sexual act has often been thought to be "dirty" and only necessary for the ongoing propagation of the human race. When Freud and others began to discuss sex openly and even suggest that human behavior can be strongly tied to our sexual needs, this was a direct, immoral affront to Christian "decency" and more than many morally upright Christians could tolerate.

The Development of Two Criticisms

Darwin and Freud were two of the perceived external threats to the faith. However a third threat was brewing within Christianity itself. It would prove to create a perfect storm, which is still resonating today: the development of Higher Criticism or Textual Criticism as opposed to Lower Criticism. Generally these terms are reserved for seminary classrooms as most rank and file Christians have little use for the type of heady discussions these subjects produce. They are very important, however, because these concepts play significantly into the new Re•Formation the church is experiencing.

- Lower Criticism

Lower criticism is the study of the ancient manuscripts of the Bible. Over the last few centuries, thousands of these manuscripts (generally small bits and pieces of various books) have been uncovered. Lower criticism seeks to look at these manuscripts, compare them, note minor textual, grammatical, and other small differences, and then try to reconstruct what the original document may have said based on a careful study of all the variations in these copies.

As an example, let's take one of the letters of the Apostle Paul: Romans. The original letter to the Romans would have been written (usually with the help of a scribe, taking down what Paul was saying) on parchment or vellum (animal skin). Once completed, the letter would have been sent off to Rome where the community of believers would have read it. The early Christians wanted to have copies of that letter, so the process of duplicating it would begin. Before the days of copy machines, this was a very time intensive, laborious process that could result in numerous human errors being made in the transcription process. Over the centuries, many hundreds of copies may have been made and distributed to various churches. As those documents are discovered in modern times, lower criticism compares all these documents against one another to see what differences there may be. From this study scholars seek to determine what the original letter may have actually said.

It's important to note that every modern version of the Bible makes use of lower criticism in order to determine which Hebrew (Old Testament) or Greek (New Testament) manuscript would be the best one to use in order to translate the Bible into English. Obviously this becomes a subjective decision based on the thoughts of the scholars making the translation.

- Higher Criticism

Higher Criticism is significantly more complicated. This particular approach of studying the Bible had been developing in Europe long before it hit the United States, but Bible scholars in America began using this approach in earnest in the 1880s.

Higher criticism is part of the historical-critical method for studying the Bible. Scholars assumed that one could study the Bible like one would any other ancient book by applying all the scientific and critical methods to the study. In this approach there would be the attempt to establish the authorship, date, and place of composition of the original text. Attempting to place a passage of Scripture or a book of the

Bible in its historical and cultural context is extremely important in Higher Criticism.

An example might be helpful.[1]

Basics of the Historical-Critical Method

What Happened in History	Stage	How We Study It
	Jesus uses parables (example, parable of the sower Matthew 13.3-9)	
Various hearers repeat the parable to one another, possibly for more than one generation. For example person A tells it to person B who then tells person C and so forth.	↓	Form Criticism
	An oral tradition exists of what Jesus said	
The collection of parables is written down and circulates apart form any gospel--all the parables in Matthew 13, for example.	↓	Source Criticism
	A written collection of parables is in circulation	
An author takes the collection of parables, other collections of sayings or deeds, and information from his own knowledge, and creates a final gospel text, putting the material in order, placing emphasis on certain topics, creating transitions, and modifying specific vocabulary to fit his themes.	↓	Redaction Criticism
	A final gospel text (Matthew)	
Matthew is copied by hand many times, with some copies preserved. Different copies contain different errors	↓	Textual Criticism
	A copy of the Greek text of Matthew is prepared for a translator, such as in a modern Greek New Testament	

1. The parables are commonly thought to have been collected first in Mark or in a source before Mark, and then copied to Matthew and Luke. There were some independent parables (Luke 16, for example).

Higher Criticism is focused on a careful study of the text of the Bible to look for sources behind the documents as we have them. For instance, it is generally agreed that Matthew, Mark, and Luke share common material, but who borrowed from whom, and did they have common sources they each used? And why, if they did have common sources, do their stories at times disagree significantly from one another?

As Higher Criticism evolved over the last 100 years it has been used to make some extreme pronouncements and come to some alarming conclusions.

> "The Bible was often seen by higher critics as a merely human document that had undergone various revisions over time, as was true of other ancient books. More radical higher critics questioned the authorship of virtually all of the books of the Bible and determined that many were written long after the events described in the books, and that they may have included a significant amount of material that was not historical at all. In other words, much of the Bible was thought, by the radical higher critics to be mythological in nature. This in turn, called into question virtually every doctrine of the Christian faith."[2]

The Rise of Fundamentalism

As this method of studying the Bible became more widespread especially as the more radical higher critics began publishing their ideas, it is easy to understand how a backlash would develop among more conservative Christians. This approach to understanding the Bible was perceived as a huge threat to Christians who took the Bible literally and accepted at face value everything that was written within its pages.

In response, a conference was held. In 1895 the Conference of Conservative Protestants met in Niagara Falls and they issued a statement of five principles they said were absolutely necessary to claim true Christian belief. These five beliefs were further developed and expanded when *The Fundamentals: A Testimony of the Truth* was published between 1910 and 1912. It was a set of 90 essays in 12 volumes outlining the core beliefs that were supposed to be required of all Christians. For our purposes, the first five principles are the only ones we need to review. The first principle focused on the Bible itself, the other four centered on the person and work of Jesus:

1. Inerrancy of Scripture

The idea is that the Bible is fully inspired by God with every word placed in the minds of the writers by God's Spirit. This is known as "verbal, plenary (full) inspiration." Consequently the Bible is without error *in the original manuscripts.* This last phrase had to be added because it was already apparent through the study of lower criticism that there were differences in the manuscripts that had already been unearthed, so the idea of inerrancy had to apply to the "original autographs," the first writings of the biblical documents—ones that no one now possesses.

For example the doctrinal statement of one of the evangelical seminaries in the United States says, "We believe the Scriptures of the Old and New Testaments are the inspired Word of God, inerrant in the original writings, complete as the revelation of God's will for salvation, and the supreme and final authority in all matters to which they speak."[3]

2. Divinity of Jesus

The idea that Jesus was fully and completely God.

3. Virgin birth of Jesus

The idea that Jesus was actually born of a virgin girl named Mary. The Holy Spirit conceived the child within her and thus no human male was Jesus' biological father.

4. Substitutionary nature of the atonement

The idea that the death of Jesus Christ was an atonement (an act that paid for the sins of the human race). We deserved to die because of our sin, but Christ stood in our place and took God's punishment for our sin. Thus Jesus became our substitute.

5. Bodily return of Jesus

The idea that Jesus is literally and bodily going to return to earth someday to establish the Kingdom of God.

These five principles became known as "the fundamentals" from which **Fundamentalism** was born. Sometime later, a new group began to emerge from Fundamentalism and they added two other items to this list:

6. The necessity to evangelize

While it has long been the belief that Christians have the privilege of taking the good news of Jesus Christ to those who had not yet heard, this codified the idea. It made it a requirement for being a genuine Christian. If people weren't sharing their faith, their salvation was questionable.

7. A belief in Jesus as a personal savior

This idea became a unique development. Rather than having the belief that Jesus Christ is the Savior and people should seek to submit to his authority over their lives and live their lives according to his teachings in the context of a community of faith, this made the Christian faith very individualistic, personal, and frequently emotional. The way you became a Christian was by reciting what became known as the "sinner's prayer." It was a prayer where people verbally acknowledged their sin and separation from God, repented of it, and asked Jesus Christ to come into their life and be their personal savior from sin. Rather than making a confession of faith that stated, "I believe that Jesus Christ is the Son of God, the Savior," it became "Yes, BUT–is Jesus *your personal* savior?" This unique way of experiencing salvation was widely popularized by evangelist Billy Graham.

With the addition of these two principles, a new version of Christianity was birthed out of fundamentalism: **Evangelicalism.** These seven tenets have been the bedrock of fundamental and evangelical Christianity ever since.

Earlier I also mentioned the Pentecostal or Charismatic movement that has also been a significant part of Christianity over the last 100 years. Tickle perceives it to be one of the major religious shifts of the 20th Century because currently Pentecostal and Charismatic Christians number over 500 million, making it second only to Roman Catholicism as the world's largest Christian body.

It might be well to briefly touch on it here. The current Charismatic movement can trace its roots back through Pentecostalism to the Azusa Street Revival that took place in Los Angeles, California. It started with a meeting on April 14, 1906, and continued until roughly 1916. The revival was characterized by ecstatic spiritual experiences, miraculous healings, speaking in tongues, dramatic worship services, and inter-racial mingling (something quite foreign within churches at the turn of the century). At the time participants were strongly criticized by the secular media as well as Christian theologians for behaviors that were considered to be outrageous and unorthodox. Here's an example from the *Los Angeles Times:*

> "Meetings are held in a tumble-down shack on Azusa Street, and the devotees of the weird doctrine practice the most fanatical rites, preach the wildest theories and work themselves into a state of mad excitement in their peculiar zeal. Colored people and a sprinkling of whites compose the congregation, and night is made hideous in the neighborhood by the howlings of the worshippers, who spend hours swaying forth and back in a nerve-racking attitude of prayer and supplication. They claim to have the 'gift of tongues' and be able to understand the babel."[4]

The Pentecostal movement holds to five key beliefs:

1. Salvation by faith
2. Sanctification (or holiness) of the believer
3. Speaking in tongues as evidence of the Baptism of the Holy Spirit
4. Faith healing as part of God's redemption
5. The very soon return of Christ

Today, the revival on Azusa Street is considered by historians to be the primary catalyst for the spread of Pentecostalism in the 20th Century. From this initial Pentecostal revival, the Charismatic movement was birthed and for a significant part of the 20th century had been one of the fastest growing segments of the Christian church both in America and worldwide.

Fundamentalism, Evangelicalism, and Pentecostalism—these three groups have become the primary contingent of the conservative wing of Christianity. As mentioned previously, it is these three versions of the Faith that most Americans are familiar with because their development and growth coincided with the first two significant mass media tools of the 20th Century—radio and television. That's why today, most of the religious programming you'll find will be highlighting one of these three faith expressions.

It is also significant to note that it has been within these three faith traditions that another 20th Century phenomena took place—the rise of the mega-church. These are churches with thousands of attendees at weekend services, multiple programs and ministries, huge staffs, large payrolls, and many millions of dollars invested in land and buildings. They are churches based on the ABC's of church growth—attendance, buildings, and contributions. By business standards, mega-churches are the epitome of success in a religious endeavor. Depending on one's theology some might say, "See, these churches are growing and successful because they are preaching the truth." However, beneath all the external trappings of success, the foundation is not as stable as one might think.

So What?

What difference does all of this historical review make to our discussion concerning the new Re•Formation? A great deal. For many years the conservative wing of Christianity has somewhat arrogantly highlighted the continuing decline of the liberal denominations. Pointing to groups like the Episcopalians, Presbyterians, Methodists, and others, leaders of the conservative Christian movement have maintained that the reason these denominations are in such numerical free fall is because they have forsaken the basic tenets of the faith while they (the conservative churches) are experiencing phenomenal growth because they've stayed true to the core Christian beliefs.

Consider the following:

- At its peak in the 1960s the Episcopal Church had over 3.4 million members. As of 2009 the membership was just a little over 2 million.
- Since 1965 the Presbyterian Church USA has lost 1½ million members.
- According to one calculation, the United Methodist Church has lost 1,000 members a week for the last thirty years. When the United Methodist Church was formed in 1968 by the joining together of Evangelical United Brethren Church and the Methodist Church, it had over 11 million members. Today in America that number is around 8 million.

The obvious conclusion that has been drawn by these startling statistics is that the mainline churches are in crisis. This is not news. In 1996 Thomas Reeves published a book which examined this American crisis: *The Empty Church: The Suicide of Liberal Christianity.* The book documents the decline and possible extinction of these historic churches. Reeves said, "Churches today are all too often, very predictable, very liberal, very permissive, and without any sort of demands being made on the people. And for millions of Americans there seems to be simply, no reason to go."

However, while it is true that conservative churches have experienced phenomenal growth over the last 40 years, that growth now seems to have stalled and indeed, is now headed down. The conservative churches are beginning to experience a decline similar to what the liberal denominations began to encounter 50 to 60 years ago—it's just that we're viewing the beginning of this trend. It will become much more apparent over the next 20 to 30 years.

Consider the following:

- The 2009 *Yearbook of American and Canadian Churches* chronicled a loss of 40,000 members in the behemoth (and seemingly resilient) Southern Baptism Convention. Now, that's a very small decline, but it was a jolt that produced panic among some Baptists. Over the last decade the SBC has dropped from 18 million to 16 million members. And according to journalist Christine Wicker,[5] the internal number of active members may well be around five million.
- The Lutheran Church Missouri Synod, which has been run by what moderates saw as a quasi-fundamentalist take-over party in the 1970s, always advertised that it was blessed because it was conservative and firm. In 1970 the church reported 2.8 million members. As of 2006, membership was reported at 2.4 million members.
- The conservative branch of the Presbyterian Church (the PCA—Presbyterian Church in America) lost members in 2009 for the first time in its 37-year history.

Taken individually, these numerical regressions might seem sketchy at best. But when taken with other examples, they become snapshots of what quantitative surveys have been pointing out for the last few years—membership decline isn't only the struggle of liberal churches.

In the April 4, 2009, *Newsweek* cover story, Jon Meacham wrote an article entitled, "The End of Christian America." In the article he shows that many conservative Christian groups aren't doing that well. The old accusation—and theological threat used by conservatives against mainline denominations—that the denominations have failed because they are too liberal—is now being proved false by both qualitative journalists and quantitative researchers. Almost *all* Christian institutions are experiencing slowing growth and/or membership declines. The only growing Christian churches in North America are "non-denominational," and those congregations are difficult to classify theologically because they are so diverse.

The article quotes the 2009 "American Religious Identification Survey" that discovered that the number of Americans who claim no religious affiliation has nearly doubled since 1990, rising from 8 to 15 percent. The president of the Southern Baptist Theological Seminary, R. Albert Mohler Jr. said, "A remarkable culture-shift has taken place around us. The most basic contours of American culture have been radically altered. The so-called Judeo-Christian consensus of the last millennium has given way to a post-modern, post-Christian, post-Western cultural crisis which threatens the very heart of our culture. Clearly there is a new narrative, a post-Christian narrative that is animating large portions of this society."

On www.beliefnet.com, Diana Butler Bass wrote an article, *The Real Decline of Churches.* Here's part of what she says:

> "What is causing the erosion of Christianity in North America? Most North Americans look at Christianity--especially as embodied in religious institutions–and find it wanting. I suspect that Christianity is in decline because it appears both hypocritical and boring. Although young North Americans express deep longings for a loving, just, and peaceful world, they don't find an equal passion for transforming society in meaningful ways in most congregations. And, sadly, many churches simply lack the imagination and passion that many spiritual people are searching for. Folks aren't looking for answers nearly as much as they are trying to clarify their questions and are hungry for accepting communities in which to ask them.

> If you think about it, mainline liberal churches embody a theological vision of God's reign that resonates with contemporary hopes for social transformation. But they often lack passion, acting on God's dream for the world in business-as-usual ways. Conservative churches are chock-full of passion. But they are often passionate about all the wrong stuff–like excluding people and supporting the military-and-economic status quo that is destroying the planet.
> Perhaps North American Christians are smarter than anyone suspects—that we are looking for congregations, communities and denominations that put the pieces together—passionate, imaginative, open, justice-seeking, inclusive, and loving gatherings of faith that actually live, as Jimmy Carter put it, 'the teachings of Jesus Christ.' If progressive faith communities can be both—transformative and passionate—we may be better poised to reach a new generation than the 'decline' bellyaching of recent decades suggests. With the waning of conservative churches, it may well be the historical moment for the rest of us to step up to the spiritual plate."[6]

In 2009, shortly before his death, Michael Spencer wrote a number of blogs on the coming collapse of evangelicalism. Taken together, they convey a powerful message:

> "We are on the verge—within 10 years—of a major collapse of evangelical Christianity. This breakdown will follow the deterioration of the mainline Protestant world and it will fundamentally alter the religious and cultural environment in the West. Within two generations, evangelicalism will be a house deserted of half its occupants. (Between 25 and 35 percent of Americans today are Evangelicals.) In the 'Protestant' 20th century, Evangelicals flourished. But they will

soon be living in a very secular and religiously antagonistic 21st century.

This collapse will herald the arrival of an anti-Christian chapter of the post-Christian West. Intolerance of Christianity will rise to levels many of us have not believed possible in our lifetimes, and public policy will become hostile toward evangelical Christianity, seeing it as the opponent of the common good.

Millions of Evangelicals will quit. Thousands of ministries will end. Christian media will be reduced, if not eliminated. Many Christian schools will go into rapid decline. I'm convinced the grace and mission of God will reach to the ends of the earth. But the end of evangelicalism as we know it is close.

Why is this going to happen?

1. Evangelicals have identified their movement with the culture war and with political conservatism. This will prove to be a very costly mistake. Evangelicals will increasingly be seen as a threat to cultural progress. Public leaders will consider us bad for America, bad for education, bad for children, and bad for society.

The evangelical investment in moral, social, and political issues has depleted our resources and exposed our weaknesses. Being against gay marriage and being rhetorically pro-life will not make up for the fact that massive majorities of Evangelicals can't articulate the Gospel with any coherence. We fell for the trap of believing in a cause more than a faith.

2. We Evangelicals have failed to pass on to our young people an orthodox form of faith that can take root and survive the secular onslaught. Ironically, the billions of dollars we've spent on youth ministers, Christian music, publishing, and media has produced a culture of young Christians who know next to nothing about their own faith except how they feel about it. Our young people have deep beliefs about the culture war, but do not know why they should obey Scripture, the essentials of theology, or the experience of spiritual discipline and community. Coming generations of Christians are going to be monumentally ignorant and unprepared for culture-wide pressures.

3. There are three kinds of evangelical churches today: consumer-driven mega churches, dying churches, and new churches whose future is fragile. Denominations will shrink, even vanish, while fewer and fewer evangelical churches will survive and thrive.

4. Despite some very successful developments in the past 25 years, Christian education has not produced a product that can withstand the rising tide of secularism. Evangelicalism has used its educational system primarily to staff its own needs and talk to itself.

5. The confrontation between cultural secularism and the faith at the core of evangelical efforts to 'do good' is rapidly approaching. We will soon see that the good Evangelicals want to do will be viewed as bad by so many, and much of that work will not be done. Look for ministries to take on a less and less distinctively Christian face in order to survive.

6. Even in areas where Evangelicals imagine themselves strong (like the Bible Belt), we will find a great inability to pass on to our children a vital evangelical confidence in the Bible and the importance of the faith.

7. The money will dry up.

What will be left?

- Expect evangelicalism to look more like the pragmatic, therapeutic, church-growth oriented mega churches that have defined success. Emphasis will shift from doctrine to relevance, motivation, and personal success—resulting in churches further compromised and weakened in their ability to pass on the faith.

- Two of the beneficiaries will be the Roman Catholic and Orthodox communions. Evangelicals have been entering these churches in recent decades and that trend will continue, with more efforts aimed at the 'conversion' of Evangelicals to the Catholic and Orthodox traditions.
- A small band will work hard to rescue the movement from its demise through theological renewal. This is an attractive, innovative, and tireless community with outstanding media, publishing, and leadership development. Nonetheless, I believe the coming evangelical collapse will not result in a second reformation, though it may result in benefits for many churches and the beginnings of new churches.
- The emerging church will largely vanish from the evangelical landscape, becoming part of the small segment of progressive mainline Protestants who remain true to the liberal vision.
- Aggressively evangelistic fundamentalist churches will begin to disappear.
- Charismatic-Pentecostal Christianity will become the majority report in evangelicalism. Can this community withstand heresy, relativism, and confusion? To do so, it must make a priority of biblical authority, responsible leadership, and a reemergence of orthodoxy.
- Evangelicalism needs a 'rescue mission' from the world Christian community. It is time for missionaries to come to America from Asia and Africa. Will they come? Will they be able to bring to our culture a more vital form of Christianity?

- Expect a fragmented response to the culture war. Some Evangelicals will work to create their own countercultures, rather than try to change the culture at large. Some will continue to see conservatism and Christianity through one lens and will engage the culture war much as before — a status quo the media will be all too happy to perpetuate. A significant number, however, may give up political engagement for a discipleship of deeper impact.

Is all of this a bad thing?

Evangelicalism doesn't need a bailout. Much of it needs a funeral. But what about what remains? Is it a good thing that denominations are going to become largely irrelevant? Only if the networks that replace them are able to marshal resources, training, and vision to the mission field and into the planting and equipping of churches.

Is it a good thing that many marginal believers will depart? Possibly, if churches begin and continue the work of renewing serious church membership. We must change the conversation from the maintenance of traditional churches to developing new and culturally appropriate ones.

The ascendency of Charismatic-Pentecostal influenced worship around the world can be a major positive for the evangelical movement if reformation can reach those churches and if it is joined with the calling, training, and mentoring of leaders. If American churches come under more of the influence of the movement of the Holy Spirit in Africa and Asia, this will be a good thing.

Will the evangelicalizing of Catholic and Orthodox communions be a good development? One can hope for greater unity and appreciation, but the history of these developments seems to be much more about a renewed vigor to "evangelize" Protestantism in the name of unity.

Will the coming collapse get Evangelicals past the pragmatism and shallowness that has brought about the loss of substance and power? Probably not. The purveyors of the evangelical circus will be in fine form, selling their wares as the promised solution to every church's problems. I expect the landscape of mega church vacuity to be around for a very long time.

Will it shake lose the prosperity Gospel from its parasitical place on the evangelical body of Christ? Evidence from similar periods is not encouraging. American Christians seldom seem to be able to separate their theology from an overall idea of personal affluence and success.

The loss of their political clout may impel many Evangelicals to reconsider the wisdom of trying to create a "godly society." That doesn't mean they'll focus solely on saving souls, but the increasing concern will be how to keep secularism out of church, not stop it altogether. The integrity of the church as a countercultural movement with a message of 'empire subversion' will increasingly replace a message of cultural and political entitlement.

Despite all of these challenges, it is impossible not to be hopeful. As one commenter has already said, 'Christianity loves a crumbling empire.'

We can rejoice that in the ruins, new forms of Christian vitality and ministry will be born. I expect to see a vital and growing house church movement. This cannot help but be good for an evangelicalism that has made buildings, numbers, and paid staff its drugs for half a century.

We need new evangelicalism that learns from the past and listens more carefully to what God says

> about being His people in the midst of a powerful, idolatrous culture.
>
> I'm not a prophet. My view of evangelicalism is not authoritative or infallible. I am certainly wrong in some of these predictions. But is there anyone who is observing evangelicalism in these times who does not sense that the future of our movement holds many dangers and much potential?"[7]

When Spencer's thoughts first appeared, they created quite a buzz. Many felt he grossly overstated the seriousness of the problem that exists within conservative Christianity. I don't think so. As stated at the beginning of this chapter, I believe Evangelicalism is somewhat like that chicken my grandfather decapitated. The movement is dying, but in many ways one would not be able to discern that fact. It's still moving and shaking and touching some lives, but as a movement, it no longer is capable of addressing the issues of a post-Christian society.

One of the biggest tragedies of the entire last century has been this: the church of Jesus Christ has not been able to penetrate our society in any significant way. The vast majority of church growth that takes place in America today is really nothing more than aquarium swapping. It's the fish deciding that the aquarium they've been swimming in no longer works for them, so they hop over to another aquarium because it has prettier rocks, more fish to swim with, and bigger bubbles to keep them entertained.

In other words, seeing people who have been walking in darkness come to embrace the light of love and truth as seen in Jesus (known as conversion) has not happened. Yet pastors and leaders of growing congregations pat themselves on the back because they are "making a difference and changing the world for God." Often their churches are filled with people who have simply left another church in search of something that will meet their perceived needs in a better, more fulfilling way.

In fairness, some within evangelical circles are trying to bring new life into their churches. They intuitively sense that something is horribly wrong. But I fear they're not addressing the real issues that need to be tackled. They think that by having a different kind of music, using more video, using candles and prayer stations and other "innovative" ideas, they will be able to infuse life into a body where the death rattle has begun. Those are surface level, cosmetic changes that *might* be of some help. But this approach reminds me of Charlie Brown in the "Peanuts" comic strip. At Christmas time he has this pathetic, scraggly, almost dead Christmas tree. But it is his tree. He hangs an ornament or two on it in an attempt to make it look good. Unfortunately it doesn't work. It still is a pathetic, almost dead tree. But it is *his* tree and it brings a smile to his face. Unless cosmetic changes are being infused with systemic transformation, the future for evangelicalism is bleak.

We know the church continually needs to engage new methods in order to try and connect with an increasingly disconnected society, but church leaders are only kidding themselves if they believe those external changes will help address the fundamental shift that is taking place. There is a new Re•Formation on the horizon and candle-lit sanctuaries, relevant videos, and engaging music are not going to address the fundamental issues. We must stop thinking we can put new wine into old wineskins. New wine calls for new wineskins.

Endnotes

[1] From www.participatorystudyseries.com, "What is Biblical Criticism?" Used with permission.

[2] Adam Hamilton, *Seeing Gray in a World of Black and White,* p. 60. Used with permission.

[3] Denver Seminary

[4] Jack W. Hayford & David S. Moore, *The Charismatic Century: The Enduring Impact of the Azusa Street Revival* (August, ©2006 ed.).

[5] Christine Wicker, *The Fall of the Evangelical Nation: The Surprising Crisis Inside the Church* (HarperOne, ©2008).

[6] Read more of Diana Bass' article at: http://blog.beliefnet.com/progressiverevival/2009/07/-three-news-stories-in.html#ixzz16n9fshLC. Used with permission.

[7] Michael Spencer, founder of www.InternetMonk.com. Used with permission.

Part Two

The Issues

8

What about the Bible?

"Conflict about the Bible is the single most divisive issue among Christians in North America today."[1]

"What is the Bible? It is a book written by people who lived in ancient times, with their own biases and limitations in knowledge, who had great insights and experiences of God, yet who were also capable of misunderstandings, inconsistencies, and writing things that may have been important to their first readers, but not necessarily timeless words that apply in every situation. And it is a book through which God has spoken and still speaks, one that is 'living and active' and through which God comforts, challenges, and inspires, the very reading of which has the power to change lives."[2]

"For the past few centuries, this earlier way of seeing Christianity, what I call an 'earlier paradigm,' has been shared in common by most Christians in Western culture. It remains a major voice within North American Christianity, perhaps still the majority voice. This earlier way of being Christian views the Bible as the unique revelation of God, emphasizes its literal meaning, and sees the Christian life as centered in believing now for the sake of salvation later—believing in God, the Bible, and Jesus as the way to heaven. Typically, it

has also seen Christianity as the only true religion. The second way of seeing Christianity, the 'emerging paradigm,' has been developing for over a hundred years and has recently become a major grass-roots movement within mainline denominations. Positively, it is the product of Christianity's encounter with the modern and postmodern world, including science, historical scholarship, religious pluralism, and cultural diversity. Less positively, it is the product of our awareness of how Christianity has contributed to racism, sexism, nationalism, exclusivism, and other harmful ideologies."[3]

Over the last 100 years, some terms have come to be closely associated with the authority and role of the Bible in Christian experience. In particular three words are of great importance: **inspired**, **inerrant**, and **infallible**. Of these three, only one is used in the Bible to describe the Bible: inspired. This word was used by the Apostle Paul[4] in II Timothy 3.16 when he wrote, "All Scripture is inspired by God and is useful for teaching, for reproof, for correction, and for training in righteousness...." The word inspired literally means "God-breathed." Since none of the New Testament was canonized when II Timothy was written, a basic assumption we could make about Paul's statement is that he was referring to the Old Testament with which he was intimately familiar. For better or for worse however, this verse has become the capstone covering all of the Old and New Testaments. Further muddying the waters are the additions of two other words that are used to talk about the Bible: the **verbal**, **plenary** inspiration of Scripture.

What do these terms mean?

Inerrant: "Incapable of erring, containing no errors"

Infallible: "Incapable of erring, incapable of failing"

Verbal: "Relating to or associated with words, concerned with words only rather than content or ideas"

Plenary: "Complete in all respects, unlimited or full"[5]

As one can see, the words inerrant and infallible are almost synonymous. As they relate to the Scriptures, they mean that there are no errors or mistakes in the Bible. As mentioned elsewhere, these two terms eventually came to be applied to the original manuscripts of Scripture (none of which we currently possess), since there are obvious differences between the thousands of discovered pieces of various parts of the Bible. The words verbal and plenary are taken together and as laid out in many doctrinal statements of churches, bible colleges, and seminaries, when they say, "We believe in the verbal, plenary inspiration of Scripture," they are asserting that God inspired the complete (plenary) texts of the Bible from Genesis to Revelation, including both historical and doctrinal details. The word verbal affirms the idea that inspiration extends to the very words the writers chose.

Taken together, all of these words provide the foundation for the literal interpretation of Scripture. Common sense would seem to indicate however, that by adding additional words like inerrant, infallible, verbal, and plenary to the one biblical word, inspired to try and help us clarify how we understand the Bible, the net result has been the opposite: it has painted literalists into a corner. And like a tiger that is cornered, the only way to try and escape is to attack. Thus you have the vitriolic assault against any idea or suggestion that would seemingly undermine this sacrosanct concept.

Marcus Borg offers some insight here:

"Christianity is centered in the Bible. Of course, it is ultimately centered in God, but it is the God of whom the Bible speaks and to whom it points. God is also known in other ways and other religions, I am convinced, but to be Christian is to be centered in the God of the Bible. This is a mark not of Christian exclusion, but of Christian sacred story. Yet the Bible has become a stumbling block for many. In the last half-century, probably more Christians have left the church because of the Bible than for any other single reason. More precisely, they left because the earlier paradigm's way of seeing the Bible ceased to make sense to them. Contemporary biblical literalism—with its emphasis on biblical infallibility, historical factuality, and moral and doctrinal absolutes—is an obstacle for millions of people.

An illustrative list of the kinds of claims that people find difficult when understood literally:

- That the earth (and the universe as a whole) was created in six days and not very long ago (Genesis 1-3)
- That Adam and Eve were real people, and 'the fall' brought death into the world (Genesis 2-3)
- That God sent a worldwide flood that destroyed all life, except for Noah, his family, and reproductive pairs of all animals who were saved in the ark (Genesis 6-7)
- That all people initially spoke the same language and only later were divided into different language groups (Genesis 11)
- That God ordered the slaughter of the Amalekites, men, women, children and infants (I Samuel 15.3)
- That God regulated (and therefore legitimated) slavery (found in both Testaments)
- That God cares (or has ever cared) about whether we wear garments made of two kinds of cloth (Leviticus 19.19)

> - That God ordered the subordination of women
> - That Jesus is the only way of salvation, and that people can be saved only by believing that he literally died for our sins
> - That unbelieving Jews are children of the devil (John 8.44)
> - That the second coming of Jesus will involve the destruction of most of humankind
>
> All of these (and many more) are in the Bible. Because of these, many simply cannot believe the premise of the earlier paradigm: that the Bible is a divine product and thus, in harder or softer forms, the infallible and inerrant Word of God. It is not because of what they don't know about the Bible that they have difficulty with infallibility and literalism. It's because of what they do know."[6]

For those who are literalists, these ideas are fighting words because they undermine everything these people hold dear. These words are heresy—spawned in the pit of hell. But, how we are to understand Scripture *will be* one of the key issues of the new Re•Formation. The literalism of the last 100 years will eventually make way for a more sane and sensible understanding of a book that contains both the Word of God and the word of culture. Does the Bible have all the answers? It depends on what the questions are. Perhaps some help might be given here by focusing on a more reflective approach to the Bible.

A Reflective Approach to the Bible

> "Reflective Christianity is uncomfortable with this [a literal, simplistic, cliché] approach to the Bible.

It raises questions such as, 'Does the Bible really provide divine guidance for every important daily problem?' 'Should the Bible be regarded as a collection of divine oracles that covers every conceivable, important, pressing issue facing contemporary society?' Or is the Bible's scope and authority limited to identifying who God is (his nature and character) and what God has done for us (redemption) and wants from us in terms of spiritual living (discipleship and devotion)? Does it contain a pattern for society beyond the church? Does it even offer answers to problems of governance? Should it be considered a source book or book of guiding principles for science? Can we derive from it solutions to psychological difficulties? Is there a biblical method of counseling?

Reflective Christianity raises such questions over folk religious attitudes and treatments of the Bible. An important step from folk Christianity to reflective Christianity is gaining a more profound perspective on the Bible's historical and human nature, as well as its intended purpose. Reflective Christianity is more concerned with principles than with propositions (assertions of fact) and with transformation than with information. The Bible is not merely a book of information, and if some of its information is culturally conditioned that doesn't mean it cannot still be a soul-transforming book. The Bible lacks clear propositional statements that address many pressing contemporary issues. Abortion is almost absent from the Bible. Nothing there speaks directly to cremation. The thorny problem of modern economics finds few if any solutions in the Bible. And what about cloning? It wasn't even envisioned by biblical authors. The point is that the Bible simply does not contain all the answers. For answers to many important issues we have to turn to tradition, reason, and

> experience,[7] which we always use anyway when interpreting the Bible.
>
> In short, there are urgent and pressing matters to which the Bible does not speak. Yes, as evangelical Christians we all believe that it contains authoritative answers for doctrine and for practical Christian living in the realm of morality. But we should grow out of thinking of the Bible as the one supernatural textbook for every important issue. The Bible identifies God for us and shapes us into godly persons as we allow the Spirit to work through it, but we cannot count on the Bible solving dilemmas of every kind. We have to turn to tradition, reason, and experience to discern the best approaches in many crucial matters."[8]

How Are We To Understand It?

There is no question that there are some great difficulties found within the pages of Scripture. I'm not sure who actually said this (since it has been attributed to a variety of different people) but whoever it was said, "If there are shallows in the Bible where a little child may wade, there are oceans where an adult must swim." There are parts of the Bible that are very easy to understand and then there are parts of it that we're simply not going to be able to figure out. We try. And in our attempts to "unscrew the inscrutable" we come up with a vast array of theological suppositions, positions, and ideas—which may or may not be accurate. One of the ongoing challenges believers face is trying to figure out how this ancient book can be relevant to us today.

Rather than being a book, the Bible is actually a collection of many books—66 to be exact (at least in the Protestant Bible). There are 39 in the Old Testament and 27 in the New Testament. These books were written over a period of 1500 years, by 40 plus authors on three different continents, and in three different languages (Hebrew, Greek, and Aramaic). The individuals who wrote these books had a variety of backgrounds–from unschooled fishermen to wealthy, educated noblemen. They lived in different cultures, different generations, different historical times, and obviously, most of the writers never met each other. Their writings are quite diverse, covering the history of the ancient Israelites, prophecy, poetry, proverbs, the teachings of Jesus, as well as the musings of the early leaders of the growing Christian movement. As such, the Bible then contains both the Word of God and the word of culture.

It's also important to realize that the various cultures in which the books of the Bible were written were all based on an Eastern mindset rather than a Western one. Why does this matter? Because it means they approached life from a different worldview than we do. This is not to say that their conclusions about truth were necessarily different from ours, but it does mean that they approached Scripture and God in a way in which we are unfamiliar. The Western mindset is more logical, more "legal" if you will, with thoughts moving from point A to point B in a rational manner. The Eastern mindset was more inclined toward philosophy and mysticism—more fluid. In other words, in telling a story or relating events they weren't as concerned with getting all the details correct so much as conveying the meaning and purpose behind the words they used. That helps us understand, for example the first two chapters of Genesis, where the stories don't match up with one another.

Or, ask a Westerner to describe God and you might hear things like, "God is…love, good, omniscient, omnipresent, holy, righteous, omnipotent…" These are all terms that bring *definition* to God. We are seeking to understand God with our mind. We approach God via *ideas.* Ask an ancient Hebrew to describe God and you would more than likely hear things like, "God is a rock, an eagle's wing, a consuming fire, a shield..." These are all words that bring *imagery* to God. They are words that bring God close to us because God is strong when we are weak, God is our nurturer, and God is our protector.

Faith would be another area where this difference would be seen. To us Westerners, "faith" is mainly what we believe. Once people have agreed that they believe in Jesus, they are pronounced saved. As a result, salvation is viewed as being granted to those who agree with a given theological statement or confession of faith. What one believes is more important than what one does. The Eastern mindset would see this differently. Jesus didn't say, "You will know them by their creeds" but rather "You will know them by their fruit" (Matthew 7:16, 20). When Jesus speaks of fruit, he is talking about how one lives–one's actions. In other words, what one does is the fruit of what one truly believes, and therefore deeds not creeds would be more of an accurate measure of faith. That's not to say that confession of truth isn't crucial (see, here's my Western mindset in action…I cannot not say that) but the point would be if our lives do not conform to that confession, then what's the point? Rather than seeking to place a precise definition around some biblical idea (the Western mindset), the Eastern mindset would focus more on experiencing it.

We see this Western mindset clearly expressed when we approach the subject of prophecy. People can almost become anal in putting together very detailed, specific prophetic charts and timelines, as they pull together all the various Old and New Testament prophecies that supposedly deal with the coming end of the age. They try and make them all fit with one another. First you have the rapture of the saints, and then you have the seven-year tribulation period. During the first 3½ years of the tribulation you have such and such going on, then in the last 3½ years you have such and such happening. Then we have the great battle of Armageddon where Satan and God fight it out. God wins and throws Satan into the pit for 1,000 years, known as the Millennium. Satan is briefly loosed one more time when he is finally cast into hell forever and the Kingdom of God is ushered in with a new heaven and a new earth. All of this (and a wide variety of iterations) is based on the Western mindset and our obsession with trying to make everything fit.

There is no shortage of books that delve deeply into the topic of how we approach the Bible. For my purpose here however, I'm primarily interested in trying to help us see how the Bible will be viewed in the coming Re•Formation. I believe there will be a much more straightforward, uncomplicated approach to the Bible in coming decades. This does not mean that it will be anti-intellectual or simplistic. Rather, it will be much less focused on the details and much more focused on the broad, general themes of the Bible that will provide direction and help for those who seek to make it their guidebook. In many ways, I think this will bring a new depth, richness, and texture to our reading of Scripture than what we currently possess. It will free us up from being so focused on detail (which, if we're honest with each other, has been at the root of all the denominational differences that separate Christians) and allow us to be more generous in spirit and understanding.

How are we to understand it? There are a few principles that guide us. First of all, it is important to recognize that

Jesus Christ is the center of Scripture. Christ becomes the benchmark for us to use in discerning the difference between the Word of God and the words of culture. There are numerous broad, general themes, also known as "meta-narratives"[9] found within the Bible, a primary one being the redemptive activity of God. The Old Testament themes of a covenant that God makes with people, and the prophecies of a coming Messiah testify to this activity. The heart of the New Testament is Jesus Christ, the Word made flesh, the fulfillment of Israel's messianic hope, and the King in the Kingdom of God. When we seek to understand Scripture, keeping Christ in the center of our thoughts and discussions helps us in evaluating the significance of the problems and controversies that have always persisted in the historical life of the church. John Calvin said, "In our reading of Scripture we shall hold simply to that which speaks clearly and definitely to our conscience and makes us feel that it leads us to Christ."

I think it interesting that the early Friends (the Quakers) rejected the mainstream Protestant idea of Sola Scriptura (Scripture Only). Rather they believed that Christ, instead of the Bible, is the Word of God. Robert Barclay wrote in his "Apology" that the Scriptures "...are only a declaration of the fountain, and not the fountain itself, therefore they are not to be esteemed the principal ground of all Truth and knowledge, nor yet the adequate primary rule of faith and manners."[10]

This first principle—that of keeping Jesus central to our understanding of the Bible—is not always an easy task. It makes our interaction with Scripture much more fluid. For example, it would be much simpler for us to live according to the black and white Hebrew laws of the Old Testament. There seems to be something in human nature that cries out for having someone tell us what to believe and defining our boundaries. It is a secure feeling to live inside of a box. A box makes us feel more comfortable, protected, and sheltered. I believe this is one of the reasons fundamental churches have a certain attraction for many—they provide that kind of confined faith and belief system. People don't have to think for themselves, they just follow the rules laid down by leadership and live their lives on autopilot. Trying to wrestle with the challenging issues our generation faces by processing them through the life and teachings of Jesus becomes overwhelming for some, but even though it is a more difficult road to travel, in the long run I believe it helps us develop a living, vital, and active faith that is much more in keeping with God's heart for humanity.

Another principle in understanding Scripture is this: we have to be careful not to love the Bible more than we love Jesus. Theologian and author Jim Mulholland said, "When we focus to much on the book, we miss the relationship it invites us to." Tickle's comment, that as Protestantism has evolved over the last 500 years, all we've done is replace a people pope with a paper one, resonates greatly with me. Jesus said something interesting in the gospel of John. I'd like to quote it in three different Bible versions so that we can get a better sense of his intent.

- "You diligently study the Scriptures because you think that by them you possess eternal life. These are the Scriptures that testify about me." John 5.39 (New International Version)
- "You search and investigate and pour over the Scriptures diligently, because you suppose and trust that you have eternal life through them. And these [very Scriptures] testify about me!" John 5.39 (Amplified Version)

- "You have your heads in your Bibles constantly because you think you'll find eternal life there. But you miss the forest for the trees. These Scriptures are all about me! And here I am, standing right before you and you aren't willing to receive from me the life you say you want." John 5.39 (The Message)

Echoing the position of the Quakers, Richard Wurmbrand (an evangelical pastor) wrote,

> "The Bible is a wonderful book. It is the truth about the Truth. It is not the Truth. A sermon taken from the Bible can be a wonderful thing to hear. It is the truth about the truth about the Truth. But it is not the Truth. There have been many books written about the things contained in the Bible. I have written some myself. They can be quite wonderful to read. They are the truth about the truth about the truth about the Truth. But they are NOT the Truth. Only Jesus Christ is the Truth. Sometimes the Truth can be drowned in a multitude of words."

Robert Brinsmead remarked, "The Bible in itself is not the Word of God. The Word of God is a person (John 1:1). Neither does the Bible have life, power or light in itself any more than did the Jewish Torah. These attributes may be ascribed to the Bible only by virtue of its relationship to Him who is Word, Life, Power and Light. Life is not in the book, as the Pharisees supposed, but only in the Man of the book (John 5:39)." Admittedly, Brinsmead has been a controversial figure within Seventh-Day Adventism, but these words concerning the Bible are correct.

As helpful as the Bible is, as encouraging as it is to read it, as wonderful as it is in helping us understand a little about

God and a lot about ourselves, I believe we have done a horrible injustice to the Scriptures by our insistence on almost deifying them. The Bible is in our possession, not primarily for information, but for transformation. Karl Barth, a German theologian in the last century, described the Bible in a powerful image when he wrote:

> "The Word of God that comes to us through the Scriptures is the long, strong hand of God that reaches out after us. What will happen to us in the grip of this hand is none of our business. We only need to know that we are in the grip of his hand. He who knows this understands the heart of the Bible."

Barth's words remind us that we are not to read the Bible for information only, as we might read an encyclopedia. Ultimately we read the Bible for transformation—the transformation of our heart and mind in the image and likeness of God. We read the Bible to discover who we are so that we may open ourselves to the Holy Spirit's power to re-create us in God's image. That transformation comes through a life-changing encounter with the person of Jesus and the empowerment of the Spirit. Do all of the theological differences (based on people's different understanding of the Bible) that separate and divide the thousands of denominations and sects within Christendom *really* matter?

In one of his more famous sermons entitled "Catholic Spirit," John Wesley makes a few points I feel are valid for this discussion. Wesley was frequently pictured as a man who was not very interested in theology, an exponent of practical Christianity rather than doctrinal Christianity. A contributing factor to this impression was Wesley's admonition to "think and let think." He used the expression frequently, such as, "the distinguishing marks of a Methodist are not his opinions of any sort...we think and let think."[11] However many who use this quotation fail to understand the crucial distinction Wesley made between opinion and essential doctrines. For Wesley, opinions were many, essential doctrines were few.

"Catholic Spirit" touches on this truth. The sermon is based on II Kings 10:15 where Jehu met Jehonadab and as he greeted him Jehu said, "Is your heart right, as my heart is with your heart?" Jehonadab answered, "It is." Jehu said, "If it is, give me your hand." The fundamental issue for us is this: regardless of our theological differences, are our hearts in one accord? Wesley was under no illusions regarding the differences of opinions Christians have about a wide variety of biblical issues. However, he said there is one primary responsibility *all* Christians have—that is to fulfill the royal law of love—loving our neighbors as we love ourselves. He then went on to say that there were two great hindrances that keep us from fulfilling this law: the first is that we cannot all think alike and second, that we cannot all walk alike. Then came the statement made famous from this sermon, "Though we cannot think alike, may we not love alike? May we not be of one heart, though we are not of one opinion? Without all doubt, we may."

This was based on his understanding of both Scripture and human nature. As long as we "know in part" all Christians will not see all things alike. It is as he said, "...an unavoidable consequence of the present weakness and shortness of human understanding." Regarding human nature, he was also convinced that no individual could be absolutely certain that his or her opinions are true: "...to be ignorant of many things, and to mistake in some, is the necessary condition of humanity." The conclusion was that we should allow others the liberty of thinking as in turn, we appreciate it when others allow that of us.

Later on in this sermon, Wesley speaks of what he considers to be theological imperatives. If as Christians our hearts are one with each other, we will agree on the following:

- We will believe in God, perfect, eternal, immense, all wise, powerful, just, merciful, and true.
- We will believe in Jesus Christ crucified and resurrected dwelling in us and his likeness being formed in our hearts.
- We will believe that our faith is empowered by the energy of God's love [the Spirit] which is consuming us and that we are seeking to love God "with all our heart, and with all our mind, and with all our soul, and with all our strength."
- We will believe that the love of God is motivating us to serve God with joy and a clear conscience.
- We will believe that we should be right with others, loving them from a heart filled with good will and tender affection.
- We will believe we should serve others in love.

When I read the rather lengthy and tedious doctrinal statements that most churches have, the above list seems rather short. This list is also noteworthy because of one word that Wesley uses repeatedly: *love.*

This leads to a third guiding principle on how we are to understand the Bible: we should interpret Scripture in light of the Rule of Love, the two-fold command to love God and love others. The Rule of Love was a guiding principle used by the early community of faith dating back at least to the fourth century and probably even earlier. The idea is basically this: when we interpret Scripture in a way that is hurtful to people, we can be sure we are not glorifying God. I'm amused by Marcus Borg's comment, "...most of us have known at least one person who was born again in a remarkably unattractive way. When being born again leads to a rigid kind of righteousness, judgmentalism, and sharp boundaries between an in-group and an out-group, it's either not a genuine born-again experience or it has a lot of static in it."[12] Or as Anne Lamott said, "You can safely assume that you've created God in your own image when it turns out that God hates all the same people you do." A very practical test is to ask ourselves the question, "Is my interpretation of Scripture leading me into a deeper love for God and a practical love for others?" If not, then in all probability, our understanding of the Bible is flawed.[13]

The list for how we understand the Bible is short:

- Keep Jesus at the center of Scripture.
- Love Jesus more than we love the Bible.
- Let love be the guiding principle in our relationships with each other.

I know that many will take exception to this. They will want to add all kinds of additional ideas as to how we interpret and understand Scripture. I would simply ask that one take the time to really think about it. Is it *really* necessary to add much more? Would these three principles not sufficiently guide us into effectively loving God and loving others and thus fulfill the greatest commandment of all?

Endnotes

[1]Marcus Borg, *Reading the Bible again for the First Time,* (HarperOne, ©2001) Preface, ix.

[2] Adam Hamilton, *Seeing Gray in a World of Black and White,* p. 68.

[3] Marcus Borg, *The Heart of Christianity,* (HarperSanFrancisco, ©2003) Preface, xii. Used with permission. All rights reserved.

[4] There is an ongoing debate among scholars as to whether the three Pastoral Epistles (I & II Timothy and Titus) were written by the apostle Paul himself, or by a later disciple who sought to provide guidance for the Pauline churches. Most scholars today do regard them as pseudepigraphical (that is, ascribed to the authority of a major figure but not actually written by him, a custom which is well attested in ancient literature), although there is not complete unanimity on the question.

[5]All four of these definitions come from the *American Heritage© Dictionary.*

[6] Borg, *The Heart of Christianity,* pp. 43-44. Used with permission. All rights reserved.

[7] Scripture, tradition, experience, and reason comprise what is known as the Wesleyan Quadrilateral—a method of theological reflection credited to John Wesley. The term itself was coined by 20th century American Methodist Albert Outler. Upon examination of Wesley's sermons, Outler theorized that Wesley used four different sources in coming to theological conclusions. Those four sources are:

1. Scripture: the Holy Bible (Old and New Testaments)
2. Tradition: the two millennia history of the Christian Church
3. Experience: a Christian's personal and communal journey in Christ
4. Reason: rational thinking and sensible interpretation

The United Methodist Church asserts that "Wesley believed that the living core of the Christian faith was revealed in Scripture, illumined by tradition, vivified in personal experience, and confirmed by reason. Scripture [however] is primary, revealing the Word of God 'so far as it is necessary for our salvation.'" (*The Book of Discipline of the United Methodist Church*. Nashville, Tennessee. Abingdon Press, p. 77)

When Wesley speaks of "Tradition," he does not merely refer to ancient Church Tradition and the writings of the great theologians and Church Fathers of days past, but also of the immediate and present theological influences which contribute to a person's understanding of God and of Christian theology. "Tradition" may include such influences as the beliefs, values, and instruction of one's family and upbringing. It may also include the various beliefs and values which one encounters and which have an effect on one's understanding of Scripture.

It must be understood, however, that for Wesley, Tradition, Reason, and Experience do not form additional "sources" for theological truth, for he believed that the Bible was the sole source of truth about God, but rather these form a matrix for interpreting the Bible. Therefore, while the Bible is the sole source of truth, Tradition forms a "lens" through which we view and interpret the Bible. But unlike the Bible, Tradition is not an infallible instrument, and it must be balanced and tested by Reason and Experience. Reason is the means by which we may evaluate and even challenge the assumptions of Tradition. Reason is the first means by which we may "trim our sails" and adjust interpretations of Scripture.

But for Wesley, the chief test of the "truth and nothing but the whole truth" of a particular interpretation of Scripture is how it is seen in practical application in one's Experience. Always the pragmatist, Wesley believed that Experience formed the best evidence, after Scripture, for the truthfulness of a particular theological view. He believed Scriptural truths are to be primarily lived, rather than simply thought about or merely believed. Thus, how a particular interpretation of Scripture is lived out is the best and most viable test of our theology.

Each of the "legs" of the Wesleyan Quadrilateral must be taken in balance, and none of the other three apart from Scripture should be viewed as being of equal value or authority with Scripture. None of these should be taken in isolation without the balancing effect of the others, and always Scripture should have the central place of authority. The following chart, developed by George E. Koehler, illustrates the interdependence of the four elements of Wesley's Quadrilateral.

In United Methodist understanding, both laypeople and clergy alike share in the theological task of the ongoing effort to live as Christians in the midst of the complexities of a secular world. Wesley's Quadrilateral is referred to in Methodism as "our theological guidelines" and is taught to its pastors in seminary as the primary approach to interpreting the Scriptures and gaining guidance for moral questions and dilemmas faced in daily living.

On a personal note, it was developing an understanding of the Quadrilateral that led me to a deeper exploration of Methodism. It just made practical sense to me. Whether we acknowledge it or not, the fact is, we all use these four components in processing life's issues, but for evangelicals, Tradition, Experience and Reason are minimized because of the Reformation's battle cry of, Sola Scriptura, Scriptura Sola. Having grown dissatisfied with the inability of evangelicalism to address the challenging issues of the 20th and 21st century, the Quadrilateral has provided a way for me to think through, process, and prayerfully address complex topics. It has been a key part of my own journey into a more reflective approach to the Bible.

[8] Roger E. Olson, *Questions to All Your Answers: The Journey from Folk Religion to Examined Faith* (Zondervan, ©2008). Used with permission. All rights reserved. Roger E. Olson (Ph.D., Rice University) is professor of theology at George W.

The interdependence of the four elements of Wesley's Quadrilateral

We rely on the way of salvation given in the Bible.
We use the Bible as a touchstone in examining real or supposed revelation.
We take it as the final authority in matters of faith and practice.
Thus we need to study and interpret it carefully.
Roots: Protestant Reformation
Danger: bibliolatry

We revere the ancient church as well as our own.
We use the writings of Christians through the centuries.
Particular value is given to the early church fathers.
The standards of the Church of England are utilized: prayerbook and homilies.
Roots: Roman Catholic Church
Danger: traditionalism

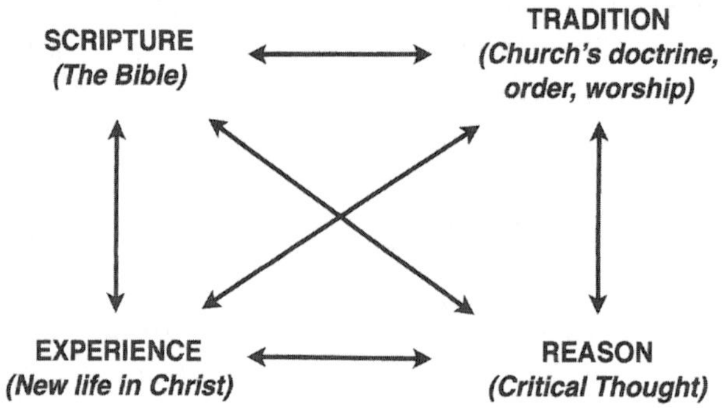

SCRIPTURE
(The Bible)

TRADITION
(Church's doctrine, order, worship)

EXPERIENCE
(New life in Christ)

REASON
(Critical Thought)

The Holy Spirit uses scripture and tradition to bring us to faith.
By God's grace we receive a personal experience of faith.
There are variations of Christian experience; none can be normative.
Thus ours is a "heart religion," but is not dependent on "feelings."
Roots: free churches
Danger: enthusiasm

Reason lays the foundation for true religion and helps raise its superstructure.
Reasons helps us order the evidence of revelation and (with tradition) guard against poor interpretation of scripture.
But reason cannot prove or disclose God.
Roots: Deism
Danger: rationalism

Truett Theological Seminary of Baylor University in Waco, Texas. He would be considered an evangelical Christian. He is the author of over 15 books with one entitled *How to be Evangelical without being Conservative.* In *Questions to All Your Answers,* he maintains that many Christian's faith exists as a loose collection of unexamined clichés and slogans borrowed from songs, devotional books, sermon illustrations, and even the Internet. Some of the clichés he addresses are, "God is in Control," "Jesus is the Answer," "God Helps Those Who Help Themselves," "Money isn't bad, but only what we do with it," "God has a perfect plan for your life." Too often this belief system (if it can be called a "system") lacks coherence and intelligibility; it can hardly be expressed, let alone defended, to others. The problem with folk religion is that it too easily withers under the onslaughts of secularism or seemingly reasonable answers provided by cults and new religions. Socrates said that the unexamined life is not worth living; great Christian minds of all the ages have believed the unexamined faith is not worth believing. Reflective Christianity is Christian faith that has subjected itself to the rigorous questioning of Scripture, tradition, reason, and experience. It is a mature Christian faith that goes on believing even as it questions what it believes.

[9] Meta-narrative. One of the ways people of the new Re•Formation will approach the Bible is by focusing on the meta-narratives–the story behind the stories. The meta-narratives focus on the larger, more all-encompassing themes of Scripture that enfold and explain all the other "little stories." A meta-narrative is an over arching theme that is often untold but one that is reinforced and unified by the specific narratives within its sub context.

Let's take the Genesis accounts of creation as an example, for even a casual reading of Genesis 1 and 2 reveals that there are definitely two different accounts of creation. My appreciation for his permission is extended to my friend, Rev. Dr. Harvey Martz, Senior Minister of St. Andrew United Methodist Church in Highlands Ranch, Colorado. This example is from a recent sermon he preached entitled, "*Can We Believe in Jesus and in Dinosaurs?"* I thought he did an excellent job of illustrating a meta-narrative.

> "The first chapter of Genesis tells us a majestic story of creation. God only had to speak and the universe was formed, beginning with light, to illuminate the chaos that God then ordered and subdued. At the end of the story, on day six, God creates human beings, male and female. Chapter Two is a different story. There are no plants, no garden, just some springs to water the ground, and the *first thing* (emphasis mine) that God creates in Chapter Two is man, a male human being. The second thing God creates is a garden. God puts the man in the garden and says, *it is not good for the man to be alone. I will create a companion or a helpmate.* So the next thing God creates...[are the] animals and brings them to man. Finally, God creates a woman from a rib. This is not, I believe, biology or science or history. It is something more important. God places the creatures in the garden, points out some boundaries so they will not try to become like gods, and then we get to the part about the talking snake. The tree of the knowledge of everything is just too tempting. This is what the metaphor 'knowledge of good and evil' means. They eat some fruit from the tree and their eyes are opened. The man and the woman become ashamed of their nakedness, they become fearful, and they hide when they hear the sound of the Lord God 'taking a walk in the garden to enjoy the evening breeze.' This is a very anthropomorphic image of God. When God asks them where they are and what they have done, the man heroically steps right up and takes full responsibility—right? No, he shifts the blame: '...the woman that YOU gave to be with me—SHE DID IT!' The woman blames the snake and by then, the snake has stopped talking! From my perspective, this is not

> history. This is something more powerful and more important and more formative than history."

It is at this point that we see in this sermon the meta-narrative approach being used. Rather than focusing on trying to resolve and reconcile all the inconsistent details of the two different creation accounts, the sermon continues,

> "What can we learn from these chapters of Genesis?

1. Our universe is an awesome and wondrous creation… Einstein had that sense of wonder. It is why he said, 'Science without religion is lame. Religion without science is blind.'
2. The universe is not an accident. There is a purposeful creator at work over billions of years.
3. The creation is good. Does this sound self-evident? Many churches have not believed in the goodness of creation and that started a hundred years after Christ in a movement called Gnosticism. Gnosticism says that Jesus could not have really been a human being because bodies are bad, flesh is bad. It says the Jesus only appeared to be human but really sort of floated along like a ghost.
4. Genesis says, the created world is good, and human sexuality is good, and we are meant for relationships with God and with others.
5. You and I are created in the image of God. That is a complex and profoundly important insight. It does not mean that God has arms and legs, it means that our capacity for creativity and compassion and justice and love are like God's. It means more, but at least that.
6. The story says that boundaries are important and when we violate some boundaries about what is really good for us, what God intends for us, we get ourselves into trouble. We are still creatures with limits, and the word for when we try to ignore those boundaries is hubris, arrogance.

7. God takes a great risk and gives us the created universe and puts us in charge to care for the earth. It is a sacred trust.
8. We are accountable to God for what we do and don't do. We see this in Genesis 3. Maybe God still asks us like those first creatures, 'Where are you? What have you done?'
9. Sometimes we try to avoid accountability. The man in the garden was the first to shift the blame. People still do that.

Finally this story teaches us about grace, about God's forgiveness even when we cross some boundaries and repent. The snake tells the man and woman in the Garden of Eden that even if they eat from the forbidden tree, they will not die. Was the snake right? God does not let them die at that time. God sends them from the beautiful garden to live 'East of Eden' (the title of the John Steinbeck book). But God also, before they go, makes new clothes for them to replace their fig leaves. Even in these early stories we see God's grace. The Bible begins and ends with a God of grace and compassion and new beginnings and second chances. Thanks be to God!"

It is my personal opinion that looking at the Scriptures through the lens of meta-narratives is a very expansive approach to the Bible. It looks for the meaning behind the words themselves, the intent of the stories given. I think it honors and elevates the Bible in a way that simple literal interpretation does not. It provides us with a richness and texture to our holy book. And rather than diminishing the Bible, it exalts it and breathes new, deep meaning onto its pages. This is what is meant when you hear people talking about "taking the Bible seriously, but not literally."

Other meta-narratives would be the themes of redemption, separation, wholeness, compassion, justice, mercy, forgiveness, and love. As one moves through the Bible rather than dissecting the Scriptures and looking at them through a microscope, the emphasis is on seeing the vast expansiveness of the Bible, as if looking through a telescope. Thus we see the power of the stories. In the creation accounts we see the power of God and the fact that God is the prime mover. As we see God interacting with people (Abraham, Isaac, Jacob, Joseph, Moses, Saul, David, Solomon, Daniel, Nehemiah, the disciples, other individuals around Jesus, Jesus himself, the Apostle Paul, and countless others) we come to understand how God might work in our lives. We focus on the inspiration of the Psalms, the practicality of the Proverbs, the mystery of God through Job, and the cry for justice from the Prophets, the life and teachings of Jesus, the power of community in the early church, and the call to righteous living in the Epistles.

[10] Robert Barclay. "Barclay's Apology, proposition 3." Quaker Heritage Press.

[11] Thomas Jackson (ed.), *The Works of John Wesley,* Third Edition (London: John Jason, 1829), VIII, 340.

[12] Borg, *The Heart of Christianity,* p. 104.

[13] In the Epilogue to *Reading the Bible again for the First Time,* Borg makes some comments regarding what a biblical vision of life with God is like. I feel his words are important enough to share with you. "The major voices of the biblical tradition, as I hear them, share three primary convictions in common: First, there is a deep sense of the reality of the sacred. God is not only real, but knowable. Moreover, the sacred is known not in a set of statements about God, but experientially, as a Mystery beyond all language. This Mystery—God—transcends all of our domestications of reality, including those generated by theology and even the Bible itself.

Second, there is a strong conviction that our lives are made 'whole' and 'right' by living in a conscious relationship with the Mystery who is alone Lord. Life with God is not about believing certain teachings about God. It is about a covenant—a relationship. More specifically, it is about becoming conscious of a relationship that already exists, for the God of the Bible has been in relationship with us from our beginning, whether we know it or not, believe it nor not. And we are not simply to become conscious of it; we are to become intentional about deepening the relationship. Christian faith is not about believing, but about faithfulness—fidelity—to the relationship. As the path of life, this relationship is the path of personal transformation. It is the path of liberation from existential, psychological, and spiritual bondage to the lords of convention and culture. It involves dying to an old way of being and being born into a new way of being.

Third, these voices are convinced that God is a God of justice and compassion. The God of the Bible is full of compassion and passionate about justice. God's passion for justice flows out of the very character of God. God cares about suffering and the single greatest source of unnecessary human misery is unjust and oppressive cultural systems.

So these three, I am suggesting, are at the core of the biblical vision of life with God: a sacred Mystery at the center of life, with whom we are to be in a conscious relationship and who is passionate about the well-being of the whole creation. We are called to participate in the passion of God.

From these three core elements flows a remarkably simple vision of the Christian life. It is not complicated, though it is challenging. It is crystallized in the very familiar twofold 'great commandment' attributed to Jesus. I prefer to think of it as the 'great relationship,' and I thus paraphrase it as follows:

The first relationship is, 'Hear O Israel: the Lord our God, the Lord is one; and you shall love the Lord your God with all your heart, and with all your soul, and with all your mind, and with all your strength.' This is the great and first relationship. And a second relationship is like it: 'You shall love your neighbor as yourself.' On these two relationships depend all the Law and the Prophets.

Thus at the center of a life grounded in the Bible is the twofold focus of the great relationship." *(Epilogue pp. 299-301. Used with permission. All rights reserved.)*

9

The Eight Hundred Pound Gorilla

"Never have people felt so strongly about something they know so little about."

-Anonymous

"To approach any of the arguments and questions surrounding homosexuality in the closing years of the twentieth century and the opening ones of the twenty-first is to approach a battle to the death. When it is all resolved—and it most surely will be—the Reformation's understanding of Scripture as it had been taught by Protestantism for almost five centuries will be dead. That is not to say that Scripture as the base of authority is dead. Rather it is to say that what the Protestant tradition has taught about the nature of that authority will be either dead or in mortal need of reconfiguration. And that kind of summation is agonizing for the surrounding culture in general. In particular, it is agonizing for the individual lives that have been built upon it. Such an ending is to be staved off with every means available and resisted with every bit of energy that can be mustered. Of all the fights, the gay one must be—has to be—the bitterest, because once it is lost, there are no more fights to be had. It is finished."[1]

As we've already seen in looking back over the centuries of Christian tradition, there have been numerous blows struck against the Protestant Reformation's battle cry of Sola Scriptura, Scriptura Sola. The concept of the ultimate authority of the Bible was challenged in this country with the fight over slavery. At the turn of the 20th century it was fought again over the role of women. The fight to end segregation further eroded the influence of Scripture. Another attack came over the battle to ordain women to ecclesiastical positions. It was again assaulted when the issue of divorce had to be addressed. All of these represented great times of struggle as people pushed through the supposed authoritative teaching of the Bible to a deeper understanding and acceptance of what is ultimately right.

It seems that the church has always had some issue with which it is struggling, some group that it seeks to marginalize. Because of that, I'm not sure I totally agree with Tickle's assessment regarding the fight over homosexuality: that once this battle is done, there will be no more fights to be had. But there are two points in her comments with which I totally agree: this matter *will be* resolved, and not in a way that is favorable to the conservative point of view. Second, there is no question that this issue *is* the 800 pound gorilla in the room for our generation. It has to be addressed and there will continue to be bloody battles fought as traditionalists seek to hold on to a thread of biblical authority. This topic will also be one of the key hinge pins as we continue to move into the new Re•Formation.

In thinking about how our views regarding homosexuality are developed, there seems to be many streams flowing into our conscious and unconscious minds that shape our attitudes toward this subject. We are influenced by the society around us, and the general sense from others as to their perceptions of right and wrong. We are strongly swayed by our parents and the thoughts and prejudices they exhibit. The friends we associate with help mold our values. What we see and read through television, movies and on the Internet have a huge effect on our ethics. And, for those who have been raised in a church culture, the teaching of our particular church, its pastor and leaders, and the words of Scripture become influential forces that help sculpt our thoughts and attitudes.

At this point it is important for me to share a bit of my story. As a teenager growing up in the 1960s there was very little information available regarding the subject of homosexuality. At that time, in the DSM (the *Diagnostic and Statistical Manual)* of the American Psychiatric Association, homosexuality was classified as a mental disorder. The kids I hung around with would frequently make disparaging comments about "fags." My own family of origin, though not overly religious, was strongly moral and it was made very clear that those kinds of people were not normal. During those years my perception of homosexuality was that it was wrong.

At the age of 17 I had a very profound, life-changing and emotional experience with God. In evangelical terms, I was "born again." I immediately got involved in an interdenominational church, which had its roots in Pentecostalism. I attended a conservative Christian college and ultimately went to a very conservative evangelical seminary. Then I became the pastor of an evangelical church, where I stayed for 28 years. In that role my belief in the authority of Scripture was part of the bedrock of my faith. I took the Bible literally and presented it as such to my congregation. In my private moments however, I struggled deeply with many of the inconsistencies and contradictions that are found in Scripture. But as a busy pastor, those questions had to be kept in the back of my mind—I had more urgent and pressing matters to focus on.

The reason I wanted to share with you a little of my own story is because as we come now to address the issue of homosexuality, I want you to know that basically my entire adult life has been spent as an evangelical holding to a very high and literal view of Scripture. As we take this in-depth look at the Bible passages that seem to speak to the issue of homosexuality, the conclusions may be disturbing to some, or comforting and perhaps even liberating to others. My understanding of these passages has evolved from a casual, surface reading of these verses to one which I believe does much greater justice to the texts themselves, and actually honors Scripture as words inspired by God. I desire to "do my best to present myself to God as one approved, a worker who does not need to be ashamed and who correctly handles the word of truth." (II Timothy 2.15)

This gradual change has not been easy for me nor without cost. But intellectual integrity requires that I continue to move down this path for you see, I've been going through an individual re•forming process. Gail Sheehy said, "If we don't change we don't grow. And if we don't grow, we aren't really living." I realize that I won't be able to keep some of you from thinking what you will about me and about the following material. But if you can, I would ask that you be willing to approach this with an open mind, a teachable spirit, and a sensitive heart.

I can't do much to help you work through the influence of society, friends, parents, the media, your church's teaching on this subject, or your own emotional reactions. Others will have to step up to the plate to address those issues. But I am hopeful that I can be of service in helping you wrestle with what the Bible says and doesn't say about homosexuality. My desire is that you could come to realize that there are very legitimate and accurate ways of understanding these passages other than just taking them literally and at face value. In fact, I contend that the literal approach actually dishonors God's Word because it doesn't take into full consideration the cultural, historical, and grammatical nuances of the verses we will be focusing on. If nothing else, I hope to show that these passages are not as black and white as one might think them to be.

The Literal Approach to the Bible

Understanding and interpreting the Bible literally is one way of approaching Scripture. But it's important to realize that it is not the only way and, in fact, when the Bible is taken literally, it creates some huge issues that usually are brushed under the carpet and virtually ignored by those within the conservative Christian communities.

The Bible presents us with many difficulties, contradictions, various dates for the same event, chronological differences, and other internal inconsistencies. These things have not gone unnoticed by conservatives, but generally they are ignored. Occasionally an author will bring out a book that seeks to address the biggest contradictions in the Bible, but those are few and far between, and often, they really don't address the root problems.

By conveniently ignoring the obvious difficulties a literal approach to Scripture creates, conservatives basically end up becoming "cherry pickers." They go through the Bible like they're going through a cafeteria line, picking and choosing the verses, topics, and teachings they want to focus on while disregarding the ones they don't particularly like or can't explain. Today, rather than having the Bible be the authoritative guidebook for Christian living, it has become subject to a more supreme commander—the individual Christian's personal persuasions. The Christian then decides which teachings of the Bible to apply as valid for today and which ones to ignore.

One of the basic problems we have when we approach the Bible is that we can make it say just about anything we want it to say. We can use the Bible to support just about any kind of position we want to support. As noted in a previous chapter, that is exactly what has happened down through the centuries. The book I've previously referenced, *The Bible Tells Me So,* addresses this issue. The back cover says the following:

> "Does the Bible justify slavery—or its abolition? Support or oppose capital punishment? Prove the inferiority or superiority of one race or another? Justify hatred and persecution of homosexuals or advocate their acceptance just as they are? Condone or condemn prayer in public schools? Depending on your point of view, the Bible does all these things—and more. Throughout history preachers, politicians and pundits have selectively used the Bible to reach often contradictory conclusions on the great issues of morality and politics: from women's rights, abortion, and celibacy for the clergy to war, civil rights, the environment, and the separation of church and state—even appropriate hairstyles. Now, as much as ever, those in control are convinced they have all the right answers. The Bible tells them so."[2]

Some General Observations

Let me give a handful of examples of the problems encountered when the Bible is taken literally:

1. Gluttony is talked about at least as many times in Scripture as homosexuality and the Bible even calls it a form of idolatry in Philippians 3.19. If churches are going to exclude or marginalize gay men and women from their fellowship, why shouldn't those same congregations exclude gluttonous idolaters? A USA Today article (October, 2005) reported on the results of a study that found that 62 percent of adult Americans are overweight. With this kind of information in hand, we can understand why it's doubtful that any church would be willing to exclude almost two-thirds of its congregation. Even more intriguing is the fact that it's in the Bible Belt—the conservative Southeastern part of the United States—where obesity levels and adult diabetes levels are the highest.[3]
2. Slavery has already been addressed, but it is worth repeating that both the Old and New Testaments seem to approve of slavery. In fact, this issue split the Baptist Church in 1845 between the North and the South. It took until 1995 (150 years later) for the Southern Baptist leadership to issue a formal apology for their earlier support of slavery and segregation and repent of their bigotry and racism. Like a mighty glacier moves the church of God.
3. If the Bible is taken literally, women should be prohibited from wearing gold jewelry, braiding their hair, and wearing expensive clothing (I Peter. 3.3). They should be silent in churches (I Corinthians 14.34) and they are to have their heads covered and their faces veiled (I Corinthians 11.5-6).

4. Fasting is repeatedly discussed in the Bible as being a spiritual discipline, but in many congregations it is almost never talked about or encouraged.
5. Concerning the gift of tongues: Paul warned the church at Corinth to "not forbid the speaking in tongues," (I Corinthians 14.39) but rarely is that behavior allowed in our churches. The Charismatic churches are about the only ones that encourage the use of this gift.
6. In I Corinthians, Paul encouraged those who are unmarried to remain that way, saying that being single is better than married life (I Corinthians 7.8). His plain advice was: don't seek to be married. And then, the reason he gives for getting married is—if you can't control your lust (I Corinthians 7.9). This advice seems to reduce the beauty, holiness, and sanctity of marriage to a very carnal, almost animal level. From this passage it would appear that the New Testament foundation for marriage is an uncontrollable sexual appetite.
7. People headed for hell: the subject of hell, while a topic of much pulpit time in many fundamentalist churches really isn't talked about that much by Jesus. When he does mention it however, he explicitly names the kinds of people who are going to be headed there. The folks on his hit list include: those who call their neighbor a "fool" (Matthew 5.22); those who lust after women in their hearts (Matthew 5.27-30); those who are not good stewards of the gifts God has given them (Matthew 25.14-30); and those who do not provide food for the hungry or drink for the thirsty; people who do not welcome strangers or provide clothing to the naked; and people who don't visit the prisoners (Matthew 25.41-46). This last one is intriguing to me. If those are the folks Jesus says are headed for eternal damnation, it

seems that a church should place a much greater emphasis on making sure that its people are engaging in social justice issues and caring for the disenfranchised people of society—for the sake of their own souls. Perhaps social involvement should be the number one priority of a church and its members.

These are just a few examples, but the point that I'm trying to make is that there are dozens and dozens of very plain stipulations in the Bible that are routinely ignored by folks who insist on a literal interpretation of Scripture. This becomes a critical point in examining the passages of Scripture that seem to speak to the issue of homosexuality. While conveniently ignoring a wide variety of other issues, here is where the literalist suddenly becomes willing to get quite literal. "The Bible says it's wrong. It's an abomination. Those people are perverts. They're going to hell. Period. End of discussion." However, as I hope to show, this issue is not that cut and dried.

After I came to faith, I remember reading some of the few books or articles that were addressing this issue from a Christian perspective back in the 1960s and early 1970s. First of all, there was a dearth of information. It was still a subject very much in shadows—especially for the Christian community. People who were writing back then were grasping at straws, trying to pull out all the gay innuendos from Scripture that they could in order to garner support. They developed theories saying Naomi and Ruth were gay, David and Jonathan were gay, Jesus and John were gay, and Paul and Timothy were gay. The Roman Centurion and his young boy servant had a gay relationship (this one by the way, may have actually had some basis in historical fact—more on that later). The subject of homosexuality was not that big of an issue 40 years ago, so there was very little research being done on it from a solidly biblical perspective.

That has changed. The time has come. The subject is out of the closet or perhaps I should say the gorilla is now standing in the middle of the room. This is the issue of the moment. This will be a defining issue as the church continues its evolution into the new Re•Formation. The church is now being forced to look at this subject and it's amazing how much is being written about it from a scholarly, biblical perspective. Having said that, however, it doesn't make the issue any less volatile, emotional, and divisive.

Our Options Regarding Homosexuality

Basically there are four different options we can choose from when it comes to how we view and understand homosexuality:

- Homosexuality is a conscious choice. A person chooses to be attracted to a person of their same sex. This approach is a bit of a double standard however, because why do we not then say that heterosexuality is a conscious choice and that people choose to be attracted to members of the opposite sex? Regardless, this is the primary option that will continue to create emotional discussions around this subject. As long as people feel that homosexuality is a choice, the battle lines will be drawn and it will be very hard to come to a meeting of the minds.
- A second option says that homosexuality is an illness—a mental illness. Remember this is how it was classified in the *Diagnostic and Statistical Manual* (DSM) up until 1973, when it was removed from the list of mental disorders. The basic thought here is that for whatever reason, things just aren't functioning quite

normally in the brain. This involves the discussion of nature versus nurture, an idea that something happened in childhood, in the way a person was raised, that created a dysfunction in how that person views sexuality. Perhaps it was an overbearing mother and a passive father or maybe it was a passive mother and an overbearing father. Maybe it was sexual abuse. Yet, when gay men and women are studied there is no real pattern to justify this kind of thinking. Gay people come from all walks of life with all kinds of different backgrounds. Some from normal, healthy families, others from troubled homes. There is no common thread that ties all gay men and women to a shared source for their sexual orientation.

- A third option is that homosexuality is a tragedy in nature, something that is not in harmony with God's will, but it exists. The thought is that sexuality is a very complex and confusing part of the human experience and for reasons unknown, some people's sexuality gets messed up. There is no doubt that human sexuality is a complex subject—heterosexuality itself is very complicated. There's a reason why John Gray's book, *Men are from Mars, Women are from Venus* was such an off the charts best seller.

Underlying all three of these options is a fundamental premise: homosexuality is wrong. In some way, shape, or form, homosexuality is not what God intended for the human race and those individuals who have SSA (same-sex attraction) need to do whatever is necessary to develop a normal opposite sex attraction or at least figure out how to minimize their same sex desires.

- There is a fourth and final option. This one states that homosexuality is simply a variety in nature. In this complicated issue of human sexuality we have a broad spectrum of sexual orientations, and on one end you have heterosexuality (people only attracted to members of the opposite sex) and on the other end you have homosexuality (people only attracted to members of the same sex). In between these two extremes you have varying degrees of bisexuality (people who can be attracted to both sexes). Obviously the whole issue of bisexuality is one that many cannot even fathom and for our purposes here, it's not necessary to discuss at this time.

The basic idea however is that while heterosexuality is the predominate orientation of the human race, homosexuality, while not the norm, is not abnormal. It's just one of those differences that appear in human nature. One of the interesting facts being uncovered as more research is being done on the subject is that in cultures around the world, there appears to be about 3 percent of the population in each culture that can be classified as homosexual.

Viewing homosexuality as a normal variant of sexuality could be compared to left-handedness, a minority condition in a world where most people are right-handed and a few are ambidextrous, but a natural variation having its own contributions. There was a time when society considered left-handedness so deviant it had to be punished and changed. I was discussing this issue of left-handedness in a class I was teaching. At that point a woman in her 70's raised her hand and said, "That's exactly what happened to me." She then proceeded to tell the class how, as a child, her parents bound her left hand in burlap and made her go to school with that hand bound so she would learn to write with her right hand. Apparently it didn't work. She's left-handed to this day.

In trying to force such a change something was discovered that we're finding is also true with gays and lesbians today: attempts to alter sexual orientation don't succeed, but only cause more serious problems. While some groups promote their successes in "turning" gays into straights, their success rate is spotty at best and often not effective long term. Once it became clear that left-handedness is simply a variety of nature, we were freed to discover some of the positive benefits southpaws offer the world. My hope is that once the issue of homosexuality is settled and people come to understand it as the variety of nature it is, we will be able to fully appreciate all the contributions to society gay men and women have made through the years.

Since there are as of yet no experts who know exactly what causes sexual preferences, all we can do is find the best information available from the testimonies of gay and lesbian people, the ongoing results of scientific research, and the insights of serious biblical scholarship, praying that the Holy Spirit will lead us into a deeper understanding of this issue. Each of us will choose to believe one of these four options and we each will have to take responsibility for the outcome of our choice.

Endnotes

[1] Tickle, *The Great Emergence,* p.101

[2] Hill & Cheadle

[3] The top five states with the highest obesity levels in the country are as follows: Mississippi (32.5%); West Virginia (31.2%); Alabama (31.1%); Tennessee (30.2%); and South Carolina (29.7%)

10

The Old Testament Passages on Homosexuality

Someone once remarked, "The Bible contains six supposed admonishments to homosexuals and 362 admonishments to heterosexuals. That doesn't mean God doesn't love heterosexuals...they just need more supervision."

As we look at the passages of Scripture, which seem to speak to the issue of homosexuality, it must be said that when it comes to how we understand Scripture, we have to be careful not to force the Bible to answer questions that it does not address. What I mean is this: the distinction that we now routinely make between heterosexuality and homosexuality was not made in the ancient world. Sexuality in the ancient times lacked the modern categories of "heterosexual" or "homosexual." Instead the differentiating characteristic was activity versus passivity, or penetrating versus being penetrated.

The actual word "homosexual" was not coined until the mid 19th century. The first known appearance of the term homosexual is found in a 1869 German pamphlet, the title of which is a mouthful: *143 des Preussischen Strafgesetzbuchs und seine Aufrechterhaltung als 152 des Entwurfs eines Strafgesetzbuchs für den Norddeutschen Bund* (Paragraph 143 of the Prussian

Penal Code and Its Maintenance as Paragraph 152 of the Draft of a Penal Code for the North German Confederation). The pamphlet was written by Karl-Maria Kertbeny, but published anonymously. The first known use of *homosexual* in English is in Charles Gilbert Chaddock's 1895 translation of Richard von Krafft-Ebing's *Psychopathia Sexualis,* a study on sexual practices. The term was popularized by the 1906 Harden-Eulenburg affair, which was the controversy surrounding a series of court-martials among prominent members of Kaiser Wilhelm II's cabinet and entourage during 1907-1909, and five civil trials regarding accusations of homosexual conduct, and the accompanying libel trials.[1]

Many are also unaware of the fact that there is no word in biblical Greek or Hebrew that is equivalent to the English word, *homosexual.* Up until very recently other phrases or words were used to translate the Hebrew or Greek words that seemed to be talking about some kind of same sex experience. Now, numerous modern translations have begun using the word *homosexual* as part of their translation: New American Standard Bible (NASB, 1963); New King James Version (NKJV, 1982); New International Version (NIV, 1984); Contemporary English Version (CEV, 1995); and the English Standard Version (ESV, 2001).

This use of the word *homosexual* to translate a Hebrew or Greek word is misleading. It reflects a bias on the part of the translator, as well as a flagrant overgeneralization of a concept that has multiple nuances in ancient society, confusing this issue tremendously. More on that later.

There are only a few places where same-sex practices of some kind are mentioned in the Bible, and when they are, they are not the topic of extended discussion—only passing references or allusions. I, as well as others, call these the

"CLOBBER" passages, so named because that's how conservative Christians have used these various verses—to clobber people over the head with them in an attempt to get them to see that the Bible says quite clearly that homosexuality is wrong. As with anything that gets clobbered, this is generally done with a lot of force and little compassion.

Taking Scripture as a whole, it is also important to note that there are many other issues that stand far higher on the Bible's moral agenda than the issue of homosexuality. Subjects such as: deceitfulness, transgression of the rights of others or indifference to their needs, greed, sloth, self-interest, injustice in the marketplace, oppression of the weak, exploitation of the poor and needy, proud religious posturing, self-righteousness, lust for those of the opposite sex, and other topics all have dozens, hundreds, or thousands of verses that speak to those issues. For example, there are over 2,000 passages in the Bible that deal with wealth, how we use material possessions, and our responsibility toward the poor. In reading those verses, it's not hard to miss where the writers of Scripture focused their attention on what they considered supremely important.

I have come to the conclusion that there has been a great deal of misinformation disseminated by leaders within the Christian movement regarding the subject of homosexuality. Some of that misinformation has been intentional, and some spread out of ignorance and fear. Regardless of the initial motivation, it has helped create a large contingent of self-assured believers who speak with unabashed confidence and authority that their interpretation of the Bible is totally and completely right.

If we are going to have a healthy understanding of this topic, we are going to have to dig deeper into the Scriptures than many people have done before. I hope you'll consider it a worthy expedition. Let's view our study of these passages as if we are prospectors panning for gold—a very tiring and time consuming task, but once those nuggets are found, very rewarding. There are three passages in the Old Testament and three in the New Testament that are referenced in regard to homosexuality. This chapter looks at the Old Testament passages.

Genesis 1-2: The Creation Narrative

Genesis chapters one and two give us two different accounts of creation. It's interesting that we only have to get into the first two chapters of the Bible to see some of the problems associated with literal interpretation. These two different creation accounts do not line up with one another. Rather than being willing to take the Bible seriously but not literally, the literalists have had to propose some theories which would seek to do away with these differences. Taking the Bible seriously means we look at a bigger question that overshadows these two chapters: what was the intent and purpose for the writer(s) of Genesis in including creation accounts? The obvious answer is they wanted to show that God was the creator of all things. They desired to have people understand where everything that they saw and interacted with came from—including humankind.

> Genesis 1.27-28 in the TNIV says, "So God created human beings in his own image, in the image of God he created them; male and female he created them. God blessed them and said to them, 'Be fruitful and increase in number; fill the earth and subdue it. Rule over the fish in the sea and the birds in the sky and over every living creature that moves on the ground.'"

As any good student of Bible study will affirm, an important principle of biblical interpretation is that you seek to interpret a particular passage of Scripture in light of the entire Bible.

With that being the case, we need to ask ourselves, what was the intent of the writer(s) of Genesis—the book of beginnings? Peter Gomes in his book, *The Good Book,* writes,

> "...the authors of Genesis were intent upon answering the question 'Where do we come from?' Then, as now, the only plausible answer is from the union of a man and a woman. The creation story in Genesis does not pretend to be a history of anthropology or of every social relationship. It does not mention friendship, for example, and yet we do not assume that friendship is condemned or abnormal. It does not mention the single state, and yet we know that singleness is not condemned, and that in certain religious circumstances it is held in very high esteem."[2]

In other words, a man and a woman, Adam and Eve, are the only possible relationship that would make sense for this specific account. It is a story about creation and the propagation of the human race and only a procreative (i.e. heterosexual) relationship would be appropriate for this particular story. I personally do not think this passage even has that much bearing on the whole subject of homosexuality; however, it comes into play when it is used by people saying, "God made Adam and Eve, not Adam and Steve." Attempts at smug humor or the desire to get a laugh at someone else's expense are demeaning and marginalizing and reveal more about the people who say that than the group they are attempting to humiliate.

Genesis 19: The Story of Sodom

This story requires a great deal more exploration.

"The two angels came to Sodom in the evening, and Lot was sitting in the gateway of Sodom. When Lot saw them, he rose to meet them, and bowed down with his face to the ground.[2] He said, 'Please, my lords, turn aside to your servant's house and spend the night, and wash your feet; then you can rise early and go on your way.' They said, 'No; we will spend the night in the square.'[3] But he urged them strongly; so they turned aside to him and entered his house; and he made them a feast, and baked unleavened bread, and they ate.[4] But before they lay down, the men of the city, the men of Sodom, both young and old, all the people to the last man, surrounded the house;[5] and they called to Lot, 'Where are the men who came to you tonight? Bring them out to us, so that we may know them.'[6] Lot went out of the door to the men, shut the door after him,[7] and said, 'I beg you, my brothers, do not act so wickedly.[8] Look, I have two daughters who have not known a man; let me bring them out to you, and do to them as you please; only do nothing to these men, for they have come under the shelter of my roof.'[9] But they replied, 'Stand back!' And they said, 'This fellow came here as an alien, and he would play the judge! Now we will deal worse with you than with them.' Then they pressed hard against the man Lot, and came near the door to break it down.[10] But the men inside reached out their hands and brought Lot into the house with them, and shut the door.[11] And they struck with blindness the men who were at the door of the house, both small and great, so that they were unable to find the door." (Genesis 19.1-11, NRSV)

This passage is crucial in our exploration of homosexuality in the Bible because of how it has been used down through the centuries as a metaphor for homosexual deviation. Let's explore what is happening. Two angels come into the town of Sodom to pay Lot a visit. Their purpose is to inform Lot of the impending doom of Sodom and instruct Lot to take his family and get out. A mob of men come to storm the house of Lot in order to "know" the two strangers in their midst. Basically this group of men should be likened to a group of thugs who are angry that some strangers have come on to their turf.

With this as a background, note the following observations:

- Sodom is already under judgment *before* this incident happens (Genesis 18.16-33). The angels come to reveal to Lot that God has already judged the city and their mission is to destroy it. Lot is being forewarned, thus giving him and his family time to escape. Whatever the reason for God's judgment (Genesis 18 does not say, other than for their "very grave sin") this city was already under sentence *before* this event in Genesis 19.
- Everyone participates: "...the men of the city, the men of Sodom, both young and old, *all the people to the last man*, surrounded the house..." (vs. 4, emphasis mine). It's totally implausible and absurd that *all* the men of the city were homosexual. This one fact in itself should reveal to us that there must be something else going on here than the traditional interpretation of homosexual lust.
- The text makes it clear that the men of Sodom intend to have sexual relations with the guests. The traditional concept of the sin of Sodom arises from the fact that the Hebrew word translated "to know" (yadha) is used by itself in ten places in the Old Testament

> to denote heterosexual intercourse. In five additional texts it is used in conjunction with mishkabh (in this context, "to lie") to mean the same thing. But yadha appears by itself no less than 943 times in a nonsexual connotation, to simply mean, "get acquainted with" or "learn of."

With that being the case, an alternate theory has been developed by some biblical scholars. Since yadha commonly means, "to get acquainted with," the demand to "know" the visitors may well have implied some serious breach of the rules of hospitality. Several considerations provide some support for this view.

In the first place, Lot was not a native of Sodom, but had the status of resident alien. As such, he may not have had the right to admit unidentified foreigners to the city. City gates were closed at night expressly to prevent lawless or subversive aliens from entering on unknown errands, and travelers carried credentials because they might at any time be asked to prove that they were in a town on legitimate business. Thus we might translate "Bring them out to us, that we might know them" as "We wish to know whom you are bringing into our city." Lot's refusal to turn his visitors over to this horde of vigilantes is totally in keeping with the then contemporary laws of etiquette, because in those days no civic police force protected strangers in a city. Any kind of robbery or physical abuse could have been meted out to the two angels if he had agreed to surrender them, but in his home they were safe. He was obliged to protect them as honored guests.

While I think this idea may have some merit, I'm more inclined to accept the idea that the men of the city were intending to have sex with the strangers—but these men of

Sodom were heterosexual. This thought is further supported when Lot offers his own daughters "...who have not known a man..." to the mob.

However, here is the key point: the intention of the men from Sodom was not to have sex with the angels because all the men of the city were homosexual, but their purpose was to humiliate and dominate them—to rape them. And the principle impulse in rape—whether homosexual or heterosexual—is not about sex. It's about power.

This threatened rape of the guests is far more likely to be a way of asserting the power of the residents of Sodom over "outsiders" than it is an expression of homosexual lust. In that culture, to subject another male to rape—to force him to be sexually submissive, as women were supposed to be—was a way of asserting or maintaining dominance over him. In the ancient world, the most humiliating experience for a man was to be treated like a woman, and raping a man was the most violent of such treatment. Dale Martin, professor of religion at Duke University says, "To be penetrated was to be inferior because women were inferior."

It also was more frequent than some might imagine. Male rape of other males was a common form of humiliation and domination committed against defeated armies in the ancient world. It was a way of degrading a defeated soldier because again, it put the man in the inferior position of being like a woman and showed the dominance of the conquering army. This is no different than what happens in our prisons today. Prisoners who rape other prisoners do so not because they are homosexual, but because it is a way of asserting control and dominance and forcing another man into a submissive position.

- There is another Old Testament passage that is relevant at this point—Judges 19. It is a very grim story. It bears a striking resemblance to the Sodom narrative. A man (a Levite) arrives in the town of Gibeah. There he meets an old man who is, like Lot, a resident alien. The old man warns the Levite that he should not stay in the town square, and he extends the hand of hospitality, inviting him to share his home for the night. The men of the city surround the old man's house and demand that the Levite be sent out so "that we may know him" ("yadha" again). The old man refuses, but offers his virgin daughter and the Levite's concubine to the mob instead. When the mob refuses the offer, he throws the Levite's concubine outside as a diversion, whereupon this "perverse lot" (NRSV) rape and abuse her all night, leaving her dying on the doorstep. When the Levite arises the next morning to continue on his journey and sees his concubine, lying dead on the doorstep, he cuts her body into twelve pieces and sends the pieces to all of the twelve tribes of Israel at which point the tribes of Israel rise up and destroy Gibeah.

Some parts of the Bible are very difficult to understand.

It says in this passage that the men were a *perverse* lot. Our understanding of perversity is generally related to sexual perversion, but the word actually means "sons of worthlessness." In other words they were just a bunch of thugs. The word is not a comment on their sexual orientation.

In both of these stories the hosts attempt to placate the threatening gangs by offering women to them to abuse. Notice again the cultural emphasis on the superiority of men over women. In the ancient Near East, the critical issue was not sexuality but gender—it was important that the superior position of men over women be maintained. In that culture, the hosts felt that it was more important to protect the male visitors in their house than to protect women, even their own daughters or a common-law wife (a concubine). The hosts obviously do not think of the attackers as primarily homosexual or they would not offer women for them to abuse.

It is fascinating that the very phrase "the sin of sodomy" has come to refer to same-sex relations. That seems to be the primary thing people focus on when they address this passage. For example, very little is said about the wickedness and utter depravity of Lot in offering his own daughters to these men in lieu of the guests in his home. To me, *that's* perverse. In our culture today, it makes absolutely no sense that hospitality was such a sacred, revered concept in biblical times—so much so that you would be willing to give your daughters over to a group of men to be violently raped rather than have the guests in your home dishonored. But that's exactly the distinction Lot expresses: the visitors are my guests, so please don't harm them. Instead, take my daughters.

In addition to maintaining the superiority of men over women, this elevated hospitality code that was prevalent in the ancient world is also worth noting. An example of the significance of the hospitality code is found in the book of Joshua. Prostitution was condemned in the early writings of the Old Testament, yet Joshua spared the life an admitted prostitute before destroying the city of Jericho in return for her hospitality to a pair of Joshua's spies who were being pursued by agents of the King of Jericho. "They burned the whole city and everything in it...But Joshua spared Rahab the prostitute, with her family and all who belonged to her, because she hid the men Joshua had sent as spies to Jericho." (Joshua 6:24-25)

There is one final point to make. You would assume that if Sodom's sin was homosexual relations, other authors in the Bible would make that connection. But nowhere does that happen:

- **Ezekiel 16.49-50**: "Sodom's sins were pride, gluttony, and laziness, while the poor and needy suffered outside her door."
- **Amos** warns that Israel will be overthrown just as God overthrew Sodom and Gomorrah (4.11) and for the same general reason: the poor are oppressed and the needy are crushed (4.1).
- **Isaiah** says the people of Jerusalem and Judah "proclaim their sin like Sodom" (3.9). The charge? "Your hands are full of blood" (1.15); "the spoil of the poor is in your houses" and for "grinding the face of the poor" (3.14-15). "The daughters of Zion are haughty" and are "glancing wantonly with their eyes" (3.16).
- **Zephaniah** states, "Moab shall become like Sodom, and the Ammonites like Gomorrah" (2.9) for these have filled houses "with violence and fraud" (1.9).
- **Jesus** himself predicts judgment (like Sodom) to those towns that do not welcome and care for his disciples who are traveling the countryside (Mt. 10.14-15; Luke 10.12). It's interesting that when recalling the doom of Sodom, Jesus says nothing of any sexual improprieties. Instead he speaks of these cities as exemplifying the fate of those towns that refuse hospitality to his disciples.

There is one other passage that needs to be noted. **Jude 1.4-7** says,

> "For certain intruders have stolen in among you, people who long ago were designated for this condemnation as ungodly, who pervert the grace of our God into licentiousness and deny our only Master and Lord, Jesus Christ. Now I desire to remind you, though you are fully informed, that the Lord, who once for all saved a people out of the land of Egypt, afterward destroyed those who did not believe. And the angels who did not keep their own position, but left their proper dwelling, he has kept in eternal chains in deepest darkness for the judgment of the great day. Likewise, Sodom and Gomorrah and the surrounding cities, which, in the same manner as they, indulged in sexual immorality and pursued unnatural lust, serve as an example by undergoing a punishment of eternal fire."

This is an incredibly unclear passage of Scripture and it is very dangerous to develop any kind of significant moral teaching from it. What Jude seems to be saying however, is that God will punish those who have abandoned belief in Jesus as Lord (vs. 4) and will judge them as severely as God judged the angels who came down from heaven and had intercourse with human women (see Genesis 6.1-4)[3] and those inhabitants of Sodom and Gomorrah who wished to have intercourse with the angelic visitors of Lot (Genesis 19). If this is even close to a proper interpretation of these verses, the condemnation here seems to be of those who want to have intercourse with angels, not those who want to have same-sex relations. To use this extremely vague passage as a support to condemn homosexuality is totally inappropriate.

As the story of Sodom relates to us today, I think it is absolutely tragic that this term "sodomy" has become synonymous with homosexuality. We have "sodomy" laws and people who engage in same sex relationships are "sodomites." It is a disastrous and unwarranted distortion of what was going on in Genesis 19. A Sodomite was nothing more than a resident of Sodom, like an Edomite was from Edom, a Moabite was from Moab, or a Canaanite was from Canaan. That is all that the word "sodomite" meant. That's all it *should* mean for us today.

Yet metaphorically, it has devolved to refer to homosexuality. A careful study of Genesis 19 reveals that homosexuality, as we understand it today, isn't even in the passage. Rather it is a passage that speaks of heterosexual rape, sexually dominating strangers as a form of humiliation, and exercising authority and power.

Tragically, however, Genesis 19 is one of kingpin passages that literalists use to say, "See God hates homosexuality, and those perverts in Sodom were destroyed because they were homosexual." It would seem those who take the Bible literally might do well to spend a little more time in researching the cultural and historical situations of the ancient Middle East as well as carefully looking at other passages within the Bible itself that describe Sodom.

Leviticus 18.22 and Leviticus 20.13: The Holiness Code

Some of you might be familiar with Dr. Laura Schlesinger, the talk radio host, author, and socially conservative commentator. Being an observant Orthodox Jew, she has said that homosexuality is an abomination according to Leviticus 18.22 and cannot be condoned under any circumstance. The following response is an open letter to Dr. Laura, penned by a U.S. resident, which was posted on the Internet. It's humorous as well as informative:

> Dear Dr. Laura:
>
> Thank you for doing so much to educate people regarding God's Law. I have learned a great deal from your show, and try to share that knowledge with as many people as I can. When someone tries to defend the homosexual lifestyle, for example, I simply remind them that Leviticus 18.22 clearly states it to be an abomination...end of debate.
>
> I do need some advice from you, however, regarding some other elements of God's Laws and how to follow them.
>
> 1. Leviticus 25.44 states that I may possess slaves, both male and female, provided they are purchased from neighboring nations. A friend of mine claims that this applies to Mexicans, but not Canadians. Can you clarify? Why can't I own Canadians?
> 2. I would like to sell my daughter into slavery, as sanctioned in Exodus 21.7. In this day and age, what do you think would be a fair price for her?
> 3. I know that I am allowed no contact with a woman while she is in her period of menstrual uncleanness — Leviticus 15.19-24. The problem is how do I tell? I have tried asking, but most women take offense.
> 4. When I burn a bull on the altar as a sacrifice, I know it creates a pleasing odor for the Lord — Leviticus 1.9. The problem is my neighbors. They claim the odor is not pleasing to them. Should I smite them?
> 5. I have a neighbor who insists on working on the Sabbath. Exodus 35.2 clearly states he should be put to death. Am I morally obligated to kill him myself, or should I ask the police to do it?

6. A friend of mine feels that even though eating shellfish is an abomination, Leviticus 11.10, it is a lesser abomination that homosexuality. I don't agree. Can you settle this? Are there "degrees" of abomination?
7. Leviticus 21.20 states that I may not approach the altar of God if I have a defect in my sight. I have to admit that I wear reading glasses. Does my vision have to be 20/20, or is there some wiggle-room here?
8. Most of my male friends get their hair trimmed, including the hair around their temples, even though this is expressly forbidden by Leviticus 19.27. How should they die?
9. I know from Leviticus 11.6-8 that touching the skin of a dead pig makes me unclean, but may I still play football if I wear gloves?
10. My uncle has a farm. He violates Leviticus 19.19 by planting two different crops in the same field, as does his wife by wearing garments made of two different kinds of thread (cotton/polyester blend). He also tends to curse and blaspheme a lot. Is it really necessary that we go to all the trouble of getting the whole town together to stone them? (Leviticus 24.10-16) Couldn't we just burn them to death at a private family affair like we do with people who sleep with their in-laws? (Leviticus 20.14)

I know you have studied these things extensively and thus enjoy considerable expertise in such matters, so I'm confident you can help.

Thank you again for reminding us that God's word is eternal and unchanging.

Your adoring fan.

—James M. Kauffman, Ed.D.
Professor Emeritus, Dept. of Curriculum,
Instruction and Special Education
University of Virginia

> P.S. It would be a damn shame if we couldn't own a Canadian.

In a lighthearted way, Dr. Kauffman points out a very significant issue: what in the world was going on in the ancient community of Israel with regard to these unusual laws and regulations that God prescribed for them?

As mentioned earlier, people can make the Bible say just about anything they want it to say. Many have used various portions of Scripture to support their own peculiar version of the Christian faith. We see this happening all the time in the field of theology. Verses are pulled out here and there and all of a sudden you find support for Calvinism. Other verses are used to support Arminianism. String together some other verses and you become a Dispensationalist, while other verses will lead you to believe in Covenantalism. A few verses put together and you become a believer in adult baptism by immersion. Other verses will lead you to believe in baptism for an infant by sprinkling. This list can go on and on and on. Also, this is the reason why (according to the World Christian Encyclopedia, 2001) there are about 34,000 different Christian groups in the world since CE 30. Each of these groups has some major or minor disagreement(s) with the other factions based on their own unique understanding or interpretation of the Bible.

What is important to me is that we try to approach the Scriptures with some sense of integrity and honest scholarship to see what it says about this issue.

- **Leviticus 18.22** says, "Do not lie with a man as one lies with a woman; that is detestable (an abomination)."
- **Leviticus 20.13** says, "If a man lies with a man as one lies with a woman, both of them have done what

> is detestable (an abomination). They must be put to death; their blood will be on their own heads."

From these two similar passages it would seem quite clear that homosexuality is wrong. However, let's look behind the words to see if we can understand what is actually being said here. I have some comments regarding these verses:

If God inspired the Bible (which means that in some way God helped the writers of the Old and New Testaments to put down in writing eternal truths and principles) and God intends it to be a manual for how to live life most effectively by loving God and others, could it not have been written a little more clearly? Presumably God can do anything—including helping authors write plainly—but the fact is human authors were used in this process. Partly as a result of that and partly as a result of how the Bible was put together, it can be complex and hard to understand in places.

As it relates to these two verses, it would have been so simple if the writer of Leviticus would have just said, "Do not lie with a man. That is an abomination." Again, in chapter 20 if he would have just said, "If a man lies with a man, both of them have committed an abomination." Obviously he was writing to the men here—since nothing is said about the women. If I wanted to be a bit flippant about the whole thing, I'd be inclined to say that God is giving the women a get out of jail card when it comes to their sexual behavior. Sadly, that's not the case at all. Again in the male dominated hierarchy of the ancient Middle East, women didn't matter enough to write about them.

Had the writer of Leviticus written it as just I noted, it would have made our understanding of these verses much easier. The term translated "lie" is an English word that is often used to translate a Hebrew word for sexual relations and it would have been very clear what was being said. But no, the writer had to go and throw in a qualifying phrase in both passages, "…as one lies with a woman." That qualifying phrase actually makes the whole issue more complex.

Let's put these verses in their broader context. The Israelites had been slaves in Egypt for 400 years. Moses delivered them out of the hands of the Egyptians, at which point they wandered around in the desert for 40 years. During this time they were subject to attacks from other tribes, had sanitation issues to be concerned with, food issues, infectious diseases were a potential problem, and there was continual internal disunity, quarreling, and fighting going on. When they finally entered the Promised Land they needed to evolve from a wandering tribe of former slaves to a united nation. They needed cohesiveness, guidelines for personal cleanliness, regulations for living together as a community, and order in every aspect of their lives. They were to stay pure in their manner of worshipping God. They were struggling for their own identity, as a people of God, surrounded by pagan communities.

In response, the Holiness Code was developed to guide the nation in all aspects of its existence. There are over 600 rules and regulations that were given to govern the life of the Israelites. We have trouble trying to keep the Ten Commandments. Can you imagine trying to live your life in such a way that you don't violate over 600 commandments? There were three parts to the Holiness Code: moral, civil, and religious. The Book of Leviticus contains a good portion of the Holiness Code and Leviticus 18.22 and 20.13 are part of that Holiness Code. It is this code to which Dr. Kauffman's letter refers.

The Code's function was to help achieve and maintain the "holy purity" (Leviticus 19.2) that God wanted for the nation. The underlying theme of the Holiness Code was that the people of Israel must be separate. They were to be different from the Egyptians from whom they had escaped and different from the Canaanites in whose land they were now living.

There were three primary ways that the fledgling nation of Israel was to be distinct and achieve this holy purity.

1. Israel's worship had to be different from those of the tribes or nations around them. The other nations were polytheistic. The people of Israel were to worship one God. To become like the Canaanites and start worshipping multiple deities would make them impure and defiled.
2. Second, if they were to remain pure, they could not mix with any of the other surrounding nations or adopt alien customs. The word "pure" is a key concept to understand, because it's not so much referring to moral purity, as it is ritual purity. In other words, what kept the nation of Israel distinct from all these other impure nations around them was this cumbersome Holiness Code, which regulated all aspects of their life together.

I'll describe the third way for achieving holy purity later. For now, as it relates to this second point, we need to spend some time on a very important word: abomination. The Hebrew word for abomination is "to'evah" and it does not have a very precise meaning—at least one that is known today. We do know that it denoted something abhorrent, something to be avoided, something that was forbidden, or something that is detestable or disgusting. It occurs over 100 times in the Hebrew Old Testament and in nearly every occurrence outside these verses that we are looking at, the word is generally applied to an unacceptable religious practice or an unjust economic or social action. This last idea is very important and bears repeating: the word is generally applied to an unacceptable religious practice or an unjust economic or social action.

Let me give you some examples:

- Leviticus 11.13 says that eagles were an abomination (to'evah).
- It was an abomination (to'evah) for an Israelite to marry a non-Israelite (Exodus 32.12-16, Deuteronomy 7.1-4). Interestingly, Moses married a non-Israelite woman (Numbers 12.1) and God seemed to support the decision. Aaron and Miriam criticized Moses because of this and God punished Miriam by making her leprous (Numbers 12.2-16). I find it notable that Aaron received no punishment for this criticism, only the woman.
- Deuteronomy 17.1 says it was an abomination (to'evah) to sacrifice an ox or a sheep that is defective, the reason being is that by offering a defective animal to God, there was the attempt to try and cheat God by giving something that is of a lesser value to you.
- Deuteronomy 25.13-16 states it is an abomination to cheat your customers with dishonest weights and measures.
- Ezekiel is particularly suggestive in regard to this word. Israel's idolatry is symbolized by sexual immorality of a heterosexual kind. Ezekiel portrays Israel as an adulterous woman, a prostitute, and the word to'evah (abomination) occurs repeatedly (16.43, 47, 50). I've already addressed this, but it bears repeating.

In chapter 16.46 and following, Ezekiel compares the sins of Israel to those of Sodom. Here, if anywhere, we could expect the use of homosexual imagery to be used since Sodom is referenced. But notice what Ezekiel actually says about Sodom: "Sodom's sins were pride, gluttony, and laziness, while the poor and needy suffered outside her door" (Ezekiel. 16.49-50). It would appear that the word "sodomy" might be a more appropriate term for economic injustice or personal indulgence than it is to refer to some kind of homosexual practice.

- Anything that makes a person ritually unclean was an abomination (to'evah). For example having intercourse with a woman while she is menstruating. (Leviticus 15.19-24)
- Other abominations (to'evah) include: cursing, working on the Sabbath, and improperly purifying a woman after childbirth.
- It was an abomination (to'evah) to eat pork, or shellfish, or misuse incense.
- It was abomination (to'evah) to sow two different kinds of seed in the same field.
- Picking up fallen grapes during harvest was a to'evah.
- It was an abomination (to'evah) to cross breed livestock. Today that would rule out mules (horse and a donkey), ligers (male lion and female tiger), yattle (yak and a cow) yakalo (yak and a buffalo), and quite a few other mixed-breed animals.
- It was to'evah to plow a field with an ox and a donkey yoked together.

- It was abomination to wear a garment made of two different kinds of materials. Cotton/poly blends would be a no-no.
- Tattoos were an abomination.
- Long hair on a man was an abomination. (I think I know of a least one person who would take exception with that.)

Now some will say that all those above-mentioned issues are not moral issues. Homosexuality is a moral issue. How do we decide from the Bible what is moral and what is not? Does it become a purely subjective decision? Does "moral" refer only to things sexual? Is moral based on the penalty prescribed if you violate one of the commandments in the Holiness Code?

For example, the death penalty was commanded for this same-sex act mentioned in Leviticus. But the death penalty was also prescribed for working on the Sabbath. Who equates those two things today as being of equal moral value? My wife frequently has to work on Sundays and Sunday isn't even actually the Sabbath, but is she supposed to be taken out and stoned because she's supposedly breaking a moral law? The death penalty was prescribed for a rebellious child. Is that a moral issue?

3. I now come to the third point about how the nation of Israel was to be distinct and maintain holy purity. It was very important in the Israelite culture that male gender superiority be maintained, just as it is in the Middle Eastern culture of today. I'm always a bit amazed that thoughtful, intelligent people will not give this point the full weight that it deserves. In looking

at the societies of the Middle East and other parts of the world today we find continual examples of ongoing gender inequality and oppression of women. In various countries we see the following: women aren't allowed to vote; they can't drive; and they have to be totally covered, from head to toe in black (the *burka).* They're not allowed to pursue higher education and they have arranged marriages. Domestic abuse, genital mutilation, acid attacks, and female infanticide are common. This is in the 21st century! If it is still like this today, extrapolate that oppression back 2,000, 3,000, or 4,000 years and try and imagine what it must have been like for women then.

There is a pyramidal hierarchy that we see evidenced in ancient cultures—including Israel. At the top is the man. Underneath the man is the woman, considered to be the property of the man. The woman possessed some rights but was still viewed basically as chattel. Underneath the women were the children, having few rights and again considered to be the property of the man. Male children were of course more valued and privileged than female children. Finally, at the bottom of the pyramid were the slaves. They had no rights at all and could be treated in any way the owner chose.

This hierarchy is noted, both in the pagan cultures as well as the Israelite culture of the Old Testament. As we read through Leviticus what we find is that any action that undermines male gender superiority incurs the death penalty.

- A rebellious child could be put to death—that was an abomination (to'evah), in that it threatened the social order in a patriarchal society.

- Adultery was punishable by death—that was an abomination (to'evah) because it was an unlawful use of a woman who was the property of the man, and therefore jeopardized lines of ownership and inheritance.
- Engaging in a homosexual act where one of the men would take the passive role (like a woman and be penetrated) was an abomination (to'evah) and was punishable by death because it undermined male gender superiority. Males were not to put themselves in a womanly position—that would be demeaning and humiliating for a man. Thus the writer of Leviticus says in both 18.22 and 20.13, "If a man lies with a man *as one lies with a woman* it is an abomination (to'evah)."

Having an understanding of how demeaned, devalued, and dishonored women were in ancient societies and how it was such an incredibly strong patriarchal society in those cultures helps us understand what's being said here. Males are dominant—they are to take the aggressive role in sex; females are subservient, passive and compliant—they are to do what the man wants; and for a male to put himself in the role of a female and be passive would be emasculating, humiliating, and undermine the male superiority principle that was the foundation of the male dominated society of the time.

I mentioned this earlier, but it is interesting to me that there is no corresponding prohibition here for a woman having sex with another woman. Does that mean same sex relationships are O.K. for women but not for men? There was probably not that kind of double standard. That should give us a clue however, that there must be something more going on here than just two men having sex.

I believe these two verses have been taken out of their historical and cultural context and are being used today to condemn an entire group of people for failing to conform to an ancient, culturally conditioned code that is not even applicable to them or their circumstance.

Think about it this way: how many of these other commands that we've just looked at, does the church consider normal for today? None of them. Do any of us believe the national symbol of America is an abomination to God? Christians today wear cotton/poly blends, eat shellfish, work on the Sabbath, curse occasionally, have sex with their wives while they are menstruating, and eat ham. Our Christian teenagers frequently have tattoos on their bodies–often of a cross or biblical verse, and we do not advocate stoning our rebellious children. None of those aspects of the Holiness Code do we take today as being normative for us. Yet, we pull this particular command out regarding a man taking a passive role like a woman and say, "But this one *is* applicable for us today."

Let's leave the Holiness Code *in its entirety* where it belongs—in the Old Testament—as a set of guidelines God gave the ancient Israelites as they sought to become a nation distinct from their pagan neighbors.

Finally, let's remember that Jesus condensed the entirety of all the Old Testament laws, commandments, and prohibitions into just two: "One of them was an expert in the Jewish Law. So he tried to test Jesus by asking, 'Teacher, what is the most important commandment in the Law?' Jesus answered: 'Love the Lord your God with all your heart, soul, and mind.' This is the first and most important commandment. The second most important commandment is like this one. And it is, 'Love others as much as you love yourself.' All the Law of

Moses and the Books of the Prophets are based on these two commandments." (Matthew 22.35-40, CEV)

Conclusion

What does the Old Testament have to say regarding homosexuality, as we understand it today? As best as I can conclude—nothing.

It does focus on the heterosexual relationship as being the normal one for the purpose of procreation and populating the world. The human race has done a very good job of that (Genesis 1 and 2).

It focuses on heterosexual men wanting to violently rape other men for the purpose of domination and control (Genesis 19).

And it focuses on men undermining the male superiority principle of the ancient world by humiliating themselves and taking on a passive role in the sexual relationship—like a woman (Leviticus 18 and 20).

Perhaps the New Testament will clear this up for us.

Endnotes

[1] Wikipedia article, *Terminology of Homosexuality,* and *Harden-Eulenburg Affair.*

[2] Peter Gomes, *The Good Book, Reading the Bible with Mind and Heart* (Harper SanFrancisco, ©1996) pp. 149-150.

[3] The passage in Genesis 6 speaks of the sons of God (whom some Bible scholars say were angels) coming to earth and having intercourse with human women. These women then bore children who became mighty warriors—the Nephilim. This is just another part of the Bible that is very difficult to understand. But connecting two very difficult parts of the

Bible together and then jumping to the conclusion that those passages are talking about homosexuality is a prime example of a very poor hermeneutic.

11

New Testament Passages on Homosexuality

"When you introduce yourself as a Christian to a friend, neighbor, or business associate who is an outsider, you might as well have it tattooed on your arm: anti-homosexual, gay-hater, homophobic. I doubt you think of yourself in these terms, but that's what outsiders think of you."[1]

"The one thing the New Testament forbids us to do is to treat it as a static document to be used as a set of proof-texts for instant solutions to complex and controversial contemporary problems. To misuse the New Testament in this way is to deny its dynamic character and to fail to realize that the Word has to be applied in a specific context...A static interpretation of the New Testament is dependent on a frozen Christology."

—Karl Paul Donfried

The Changing Meaning of Words[2]

It used to be that,
"grass" was mowed,
"coke" was a cold drink,
"pot" was something your mother cooked in, and
"rock music" was your grandmother's lullaby.
"Aids" were helpers in the Principal's office,
"chip" meant a piece of wood,

"hardware" was found in a hardware store, and
"software" wasn't even a word.

Life before the Computer[3]

"Memory" was something you lost with age
An "application" was for employment
A "program" was a TV show
A "cursor" used profanity

A "keyboard" was a piano
A "virus" was the flu
A "CD" was a bank account

A "hard drive" was a long trip on the road
A "mouse pad" was where a mouse lived
And if you had a "3½ inch floppy"
...you just hoped nobody ever found out.

With the intense seriousness of this chapter, I thought beginning with a little levity might be helpful. However, there is a point to be made: over time the meaning of words change. Language is fluid. We routinely now use words that weren't even in existence a few decades ago. And many of the words that were used to mean one thing, now can have an entirely different meaning. I will elaborate more on word changes; meanwhile, in order to try and understand what is being said, we're going to have to look carefully at the Greek words that are used in the following passages in an attempt to understand their meaning.

Let me also say that this chapter has some very graphic images in it. The purpose for including these is not to be provocative or salacious—it is to demonstrate that what I'm writing about can be well documented by studying ancient Roman and Greek culture. Karl Paul Donfried's comment is extremely important: the New Testament must not be used as a set of proof texts when we are dealing with very complicated and controversial contemporary subjects. First and foremost, the Scriptures have to be applied to the specific context in which they were written. If a subject is complex, it's unrealistic to think that a solution is simple. As I wrote in the previous chapter, if we are going to have a healthy understanding of this topic, we are going to have to dig deeper into the Scriptures than many people have been willing to do up to this point.

There are three New Testament passages that seem to speak to the issue of homosexuality: I Corinthians 6 and I Timothy 1. These two similar passages are known as "The Vice Lists." The third passage is Romans 1.18-32. Let's begin by looking at The Vice Lists.

The Vice Lists

> "Do you not know that wrongdoers will not inherit the kingdom of God? Do not be deceived! Fornicators, idolaters, adulterers, male prostitutes (**malakoi**), sodomites (**arsenokoitai**), thieves, the greedy, drunkards, revilers, robbers—none of these will inherit the kingdom of God." (I Corinthians 6.9-10, NRSV)

> "Now we know that the law is good, if one uses it legitimately. This means understanding that the law is laid down not for the innocent but for the lawless and disobedient, for the godless and sinful, for the unholy and profane, for those who kill their father or mother, for murderers, fornicators, sodomites (**arsenokoitais**), slave traders, liars, perjurers, and whatever else is contrary to the sound teaching that

> conforms to the glorious gospel of the blessed God, which he entrusted to me." (I Timothy 1.8-11, NRSV)

Let's first look at the word *malakoi.*

The word *malakoi* (translated male prostitutes in I Corinthians 6) literally means "soft" and is primarily used to refer to a soft garment. It appears only four times in the New Testament. Three times it simply means "soft" and the fourth time it seems to imply some kind of effeminacy.

- Matthew 11.8: "What then did you go out to see? Someone dressed in *soft (malekos)* clothes? Look, those who wear *soft (malekos)* robes are in royal palaces."
- Luke 7.25: "But what did you go out to see? A man clothed in *soft (malekos)* garments?"

Both of these passages are referring to John the Baptist and the kind of clothing he wore. So, three of the four times this word is used in the New Testament it is literally referring to clothing. The fourth time it is used is here in I Corinthians 6 and it is translated "male prostitutes" in the New Revised Standard Version. That in itself, is quite a big leap in how this word is rendered in an English translation.

Before proceeding it might be helpful to see how this word has been understood down through the centuries:

- Strong's *Greek Dictionary of the New Testament* reads: *(malekos)* = soft (i.e. fine clothing), figuratively, a catamite—effeminate, [a boy who has a sexual relationship with a man].
- Some Greek dictionaries define it to mean morally weak.
- Martin Luther translated it "weaklings."

- Philo (a first century contemporary of Paul) applied the term to a man who had remarried his wife.
- It commonly designated any male whose behavior was less than respectable.
- Until the Reformation in the 16th century and in Roman Catholicism until the 20th century, *malakoi* was thought to mean condemning masturbation.

It's obvious that there has not been a consensus over the centuries as to just exactly what *malakoi* means, which in itself should give us pause before we jump to conclusions as to its meaning. Now let's observe how this word has been translated in various versions of the Bible:

- *effeminate* (King James Version, New American Standard Version)[4]
- *homosexuals* (New King James Version)
- *corrupt* (Lamsa Version)
- *perverts* (Contemporary English Version)
- *catamites* [call boys] (Jerusalem Bible)
- those who are *male prostitutes* (New Century Version)
- *male prostitutes* (New International Version, New Revised Standard Version)

The reason some versions translate this word as "catamite" or "male prostitute" is because some Bible scholars pair the word *malekoi* with the word that follows it: *arsenokoitai* in I Corinthians 6. This is the word to which we now turn.

Arsenokoitai

This word is even more difficult to understand because of its obscurity. We don't have any record of the word being used anywhere else before Paul uses it here in I Corinthians. These are the only two places in the New Testament where the word is used. Following Paul's two uses of it, there are a few recorded uses of the word during the next 200 years in secular Greek writings, and they refer to temple prostitutes. It may have been a "street" or "slang" word—something that common people used and that would have been understood by those reading Paul's letter.

Paul used it twice (once when writing to the Corinthians and then to Timothy—who pastored the church at Ephesus), so he must have assumed that his readers understood what he was talking about. However, that is a big assumption. Remember Peter comments in I Peter 3.16 that some things Paul writes are hard to understand, which some ignorant and unstable people distort. I don't want to be guilty of that, but I do acknowledge that some of the things Paul writes about can be a little confusing. This happens to be one of those things.

We must realize that when reading one of the letters in the New Testament, it is as if we are hearing only one side of a dialogue. As stated by Dr. R.S. Truluck, "Paul is often difficult and confusing to understand. A lot of Paul's writing is very difficult to translate. Since most of his letters were written in response to news from other people, reading Paul can be like listening to one side of a telephone conversation. We know, or think we know, what Paul is saying, but we have to guess what the other side has said." In other words, we can make some inferences based on what Paul wrote, but we need to be careful not to assume something that may or may not have been intended.

The word *arsenokoitai* is composed of two words *arsen* (male) and *kiotes* (to bed). What does that mean? *Male to bed?* We have to supply some words in order to have that even make sense: [a male taking a] male to bed [for sexual intercourse]. Those phrases represent what has to be supplied before the word can be associated with homosexuality.

Scholars correctly point out, however, that you can't put two words together and automatically assume that you've created a new term for men who have sex with men. One scholar, Dale Martin uses the illustration that the English word, "understand" has nothing to do with either standing or being under. Or take the word, *ladykiller.* A ladykiller has nothing to do with a lady who kills or a killer of ladies, but rather it's a man who knows how to charm the ladies. Or the word "butterfly" has nothing to do with either butter or a fly. He articulates a very important linguistic principle: the only reliable way to define a word is to analyze its use in as many different contexts as possible. That's the problem with this word—we only have a few contexts from which to examine it.

Here is how this word has been translated in various versions in I Corinthians and I Timothy:

Arsenokoitai

	1 Corinthians	**1 Timothy**
KJV	abusers of themselves with mankind	them that defile themselves
RSV	sexual perverts	sodomites
NIV	homosexual offenders	perverts
NASB	homosexuals	homosexuals
NAB	sodomites	sexual perverts
NEB	those guilty of perverts	homosexual perversion
Moffat	sodomites	sodomites
Luther	Knabenschaender[5] (child abusers)	child abusers

It's interesting that even the translators are not consistent in their use of the same word in the two different passages. This produces even more confusion as to the exact meaning of *arsenokoitai*. But how the various versions have translated this Greek word give some evidence to its ambiguity.

Here are two possible options that you'll find scholars discussing:

1. It is a term that refers to temple prostitution that was common in both Corinth and Ephesus. In the city of Corinth there was the Temple of Aphrodite who was the goddess of sexual fertility and in Ephesus there was the Temple of Diana. In those temples both male and female prostitution was an integral part of the worship of those deities. So the term would be referring to a man who went to the temple to worship and had sex with one of the young male prostitutes (a catamite) as part of that worship.
2. Some scholars say instead that it is a term that is referring to pederasty. What is that? The term itself means "lover of boys." It was a practice in ancient Greece and Rome for an older man to have a relationship with a pre-pubescent boy. It was a type of mentoring relationship, and although the relationship was not always sexual in nature, most of the time it was. Pederasty described an older man having this kind of relationship with a young boy who, once the boy entered puberty, was discarded for someone younger. In this situation, scholars connect the two words in I Corinthians, *malakos* and *arsenokoites* to refer to the young boy (the effeminate *malakos*) and the older adult in the relationship (the *arsenokoites*). Pederasty is child molestation, pure and simple, and is not the

same thing as homosexuality as we know it today. It is this type of relationship that some say the Roman Centurion and his boy servant might have had and why I mentioned in the chapter, "The Eight Hundred Pound Gorilla" that this definition might have some basis in historical fact.

In ancient Roman and Greek art, this kind of relationship was frequently featured in the following manner: the older man was represented by having a beard, the younger boy was clean shaven and the older man would be caressing the face of the young boy and fondling his genitals. Or, as in the case of the famous Warren Cup, it shows the older man being the one penetrating and the younger boy being the one penetrated.

Please note the following pictures.[6]

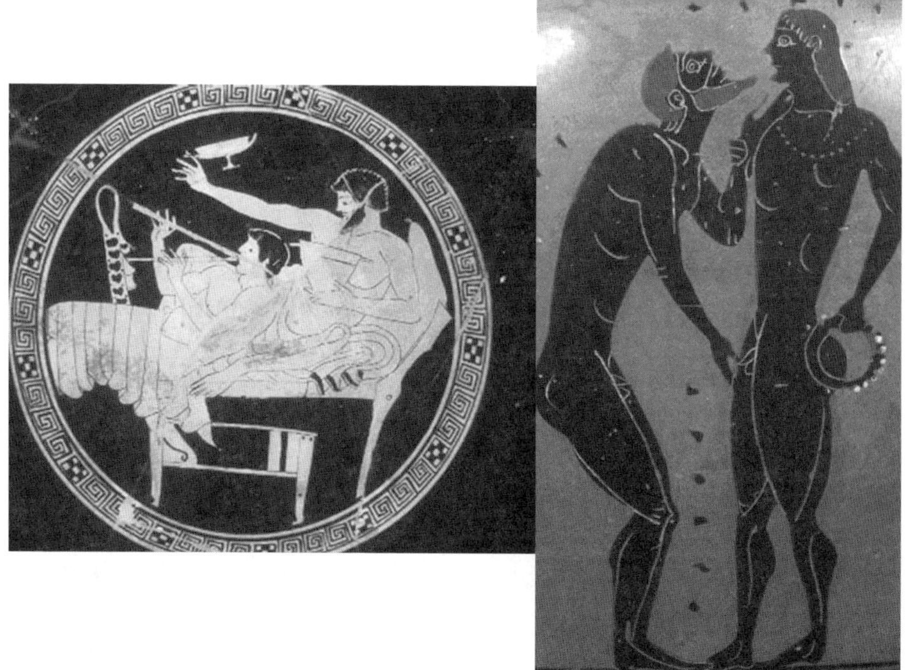

Now look again at the words used to translate *arsenokoites*: abusers of themselves with mankind (KJV), sexual perverts (RSV), sodomites (NAB), homosexual offenders (NIV). These words and phrases have a tendency to produce strong emotional reactions among people.

The phrase "abusers of themselves with mankind" is obscure enough that most people might read that and think, "What in the world does that mean?"

In our culture today the phrase "sexual perverts" could be understood in a number of different ways—none of them good.

The word "sodomite" which a few translations use, isn't even an accurate word to use in talking about this subject. As referenced earlier, the word "sodomite" is not found in the original Hebrew, nor is it found in the Greek. It was not until after the rise of the hierarchy in the institutional Church that the account of Sodom and Gomorrah began to be equated with homosexuality. It was then that the word "sodomite" came into use. The original use of this word simply referred to a person who was a resident of Sodom,[7] and the phrase "homosexual offenders" introduces a word that wasn't even used until the mid 1800s to describe a practice of some kind that was happening thousands of years earlier, and the word itself—homosexual—didn't appear in the Bible until 1958.

At this point I think it's important to repeat a few paragraphs from the preceding chapter.

"Many are also unaware of the fact that there is no word in biblical Greek or Hebrew that is equivalent to the English word, homosexual. Up until very recently other phrases or words were used to translate the Greek words in the New Testament that seemed to be talking about some kind of same sex experience. Recently, a rash of modern translations have begun using the word *homosexual* as part of their translation: New American Standard Bible (NASB, 1963); New King James Version (NKJV, 1982); New International Version (NIV, 1984); Contemporary English Version (CEV, 1995); and the English Standard Version (ESV, 2001).

The use of the word *homosexual* to translate a Hebrew or Greek word is very misleading. It reflects a bias on the part of the translator as well as a rather flagrant overgeneralization of a concept that has multiple nuances in ancient society. Sadly, using this term to translate a Hebrew or Greek word has confused this whole issue tremendously."

As ordinary Christians, we depend on Bible translators and scholars to give us accurate and clear translations of Scripture, but in this case they have failed miserably. The question before us is this: when we are confronted with a passage of Scripture that is obviously difficult to understand (even the Bible translators can't agree on exactly what it means), how should we, as 21st century Christ followers, seek to respond? Answer: with great caution, humility, and a teachable spirit.

I'd like to point out I Corinthians 6.11 that states, "And this is what some of you used to be. But you were washed, you were sanctified, you were justified in the name of the Lord Jesus Christ and in the Spirit of our God." It is not unreasonable to assume that some of men of Corinth and Ephesus who had become followers of Jesus had, at some point in their past, been part of the idolatrous temple worship of Diana and Aphrodite and in their idolatrous worship had either been the *malakoi* (the young catamite serving in the temple) or the *arsenokoites* (an older male who used the catamite) or they could have been involved in pederasty. In coming to belief in Christ, they were called to give up those behaviors because they were now washed, sanctified, and justified in Christ. Both of these behaviors however, are not in any way comparable to current homosexuality, as we understand it.

I will also remind you that women are not mentioned here. Again, we are left to wonder if women are given a free pass in regard to same sex relationships while only the men are chastised. It shows that this issue is not as cut and dried as most present day Christians have been led to believe. Looking carefully at these passages we see some behavior going on that was culturally driven. It shows the importance of looking at the Bible through the lens of culture and context before we extrapolate some teaching from the Scriptures and use it to condemn and marginalize an entire group of people in our current society.

It is an improper use of God's Word to take a few verses and use them as simplistic proof-texts for complex contemporary issues. That is misusing the Bible. When thinking through this issue more deeply it would seem that there is strong biblical justification for *not* continuing to brand gay men and women as depraved individuals on their way to hell. If someone chooses to have that attitude, they do so, not based on strong biblical support, but rather on their own emotional, cultural, or family bias.

Here is how The Message translates the verses in I Corinthians:

> "Don't you realize that this is not the way to live? Unjust people who don't care about God will not be joining in his kingdom. Those who use and abuse each other, use and abuse sex, use and abuse the earth and everything in it, don't qualify as citizens in God's kingdom. A number of you know from experience what I'm talking about, for not so long ago you were on that list. Since then, you've been cleaned

> up and given a fresh start by Jesus, our Master, our Messiah, and by our God present in us, the Spirit." (I Corinthians 6.9-11)

Romans 1.18-32

The conflict over the meaning of biblical texts becomes even more acute when we look at Romans. Some conservative scholars who are willing to dismiss the relevance of the other biblical texts that seem to address the issue of homosexuality argue that Romans 1 is a theological statement that has direct application for our time.

The New International Version of Romans 1.26-27 reads: "Because of this, God gave them over to shameful lusts. Even their women exchanged natural relations for unnatural ones. In the same way men also abandoned natural relations with women and were inflamed with lust for one another. Men committed indecent acts with other men, and received in themselves the due penalty for their perversion."

The King James Version of Romans 1:26-27 reads: "For this cause God gave them up unto vile affections: for even their women did change the natural use into that which is against nature: And likewise also the men, leaving the natural use of the woman, burned in their lust one toward another; men with men working that which is unseemly, and receiving in themselves that recompence of their error which was meet."

Other Bible translations, such as the American Standard Version, J.N. Darby Translation (1890), New American Standard Bible, New King James Version, New Living Translation, Revised Standard Version, Noah Webster Version (1833), Robert Young Literal Translation (1898), etc. do not differ significantly from the King James Version.

Here are some initial observations...

I. Again, we need to be reminded of Peter's assertion in 2 Peter 3.15-17 (NIV)

"His letters [Paul's] contain some things that are hard to understand, which ignorant and unstable people distort, as they do the other Scriptures, to their own destruction."

When approaching a very challenging, admittedly difficult and divisive subject such as homosexuality, it's important to remember that not everything Paul writes about is clear and simple. If the Apostle Peter (who was a contemporary of Paul) had trouble understanding some of Paul's writings, it's rather arrogant on our part to assert that we're able to comprehend everything he had to say some 2,000 years later. Recognizing this helps us maintain a teachable spirit and an attitude of humility.

II. We need to be sure and read these verses in context.

Many have taken these two verses (vss. 26 & 27) and developed ideas based on them apart from the context in which they were written.

Paul's thesis statement for his letter to the Romans comes in Romans 1.16 "For I am not ashamed of the gospel; it is the power of God for salvation to everyone who has faith, to the Jew first and also to the Greek." The very next sentence states this thesis in another way: "The one who is righteous will live by faith" (Romans 1.17).

No one is excluded from the possibility of receiving God's salvation. The gospel that Paul is proclaiming in Romans does not center on the issue of sexuality. It focuses on the universality of sin and the free grace of salvation through the life, death, and resurrection of Jesus Christ. That is the essence of the Christian message.[8]

Idolatry, Not Sexuality

In Romans 1.18-32, Paul is writing about idolatry, that is worshiping, giving our ultimate allegiance to anything in the creation instead of God, the Creator. Idolatry is the theme of this section of Romans. Subsequent ideas that Paul puts forth in these verses (sexual behavior, wickedness, evilness, greed, depravity, envy, murder, strife, deceit, malice, gossiping, slandering, God-hating, insolent, arrogant, boastful, parental disobedience, senseless, faithless, heartless, ruthless, etc.) are all as a result of people turning away from God and engaging in some type of idolatry.

Paul is writing from Corinth, a bustling seaport town that was notorious for vice of all kinds. Coincidently, in the Roman Empire a common name for a prostitute was "a Corinthian girl." Paul writes of people worshiping "images resembling a mortal human being or birds or four-footed animals or reptiles" (vs. 23) instead of God. Paul concludes that because people engaged in idolatry, "God gave them up to degrading passions." (vs. 26)

It seems as though Paul is "setting up" his Jewish readers (read Romans 2, where Paul addresses the Jews). It is easy at this point in the text for them to feel self-righteous. Jews didn't worship images of birds, animals, or reptiles. Those were typical idolatrous behaviors of the Gentiles. But then Paul lowers the boom on his readers by listing other sins that proceed from idolatry—covetousness, malice, envy, strife, deceit, craftiness, gossip, and slander. Idolaters could become haughty, boastful, rebellious toward parents, foolish, faithless, heartless, and ruthless (vss. 29-31). Now Paul is talking to all of us, speaking to those sins of attitude to which we sometimes succumb when we turn our ultimate allegiance away from the true God.

Paul makes this point again, in Romans 2.1. We are all without excuse, especially when we judge others. Why? Within all of us, there is the potential to idolize someone or something other than God. Paul is driving home the point that 1,500 years later became the heart of Reformation theology: no one is righteous before God. Paul had been criticizing those idolatrous Gentiles (Romans 1). Now he is saying to his Jewish colleagues (Romans 2) and to us, no one is righteous. We are all sinners. That is Paul's point in these first two chapters of Romans.[9]

III. Some important words in Romans 1:26-27

It is extremely important to understand as best we can the precise meaning of certain key words in Verses 26 & 27, as expressed in the original Greek:

About the words *shameful lusts:* The Greek phrase translated as shameful lusts in the New International Version of the Bible is also translated as:

- vile affections and degrading passions (Amplified Bible)
- dishonorable passions (English Standard Version)
- degrading passions (New American Bible, New American Standard Bible, & New Revised Standard Version)
- vile affections (King James Version)
- shameful desires (New Living Translation)
- evil things (Living Bible)
- shameful affections (Rheims New Testament)
- immoral, unnatural drives (The Great Book: The New Testament in Plain English)

In the original Greek, the phrase probably does not mean passions or lust as we understand those terms today—the type of emotion that one encounters in a marriage or sexually active relationship. Rather, it seems to refer to the frenzied state of mind that many ancient mystery cults induced in worshipers by means of wine, drugs, and music. The phrase appears to describe the results of ritual sexual orgies as performed in many pagan settings at the time. This would also explain heterosexual men and women engaging in same-sex behavior during these orgies. See the following section on the word *exchanged.* Paul could be referring here to Pagan fertility cult worship, which was prevalent in Rome and Corinth (and all over the Roman Empire) at the time.

About the words *exchanged, leaving, change, abandoned,* and *gave up*: these are the various words used in different translations. The Greek word *aphente* means, to give up, leave behind, forsake, or divorce.

> "Even their women exchanged natural relations for unnatural ones. In the same way the men also abandoned natural relations with women..." (vs. 26-27)

These words are important, because they precisely describe the people about whom Paul is talking.

- If he is actually talking about women having sexual relations with other women (even though this is not explicitly stated in the text), then he is writing about women with a heterosexual orientation, who had previously engaged in only heterosexual sex, who had exchanged their normal/inborn behaviors for same-sex activities. That is, they deviated from their heterosexual orientation and engaged in sexual behavior with other women.

- He could be talking about women taking the more aggressive, active, and dominant role with their male partners, thus violating the male gender dominance, which was the accepted social norm. When Paul talks about the natural use of the woman, he is referencing the dominant thought of his day, that the only use a woman had was to have babies to continue the man's lineage. A woman was a man's property (paid for with a dowry)—his "baby maker" so-to-speak. Any type of sexual behavior initiated and perhaps controlled by the women would not be looked upon favorably. Notice also that Paul says, "their women" (possessive). That seems to be another indication of a gender role structure.

In fact, not until the 20th Century did some in the church start teaching that sex had more than just a procreative purpose. Thus the terms, *natural* and *unnatural* in vs. 26 are to be understood in light of this cultural context.

- Similarly, in vs. 27 he describes men who abandoned or gave up their normal/inborn behaviors and engaged in same-sex activities. In this case, as with the women, he could be describing individuals with a heterosexual orientation, who were engaging in same-sex behavior–in violation of their natural desires.

About the words *natural* (vs. 26 & 27) and *unnatural* (vs. 26)—it is important to understand the key words used here: In the original Greek, the words are *physis*, "nature" and *para physin*, "against nature."

> "Because of this, God gave them over to shameful lusts. Even their women exchanged natural (physis) relations for unnatural (para physis) ones. In the

same way the men also abandoned natural (physis) relations with women and were inflamed with lust for one another. Men committed indecent acts with other men, and received in themselves the due penalty for their perversion."

According to Vine's *Expository Dictionary of New Testament Words*, *physis* means "produced by nature, or inborn." Here are some significant places where the Apostle Paul uses the word *physis*.

A. Galatians 4.8 "Formerly, when you did not know God, you were slaves to those who by nature (physis) are not gods.

Paul is referring to idols. People were enslaved by their ignorance and worshiped both animate and inanimate objects—elevating them to the level of deity. But by their very "nature" those animate and inanimate objects did not possess divine characteristics. Divinity was not intrinsically part of their nature.

B. I Corinthians 11.13-15 "Judge for yourselves: Is it proper for a woman to pray to God with her head uncovered? Does not the very nature (physis) of things teach you that if a man has long hair, it is a disgrace to him, but that if a woman has long hair, it is her glory? For long hair is given to her as a covering."

This passage is very unclear and controversial: both as to what the problem was and as to what solution Paul was suggesting.

C. Galatians 2.14-15 "I said to Peter in front of them all, 'You are a Jew, yet you live like a Gentile and not like a Jew. How is it then, that you force Gentiles to follow Jewish customs?' We who are Jews by birth (nature=physis) and not Gentile sinners..."

In this context, Paul is rebuking Peter and Barnabas for separating themselves from Gentiles at meals. Being born a Jew is not something you had a choice about—that was the nature of your biological parents—they were Jewish, so you were born Jewish.

> **D. Ephesians 2.1-3** "As for you, you were dead in your transgressions and sins, in which you used to live when you followed the ways of this world and of the ruler of the kingdom of the air, the spirit who is now at work in those who are disobedient. All of us also lived among them at one time, gratifying the cravings of our sinful nature [this is not a good translation of the word *sarke,* which means "flesh"—a better way of translating this would be: "...gratifying the cravings of our flesh] and following its desires and thoughts. Like the rest, we were by nature (physis) objects of wrath."

Paul says here that even he himself, along with the rest of humanity was an object of God's wrath. Why? Because all of humanity lives in "the flesh"—this mortal body which is subject to desires and passions that can lead us away from God. As human beings we cannot live on this earth, apart from living in this fleshly body. Because of that, by nature we are objects of wrath.

> **E. Romans 2.14** "Indeed, when Gentiles, who do not have the law, do by nature (physis) things required by the law, they are a law for themselves, even though they do not have the law, since they show that the requirements of the law are written on their hearts, their consciences also bearing witness, and their thoughts now accusing, now even defending them."

What Paul is saying here is that there is apparently some kind of awareness of the laws of God "...written on [people's] hearts." Even though a Gentile may not be aware of the laws of God, as given to the Jews, that Gentile still has some kind of internal "awareness" as part of their nature, that helps them be aware of right and wrong, good and bad. And when they violate that knowledge/awareness, their conscience accuses them (i.e. they feel guilty).

> **F. Romans 11.24** "After all, if you were cut out of an olive tree that is wild by nature (physis) and contrary to nature (para physis) were grafted into a cultivated olive tree, how much more readily will these, the natural branches be grafted into their own olive tree."

Paul uses the illustration of an olive tree to describe the process whereby God has allowed the Gentiles access to God. Symbolically, the Jews were the cultivated olive tree; the Gentiles were the wild olive tree. God "grafted" the Gentiles to the cultivated tree so that they too, could experience the kindness of God (vs. 22) and share in the "nourishing sap from the olive root" (vs. 17). It's a mystery (vs. 25) but "... Israel has experienced a hardening in part until the full number of the Gentiles has come in."

The idea here is this: by nature (just because of who they are) Gentiles are a "wild olive tree" just as the Jews by nature (just because of who they are) are a "cultivated olive tree."

In all of these passages, the use of this word *physis* points to a fundamental, underlying concept: there is something within us, part of our nature that we cannot change. It's just part of who we are. Thus as it relates to Romans 1.26-27 Paul would be saying that both men and women went against their natural, inborn heterosexual orientation and as part of their idolatrous worship, engaged in same sex behavior.

About the word *unnatural* (vs. 26):

The Greek phrase *para physin* is commonly translated into English as:

- unnatural and abnormal (Amplified Bible)

- contrary to nature (English Standard Version)
- against nature (King James Version, Rheims New Testament)
- sin with each other (Living Bible)
- unnatural (New American Bible, New American Standard Bible, New International Version, New Revised Standard Version)
- immoral, unnatural drives (The Great Book: The New Testament in Plain English)

Today, the word unnatural implies that something that is morally wrong and should be condemned. The common definition of *para physin* is: "Deviating from the ordinary order either in a good or a bad sense, as something that goes beyond the ordinary realm of experience."

So the term doesn't originally have a morally negative connotation, but rather is simply a neutral idea that could be used in either a good, bad, or neutral way. Perhaps the word *unconventional* would have been a more precise word for translators to use.

By way of example, notice again, how the phrase *para physin* is used in the passages listed above. In the above reference of I Corinthians 11.14 we see Paul use the phrase to refer to long hair on men as unusual (unconventional) and not ordinary. In the reference of Romans 11.24 Paul used the term to describe God's positive actions to bring Jews and Gentiles together. In other words, God did something very unusual (unconventional) by pruning the Gentiles from the wild olive tree, where they grew in their natural state, and grafting them into the cultivated olive tree of God's people. Since it cannot be that God sinned, to say that God did what is "contrary to nature" or "against nature" (vs. 24) means that God did something surprising, out of the ordinary, unconventional.

About the phrase *just reward:*

Romans 1.27 refers to the idolaters receiving a recompense or penalty or just reward for their perversion. The word "penalty" offers a loaded translation; it carries a negative connotation that is not in the Greek. The Greek word simply means recompense, reward, or payment that could be positive, negative or neutral. So also, the word perversion (NIV) throws in a totally unwarranted idea. The Greek word *plane* (translated, "perversion") simply means error. Using the English word "perversion" puts an extremely twisted spin on this word.

This entire last phrase in vs. 27 is extremely difficult to interpret from the original Greek. Look at how the King James translated it: "...and receiving in themselves that recompence of their error which was meet." What in the world does that mean? Later translations have also had difficulty with this phrase and have sadly used some words that are inaccurate and emotionally charged in 20th and 21st century usage.

Conclusion

In many ways, I hesitated to delve into this issue quite as deeply as I have. Being a realist, I recognize that many people will continue to maintain their beliefs about homosexuality regardless of these explanations. If a person wanted to try and convince others that their opposition to homosexuality wasn't warranted biblically, I don't know how effective it would be if they did it based on what you've just read here.

Nonetheless, for a subject as volatile as homosexuality, I think this type of study is extremely important.

As in virtually all other hot religious topics, religious conservatives and liberals take differing views on this section of Scripture.

Conservative view: Taking "the simple language of Scripture" approach brings us to the conservative view. In other words, we take our English translations of these verses as literal, and at face value, and develop our ideas about homosexuality from there.

The assertion of Bennett Sims, the former Episcopal Bishop of Atlanta, is a good example of a viewpoint that is held by many conservative Christians. He believes that these verses have done more to form Christian's negative opinion of homosexuality than any other single passage in the Bible. He writes:

> "For most of us who seriously honor Scripture, these verses still stand as the capital New Testament text that unequivocally prohibits homosexual behavior. More prohibitively, this text has been taken to mean that even a same-sex inclination is reprehensible, so that a type of humanity known as 'homosexual' has steadily become the object of contempt and discrimination."

The bottom line for the conservative view is that same-sex orientation is not a valid concept, but rather homosexuality is a choice that people make and as such it is possible to change a person. One of the ways this can be accomplished is through "reparative" or "conversion" therapy, which basically addresses the behavior.

Some conservatives are realizing that this issue is not quite that simple and they will say that while there may be a homosexual orientation (in other words, a person may "by nature" be attracted to their same sex), it is still wrong and a violation of God's ideal (a tragedy in nature because of sin) and individuals who have a same-sex orientation should seek to find ways to minimize the effects this orientation has upon them.

Liberal view: Looking behind the English words on the pages of the Bible in an attempt to understand what is being said from a grammatical, historical, and cultural context develops the liberal view. At this stage of this debate, both conservatives and liberals are attempting to do serious word studies from the original Greek language seeking to understand Paul's confusing words. So it's not just the liberals who are digging deeper. This is good and healthy, because prayerfully it will ultimately lead to a meeting of the minds. If nothing else at least it might give both sides a deeper respect and appreciation for one another.

When this is done (exploring these verses from a grammatical, historical, and cultural context) the idea that becomes apparent is that Paul is talking about people who, because of their idolatry, became unrestrained in their actions and engaged in behaviors that were accepted in their pagan belief system and encouraged as part of their worship experiences. During those rituals people went against their heterosexual nature and started engaging in sexual behavior with members of the same sex. Paul condemns such behavior. And he concludes that this type of idolatry will inevitably lead to other negative behavior: "...unrighteousness, fornication, wickedness, covetousness, maliciousness, full of envy, murder, debate, deceit, malignity, whisperers, backbiters, haters of God, despiteful, proud, boasters, inventors of evil things, disobedient to parents, without understanding, covenant breakers, without natural affection [care and love for family members], implacable, [and] unmerciful."

In this view then, there is no real connection between the issues Paul is addressing in the first century and our current understanding of homosexuality. Paul would have had no concept of same-sex orientation, as we understand it today. He was dealing with situations that he observed in his time and culture.

Conclusion

What does the New Testament have to say regarding homosexuality, as we understand it today? As best as I can conclude—nothing.

- It might focus on the sexual exploitation of young boys during the worship of pagan deities. (I Corinthians 6 and I Timothy 1).
- It might focus on the subject of pederasty—the sexual use of a young boy by an older male, which in our day is child abuse (I Corinthians 6 and I Timothy 1).
- It might focus on the consequences of idolatry—worshipping anything other than the one true God. Part of that idolatrous worship experience would be heterosexual men and women going against their nature and engaging in same-sex experiences.

But none of these situations remotely resemble our understanding of homosexuality today—that a certain percentage of the population is wired for a same-sex attraction.

None of these experiences speak to the issue of committed Christian men and women, who are not idolaters, but who are wholeheartedly serving God and wanting to honor God, yet who have a same-sex attraction.

None of these experiences remotely address the concept of two men or two women living in a loving, committed, monogamous relationship. This was a concept that would have been completely foreign to people in the first century.

None of these experiences remotely resemble the understanding that we are gaining today–that homosexuality has multiple causes: biological, psychological, and sociological. In other words, there are some gay men and women who are that way because of their natural biological inclination. Others are gay because of psychological or sociological issues, trauma, or events that have occurred in their lives. In those last two situations it might be possible through intense, long term counseling to develop a heterosexual orientation. However, trying to change the biological component would be like a black man trying to change the color of his skin or a leopard trying to change his spots (Jeremiah 13.23)—it's just who they are, and trying to force a person to change only creates greater anxiety, guilt, frustration, hopelessness, and despair.

Let me remind you how I concluded the previous chapter concerning the Old Testament passages on homosexuality: "What does the Old Testament have to say regarding homosexuality, as we understand it today? As best as I can conclude—nothing.

It does focus on the heterosexual relationship as being the normal one for the purpose of procreation and populating the world. The human race has done a very good job of that (Genesis 1 and 2).

It focuses on heterosexual men wanting to violently rape other men for the purpose of domination and control (Genesis 19).

And it focuses on men undermining the male superiority principle of the ancient world by humiliating themselves and taking on a passive role in the sexual relationship—like a woman (Leviticus 18 and 20).

Perhaps the New Testament will clear this up for us."

Then again...perhaps it won't.

Endnotes

[1] David Kinnaman, *UnChristian What a New Generation Really Thinks About Christianity*, (p. 93)

[2] "The Changing Meaning of Words," author unknown.

[3] "Life Before the Computer," author unknown.

[4] If the word is understood to mean effeminate, then the difficulty is this: the passage is condemning someone for a characteristic and not an action. In other words there are heterosexual men who speak and act effeminately. It doesn't seem proper then that this would be the intent of the word.

Just because someone doesn't "walk like a man and talk like a man" doesn't mean he isn't a heterosexual male.

[5] This word specifically refers to boys since the word "knaben" is the German word for boys.

[6] Pictures are public domain. The Warren Cup is housed in the British Museum.

[7] See Rev. Fred Pattison, founder of The Evangelical Network and his booklet "Christians Combating Homophobia Among Christians."

[8] See footnote #9 in the chapter, "Is Jesus the Only Way?" for a further expansion of this idea.

[9] See Jack Rogers, Jesus, *The Bible and Homosexuality.* (Westminster John Knox; Revised Expanded edition, ©2009).

12

Is Jesus the Only Way?

I dreamed death came the other night
And heaven's gate swung wide
A glorious angel soon appeared and ushered me inside
And there to my astonishment were folks I'd known on earth
Some I'd judged and found unfit
And some of little worth
Indignant words rose to my lips but never were set free
For every face showed stunned surprise
Because no one expected me!

As I begin this chapter, let me ask (and answer) a few questions:

1. Who will be in heaven? Answer: according to evangelical Christian theology—only those who have accepted Jesus Christ as their personal savior from sin.
2. How populated will heaven be? Again, according to classic Christianity—full, but comfortable.
3. Who will be in hell? Based on the answers to questions one and two—most of the human race.

The question Marcus Borg asks is very pertinent here: "Does it make sense that the creator of the Universe would be known in only one religious tradition?"[1] With seven billion people currently living on planet Earth and a multitude of different religious beliefs, is it not arrogant for Christians to proclaim that not only is our way the right way, it is also the only way to God?

For those who journey into the new Re•Formation this will be one of the more difficult transitions that some will have to make—particularly those from a more conservative background. Immediately some will start thinking of arguments against the idea that there might be others (besides those for whom Jesus is their personal savior) who will populate heaven. After all, Jesus did say in John 14.6, "I am the way, the truth, and the life. No one comes to the Father except through me." This is the classic proof text for what is called Christian exclusivism—the idea that salvation is possible only through Jesus and thus only through Christianity. And then there is Acts. 4.12, "There is salvation in no one else, for there is no other name under heaven given among men by which we must be saved." Then we have I Timothy 2.5, "For there is one God; there is also one mediator between God and humankind, Christ Jesus, himself human, who gave himself a ransom for all...."

One of the most fundamental tenets of Christianity over the last two millennia is the idea that Christianity is God's only way of salvation. This belief has been the prime directive for mission. Taking Matthew 28 as the marching orders from our King, we have attempted to "Go into all the world and make disciples of all nations, baptizing them in the name of the Father and of the Son and of the Holy Spirit..." (Matthew 28.19). We would be hard pressed to determine how many billions of dollars have been spent down through the centuries attempting to proselytize the heathens. Has this been money well spent? An argument I've heard for years is, "You can't put a price on a human soul. No matter what it costs, if we are able to rescue one soul from hell, it's worth it."

Now before you start gathering wood in order to burn me at the stake, let me clarify some things. Do I believe in the Great Commission? Yes, I do. Do I believe that people need to hear about Jesus Christ? Yes, I do. Do I believe that spending money on mission is important? Absolutely. Why? Because I believe that in Jesus Christ we have the fullest manifestation and revelation of God. John says, "In the beginning was the Word and the Word was with God and the Word was God… and the Word became flesh and lived among us, and we have seen his glory, the glory as of a father's only son, full of grace and truth." (John 1.1, 14)

As Christians, we share the good news of God because we believe it is the hope of the world. We share the Gospel because we believe that it is not just about heaven, but also about having true life here on earth. We share the Gospel because in it is a holistic salvation that brings to us unconditional love, mercy, and forgiveness; it is a new beginning, a new life, a mission, and purpose for our lives, and a communion with God in a way not found in any other faith. Finally, we share the gospel because Jesus asked us to. That in itself should be motivation enough. Having said that however, the question still remains–does that automatically invalidate all other religions and faith systems? This is the crux of the issue for the new Re•Formation.

John Stott said, "I have never been able to conjure up (as some great Evangelical missionaries have) the appalling vision of the millions who are not only perishing but will inevitably perish. On the other hand…I am not and cannot be a Universalist. Between these extremes I cherish and hope that the majority of the human race will be saved. And I have a solid biblical basis for this belief."[2] Up until now, there seems to have been only two options that have been talked about regarding the eternal state of the human race. At one end we have the Universalist approach to salvation—the idea that ultimately everyone will someday be saved. At the other end you have the Christian exclusivism approach to salvation—the idea that only those who have accepted Jesus Christ as personal savior will be saved (a view which condemns the vast majority of the human race to hell).

For some, this is very black and white, cut and dried. However, even those within these two camps allow for some wiggle room in their positions. The Universalists will acknowledge that there are in fact, some people who are so debased and wicked and have done such horrible, atrocious things that they won't make it to heaven. The most notable example always given is Hitler. Exclusivism also allows for some exceptions. If a baby dies before it reaches the "age of accountability," if an individual is mentally handicapped and is not able to make a decision for Christ, or the proverbial villager in a remote jungle where no missionary has ever made it—those individuals are handled with grace and compassion by God and thus they get a hall pass into heaven.

Are these the only two options? I believe that within the new Re•Formation there will be healthy dialogue focused on the idea that there will in fact be far more people in heaven than what some Christians maintain. Upon what basis do I make that kind of claim? I have to ask myself some questions, the answers to which help me process this issue. What do we do with the hundreds of millions of individuals who are on their own spiritual journey, longing to know God; who are seeking God to the best of their knowledge and ability; who pray faithfully (often putting Christians to shame) and who want to try and please God by trying to do what is right as they understand it?

I think of Mahatma Gandhi as an example. He was born a Hindu and practiced Hinduism all his life. As a common Hindu, he believed all religions to be equal, and rejected all efforts to convert him to a different faith. He was an avid theologian and read extensively about all other major religions. He had the following to say about Hinduism:

> "Hinduism as I know it entirely satisfies my soul, fills my whole being...When doubts haunt me, when disappointments stare me in the face, and when I see not one ray of light on the horizon, I turn to the Bhagavad Gita, and find a verse to comfort me; and I immediately begin to smile in the midst of overwhelming sorrow. My life has been full of tragedies and if they have not left any visible and indelible effect on me, I owe it to the teachings of the Bhagavad Gita."

Interestingly, it was Gandhi who also said of Christianity: "I like your Christ. I do not like your Christians. They are so unlike your Christ." Are we prepared to discount this man's testimony of the hope and encouragement his own religious experience brought him? Many within the Christian exclusivism camp will say, "Yes. Even though he was sincere, he was sincerely wrong." I can't. We can't just ignore these individuals, or pretend they don't exist, or worse yet take the attitude that they are all deceived. I think that is simplistic and naïve. That might have been an acceptable approach to take when people lived in their own cloistered cultures, sheltered from other world religions, but today with the entire world as our community, dismissing the religious experiences of hundreds of millions of others is not a satisfactory option.

A second question is how do we reconcile the basic message preached from pulpits all over the world with the idea of billions of people spending eternity in hell? Preachers have a tendency to say some pretty lofty things to people in order to let them know how much God loves them:

- God knows us before we were born.
- God formed us in our mother's womb.
- God cares for us like a mother cares for her child, like a shepherd watches over his sheep.
- God loves us and has a wonderful plan for our lives.
- God is our father, our protector, our shield, our supplier, our hope, our joy, and our strength.
- God sees our tears and hears our cries.
- God numbers the hairs on our head.
- God hears our prayers.
- God understands our hearts and sees our attempts to do what is right as we understand it.

If those are all accurate statements reflecting the basic character of God, is it then really the gospel (the good news) to say that God chooses to take away all that love, attention, and care once a person dies and has them spend an eternity in torment and punishment simply because though a person sought God, he or she didn't understand that Jesus was the Christ and didn't call upon him for salvation?

Something doesn't seem quite right with that. For a God whose defining characteristic is love and who also has the characteristics of justice and righteousness—for that God to draw away from hundreds of millions of people who have earnestly sought God and have them be tormented for eternity, whether God directly sends them to hell, or simply allows them to go there—seems neither loving, just, or right.

It reminds me of the game show "Let's Make a Deal," where there are three doors—doors one, two, and three. Behind door number one is a brand new car and a trip to the Bahamas. Behind the other two doors are a blender and a year's supply of toilet paper. Sadly however, on a spiritual level, if a person didn't choose door one (Jesus Christ) they are destined, not to go home with a blender or toilet paper, but rather destined to spend eternity apart from this God who supposedly cared so much about them.

In addressing this issue, my aim is not to provide an in-depth exploration, but rather to simply share a few thoughts that might generate some discussion. Specifically I would like to focus on John 14.6 since this is the primary proof text used to support the idea of Christian exclusivism. In doing so, I believe it is necessary to take a huge step back and understand the bigger picture. What I mean is this: how does John 14.6 fit in with the rest of Jesus' teaching?

A reading of the four Gospels (Matthew, Mark, Luke and John) reveals two important observations:

1. The Synoptic Gospels (Matthew, Mark, and Luke) are quite similar to one another. The Gospel of John, on the other hand, is very unique. Without getting bogged down in detail, though the three Synoptic Gospels share a considerable amount of similar material, over 90 percent of John's Gospel is unique to him. The Synoptics describe much more of Jesus' life, miracles, parables, and exorcisms. However the materials unique to John are notable, especially in their effect on the development of Christian theology.[3]

2. In his teaching ministry, Jesus frequently spoke in parables and metaphors. This was so apparent that on one occasion his disciples asked him why:

> "The disciples came and asked him, 'Why do you speak to the people in parables?' He answered, 'To you it has been given to know the secrets of the kingdom of heaven, but to them it has not been given. For to those who have, more will be given, and they will have an abundance; but from those who have nothing, even what they have will be taken away. The reason I speak to them in parables is that seeing they do not perceive, and hearing they do not listen, nor do they understand.'" (Matthew 13.10-17)

What is a parable? In a simplified way it has frequently been described as an earthly story with a heavenly meaning. Building on this idea, William Barclay stated that the parables of Jesus use familiar examples to lead men's minds toward heavenly concepts. The parables of Jesus cover a number of subjects. There are parables about the kingdom of God: the sower, the hidden treasure, the pearl of great price, the growing seed, the mustard seed, and the leaven. There are parables about loss and redemption: the lost coin, the lost sheep and the lost son. There are parables about love and forgiveness: the Good Samaritan, the two debtors, and the unforgiving servant. There are parables about prayer: the unjust judge, the friend at night, the Pharisee and the Publican, and parables about the end time (eschatological parables): the faithful servant, the ten virgins, the great banquet, the rich fool, the wicked husbandmen, the wheat and the tares, the net, the budding fig tree, and the barren fig tree. Other parables include the wise and foolish builder, the lamp under a basket, the unjust steward, the rich man and Lazarus, the talents, and the workers in the vineyard.

In harmonizing the Gospels, the parables are listed in the following chart:[4]

Number	Event	Matthew	Mark	Luke	John
1	The Growing Seed		Mark 4:26-29		
2	The Two Debtors			Luke 7:41-43	
3	The Lamp under a Bushel	Matthew 5:14-15	Mark 4:21-25	Luke 8:16-18	
4	Parable of the Good Samaritan			Luke 10:30-37	
5	The Friend at Night			Luke 11:5-8	
6	The Rich Fool			Luke 12:16-21	
7	The Wise and the Foolish Builders	Matthew 7:24-27		Luke 6:46-49	
8	New Wine into Old Wineskins	Matthew 9:17	Mark 2:22-22	Luke 5:37-39	
9	Parable of the Strong Man	Matthew 12:29	Mark 3:27	Luke 11:21-22	
10	Parable of the Sower	Matthew 13:3-9	Mark 4:3-9	Luke 8:5-8	
11	The Tares	Matthew 13:24-30			
12	The Barren Fig Tree			Luke 13:6-9	
13	Parable of the Mustard Seed	Matthew 13:31-32	Mark 4:30-32	Luke 13:18-19	
14	The Leaven	Matthew 13:33		Luke 13:20-21	
15	Parable of the Pearl	Matthew 13:44-46			
16	Drawing in the Net	Matthew 13:47-50			
17	The Hidden Treasure	Matthew 13:52			
18	Counting the Cost			Luke 14:28-33	

Number	Event	Matthew	Mark	Luke	John
19	The Lost Sheep	Matthew 18:10-14		Luke 15:4-6	
20	The Unforgiving Servant	Matthew 18:23-35			
21	The Lost Coin			Luke 15:8-9	
22	Parable of the Prodigal Son			Luke 15:11-32	
23	The Unjust Steward			Luke 16:1-13	
24	Rich man and Lazarus			Luke 16:19-31	
25	The Master and Servant			Luke 17:7-10	
26	The Unjust Judge			Luke 18:1-9	
27	Pharisees and the Publican			Luke 18:10-14	
28	The Workers in the Vineyard	Matthew 20:1-16			
29	The Two Sons	Matthew 21:28-32			
30	The Wicked Husbandmen	Matthew 21:33-41	Mark 12:1-9	Luke 20:9-16	
31	The Great Banquet	Matthew 22:1-14		Luke 14:16-24	
32	The Budding Fig Tree	Matthew 24:32-35	Mark 13:28-31	Luke 21:29-33	
33	The Faithful Servant	Matthew 24:42-51	Mark 13:34-37	Luke 12:35-48	
34	The Ten Virgins	Matthew 25:1-13			
35	The Talents or Minas	Matthew 25:14-30		Luke 19:12-27	
36	The Sheep and the Goats	Matthew 25:31-46			

The reason I wanted you to see this in visual form is because there is something very noticeable when laid out this way: there are no parables associated with the Gospel of John. In John's Gospel, metaphors are used.

What is a metaphor? It is a figure of speech in which an implied comparison is made between two unlike things that actually have something important in common. The word itself comes from a Greek word meaning to "transfer" or "carry across." Metaphors "carry" meaning from one word, image, or idea to another. Metaphors abound in our language: all the world's a stage, rug rat, couch potato, road hog, and it's raining cats and dogs—are all examples of metaphors.

One of the more familiar metaphors for a Christian would be John Bunyan's *The Pilgrim's Progress* written in 1678. This is an allegorical tale of Christian the pilgrim on his journey to the Celestial City. *The Pilgrim's Progress* is an extended metaphor that has helped millions of people make spiritual progress during the past three centuries. When we move into the Bible, there are dozens of metaphors that are used. David saying, "God is my fortress" or picturing God as a mother hen, God is our rock, Jesus is living water, the Holy Spirit is our Advocate, and the Refiner's fire. All are metaphors. Metaphors for God have long permeated our theology. In our efforts to understand that which we cannot understand, we use imagery that makes sense to us. Sometimes this imagery is very helpful in connecting us to God and gaining insight into the mystery of our faith. Sometimes these metaphors can do a disservice to God and our faith.

This becomes important when we come to the Gospel of John. In John's gospel we have the famous I AM statements of Jesus, of which there are seven. These are metaphors Jesus gives concerning himself. Jesus says, I am…

- The bread of life (John 6.35)
- The light of the world (John 8.12)
- The gate of the sheep (John 10.9)
- The good shepherd (John 10.11)
- The resurrection and the life (John 11.25)
- The way, the truth, and the life (John 14.6)
- The true vine (John 15.5)

Is Jesus literally bread? Is Jesus literally light? Is Jesus literally a gate? Is Jesus literally a shepherd? Is Jesus literally a vine? If we understand these other I AM statements to be metaphors, describing some aspect of who and what Jesus is, why do we then take this one metaphor about Jesus being the way, the truth, and the life and make it literal? Is Jesus literally the way to get to God?

Is there another way in which this could be understood? What might Jesus have been trying to tell us in using this particular metaphor? William Barclay makes the following observation:

> "In ancient Judaism there were three basic cornerstones of religious life. First, the religious life was about finding the way to God. Second, it was about discerning the fabric of moral truth. And third, it was in search of the formula that would lead to a life of blessing and prosperity. In fact, you can find those words here and there in the Scriptures of old: the way, the truth, and the life. So you can understand, then, that when Jesus identified himself with these three metaphors he was claiming to be all that both they and the world had been waiting for."[5]

Let's explore this further. If we look at the teachings of Jesus in their entirety what can we discover? Concerning Jesus being the way—what is the way that Jesus taught? The way of God is the way of death and resurrection—dying to an old way of living and being reborn into a new way—that is the only way to God. The way of God involves loving your enemies; turning the other cheek; going the extra mile; giving to those who ask of you; praying for those who persecute you; not judging others; taking up a cross and following; taking up the yoke and learning from his gentleness and humbleness and thus finding rest for our souls; doing the will of the

Father. All of those are part of the way of God. They involve a death to ourselves, our selfishness, our importance, our goals and ambitions, and being reborn as new people who seek a way other than the way of the world.

What is the truth? The truth of God is this: the way up is down. If one wants to be great in the kingdom of God, one must become a servant. The truth of God is found in humility, service, and compassion. "Whoever humbles himself as this child, he is the greatest in the kingdom of heaven." (Matthew 18.4) In Matthew 20.25-28 we read, "Jesus called them to himself, and said, 'You know that the rulers of the Gentiles lord it over them, and their great men exercise authority over them. It is not so among you, but whoever wishes to become great among you shall be your servant, and whoever wishes to be first among you shall be your slave; just as the Son of Man did not come to be served, but to serve and to give His life a ransom for many.'"

What is the life? The life of God is a life lived for others, not for oneself. It is a life where sacrifice is necessary and yet the paradox is that it is in that sacrifice that we truly find ourselves coming alive. Living the life involves the relinquishment of rights and acceptance of responsibilities. Living the life means learning how to love God with all of our heart, mind, soul, and strength, and loving others as we love ourselves. We live the life when we extend compassion to others, not rejection, condemnation, or judgment. We live the life when we live as Jesus lived. Living life like this is God's way, and it is not an easy way. Jesus said the gate is narrow and small and few find it (Matthew 7.13-14).[6] If we hear the truth of these words and act on them however, we will be like a wise man, who built his house upon the rock (Matthew 7.24). The life of God is discovered when we spend our lives learning to do what Jesus encouraged us to do: "A new command I give you: Love one another. As I have loved you, so you must love one another. By this all men will know you are my disciples, if you love one another." (John 13.34)

Marcus Borg relates the following story:

> "I once heard about a sermon preached by a Hindu professor in a Christian seminary several decades ago. The text for the day included the 'one way' passage, and about it he said, 'This verse is absolutely true—Jesus is the only way.' But he went on to say, 'And that way—of dying to an old way of being and being born into a new way of being—is known in all of the religions of the world.'"[7]

I think of the Beatitudes in relation to this:

Blessed are the poor in spirit,
Blessed are those who mourn,
Blessed are the gentle,
Blessed are those who hunger and
thirst for righteousness,
Blessed are the merciful,
Blessed are the pure in heart,
Blessed are the peacemakers,
Blessed are those who have been perse-
cuted for the sake of righteousness.
You are the salt of the earth…You are the
light of the world…Let your light shine.

Is it possible that as we seek to have these virtues manifest in our lives, we begin to live life according to the way of God, the truth of God, and the life of God?

Is it possible that the way, the truth, and the life of Jesus is a universal way, known to millions who have never heard of Jesus? This makes the way, not a set of beliefs about Jesus (that one enters into new life by believing certain things to be true), but rather the way of Jesus is the way of death and resurrection—a transition and transformation from an old way of being to a new way of being, an old way of living to a new way of living. As Borg says,

> "Finally, the language of incarnation, so central to John, is crucial for understanding the threefold affirmation of this verse: Jesus is not only 'the way,' but also 'the truth, and the life.' Incarnation means embodiment. Jesus is the way—Jesus is what the way embodied in a person looks like. Jesus is the truth—Jesus is what the truth embodied in a person looks like. Jesus is the life—Jesus is what life (real life) embodied in a person looks like."[8]

Great spiritual truths are not the exclusive domain of Christianity. Throughout the centuries, seekers of God have been able to capture the essence of genuine spirituality in a variety of faith traditions. And just because those spiritual truths came through means other than the Christian faith, that does not invalidate other faiths or the person seeking to live life according to the revelation they've received.[9] Truth is truth and all truth is God's truth. When Buddha said, "In separateness lies the world's great misery; in compassion lies the world's true strength" did he not capture the heart of God for humanity? When Gandhi said, "An eye for an eye makes the whole world blind" was he not grasping the truth that God's way is the way of loving your enemies, instead of seeking revenge? When the Dalai Lama said, "If you want others to be happy, practice compassion. If you want to be happy, practice compassion" was he not saying that it is in loving others and loving ourselves that we find the true meaning of living?

In many ways John 14.6 reminds me of the prayer of St. Francis:

Lord, make me an instrument of your peace.
Where there is hatred, let me sow love;
where there is injury, pardon;
where there is doubt, faith;
where there is despair, hope;
where there is darkness, light;
and where there is sadness, joy.
O Divine Master,
grant that I may not so much seek
to be consoled as to console;
to be understood, as to understand,
to be loved as to love.
For it is in giving that we receive,
it is in pardoning that we are pardoned,
and it is in dying that we are born to eternal life.

Is it possible that anyone who seeks to live his or her life according to a prayer such as this might actually be on the right path to God? And that even though they may have never heard of Jesus or don't know to call upon the name of Jesus might still be accepted by God? This middle position between Universalism and Christian exclusivism is called "inclusivism" (a position held by numerous individuals throughout the centuries like Justin Martyr, Zwingli, John Wesley, C.S. Lewis, and John R. Stott).

> "[Inclusivism] allows that some may reject the grace of God. It posits that Jesus' atoning work is the means by which God saves. And it maintains that salvation is not by works but by faith. It holds that in God's mercy, God will save many who sought him although they did not understand to call upon the name of Christ…I am convinced that the God whose glory fills the cosmos, who calls each of the billions

> and billions of stars by name, who sends his Son to reconcile and redeem the world, who is the Father in the story of the Prodigal Son, is not a small God. He must know that some of his children will not understand the gospel…I am reminded of the words of God to Samuel concerning King David: 'The Lord does not see as mortals see; they look on the outward appearance, but the Lord looks on the heart' (I Samuel 16.7). And just as God applies the merits of Christ's atoning work to children and the mentally handicapped, and some would say, to the faithful who lived before the time of Christ, so too, it seems to me, God can apply these merits to those who love God, seek God, and strive to serve God, but who either have never heard the gospel, or could not make sense of it."[10]

One final thought. I've tried to present a possible idea of what Jesus might have been trying to communicate through the use of the "way, truth, and life" metaphor. But it might also be helpful to understand what Jesus was not saying. I do not believe he was saying, "Different strokes for different folks." Or "Anyone can worship the god of one's choice, and it's all good, no matter whom or what one worships." An analogy that perhaps you've heard, and in the past one that I've taken great exception to, is that of hikers climbing up different sides of a mountain. The idea is that people who are on a spiritual journey are taking different routes but ultimately they'll all reach the same pinnacle. Each religious tradition has discovered a unique route for reaching the top. While they are climbing the mountain, the traditions cannot necessarily see one another. Individuals with the climbing parties may not even be aware that others are ascending the mountain. They think they alone are making the ascent. Yet when they reach the top, the climbers are surprised to find one another. Each party has reached the same goal, just by a different route.

I have come to the conclusion that this analogy is actually helpful for a couple of reasons. First, it provides a concrete way of understanding how different faiths may ultimately lead to the same place. Second, the analogy helps me understand that God may allow for different paths, each with its own integrity. Sometimes I fear that Christian liberals are overly quick to claim the unity between the world religions and get sloppy about it. They'll say things like, "They're all just saying the same things. They're really no different. All paths are legitimate." That's not true. The world's religions really are different. Their routes up the mountain engage different terrain, with different obstacles and challenges, different vistas, and different places of rest. On the other hand, sometimes Christian conservatives take the differences between the faiths to be signs that all religions but Christianity are following the wrong path. The mountain analogy helps us see how differences between faiths may be celebrated instead of either minimized (by liberals) or condemned (by conservatives). It also illustrates the fact that God's plan for the world is larger than our human minds can comprehend, because God in fact, does love all the people of the world.

Jesus makes a fascinating comment in John 10.16, "I am the good shepherd. I know my own and my own know me, just as the Father knows me and I know the Father. And I lay down my life for the sheep. I have other sheep that do not belong to this fold. I must bring them also, and they will listen to my voice. So there will be one flock, one shepherd." The mountain analogy helps shed some light on what Jesus might have been saying when he spoke of the sheep who are not of the same fold but who have the same shepherd. Jesus does not simply say, "all paths are legitimate" or "anything goes." Rather there is the affirmation that there is one God and there is one mediator between God and humankind, Christ Jesus. It is Christ who calls from the mountaintop to his sheep, who are making their way up the paths provided for them. And all sincere seekers, regardless of their spiritual tradition or faith, those who are truly seeking the way of God, once they reach the pinnacle, will find their path has ultimately led them to the Christ and in him they will find their rest.

Endnotes

[1] Borg, *Reading the Bible again for the First Time,* p. 14.

[2] David Edwards and John R. W. Stott, *Evangelical Essentials: A Liberal-Evangelical Dialogue* (InterVarsity, Downers Grove, Ill. ©1988), p. 327.

[3] There are many significant differences when one compares the Gospel of John with the Synoptic Gospels:

- Jesus is identified with the divine Word ("Logos") and referred to as Theos ("God").
- The gospel of John gives no account of the Nativity of Jesus, unlike those of Matthew and Luke, and his mother's name is never given.
- In Chapter 7:41-42, and again in 7:52, John records some of the crowd of Pharisees dismissing the possibility of Jesus being the Messiah, on the grounds that the Messiah must be a descendent of David and born in Bethlehem, stating that Jesus instead came out of Galilee; John made

no effort to refute or correct (nor did he affirm) this, and this has been advanced as implying that John rejected the Synoptic tradition of Jesus' birth in Bethlehem. F.F. Bruce sees this as characteristic Johannine irony: placing in the mouths of Jesus' opponents' statements that both the Gospel writer and his readership know to be mistaken.

- The Pharisees, portrayed as more uniformly legalistic and opposed to Jesus in the Synoptic Gospels, are instead portrayed as sharply divided; they debate frequently in the Gospel of John's accounts. Some, such as Nicodemus, even go so far as to be at least partially sympathetic to Jesus. This is believed to be a more accurate historical depiction of the Pharisees, who made debate one of the tenets of their system of belief.
- John makes no mention of Jesus' baptism, but quotes John the Baptist's description of the descent of the Holy Spirit.
- John the Baptist publicly proclaims Jesus to be the Lamb of God. The Baptist recognizes Jesus secretly in Matthew, and not at all in Mark or Luke. John also denies that he is Elijah, whereas Mark and Matthew identify him with Elijah.
- The Temple incident appears near the beginning of Jesus' ministry. In the Synoptics this occurs soon before Jesus is crucified.
- John contains four visits by Jesus to Jerusalem, three associated with the Passover feast. This chronology suggests Jesus' public ministry lasted two or three years. The Synoptic Gospels describe only one trip to Jerusalem in time for the Passover observance.
- Jesus washes the disciples' feet instead of the Synoptics ritual with bread and wine (the Eucharist).
- No other women are mentioned going to the tomb with Mary Magdalene.

- John does not contain any parables. Rather it contains metaphoric stories in which each individual element corresponds to a specific group or thing.
- Major Synoptic speeches of Jesus are absent, including the Sermon on the Mount and the Olivet discourse.
- While the Synoptics look forward to a future parousia (the second coming of Christ), John presents an eschatology that has already been realized.
- The Kingdom of God is only mentioned twice in John. In contrast, the other Gospels repeatedly use the Kingdom of God and the Kingdom of Heaven as important concepts.
- The exorcisms of demons are never mentioned as in the Synoptics.
- John never lists the Twelve Disciples and names disciples not found in the Synoptics. While James and John are prominent disciples in the Synoptics, John mentions them only in the epilogue, where they are referred to not by name but as the "sons of Zebedee."
- Thomas the Apostle is given a personality beyond a mere name, as "Doubting Thomas."

These are only a few of the many differences between John's Gospel and the Synoptic Gospels.

[4] Wikipedia article, "The Parables of Jesus."

[5] William Barclay, *The Gospel of John,* Volume 2. (Westminster Press, ©1975), p. 157.

[6] Marcus Borg reminds us that there are two distinctively different kinds of truth to consider here, two kinds of wisdom. There is, first, the notion of conventional wisdom, which reflects the dominant themes of the culture and the world — material, power, success, independence, and self-sufficiency. These are almost always entirely on the surface of life. They convey the common assumptions about the ways and workings of the world. Jesus referred to these as the broad way— the way of the great many. But there is also the narrow way and this is much closer to the heart of Jesus.

This is the worldview that looks far beneath the surface and reaches to the depths of life. It's the understanding that looks to the discerning vision of God. This is the kind of truth that is counterintuitive, subversive, and surprising — full of spirit, mystery and paradox. It's about finding life by losing it. It's about taking hold by letting go. It's about discovering love by being sacrificial. It's about becoming whole by facing brokenness. It's about trusting that the smallest seed bears the largest of trees. (Marcus Borg. *Meeting Jesus Again for the First Time.* HarperSanFrancisco, 1994, pp. 69-95. Used with permission. All rights reserved).

[7] Ibid, p. 216.

[8] Ibid, p. 217.

[9] The book of Romans presents an interesting insight into the subject of people following the revelation they have received. The theme of Romans is found in chapter 1.16-17 where Paul says that the righteous shall live by faith. This became one of the cornerstone doctrines of the Protestant Reformation. In order to drive home the powerfulness of this truth, Paul then proceeds to talk about three different groups of people: the pagan Gentiles (1.18-32); the moralistic Gentiles (2.1-16); and the Jew (2.17-3:8). Regarding the pagan Gentiles, Paul shows that people, apart from God, will fall into idolatry, which results in all types of improper behavior. However Paul says, "For even thought they knew God, they did not honor Him…." (1.21). In other words, even the pagan Gentile has some kind of knowledge of God, primarily seen through Creation (1.20). Paul then turns his attention to those Gentiles who think they are "better" because they don't conduct themselves as the idolatrous Gentiles. Of them, he says they "…are without excuse…you who pass judgment…for you who judge practice the same things." He goes on to point out that there is no partiality with God, but that when Gentiles, who do not have the Law instinctively do what the Law says, they become a law to themselves (2.14) and they show that the Law of God is written in their hearts and their conscience then either accuses or defends them (2.15). Again, there is some

kind of revelatory sense of God in the lives of these individuals. Finally, Paul proceeds to the Jews who obviously had a much-heightened revelation of God and as Paul says, the Jews "boast in God and know His will" (2.17-18) but even with this revelation the Jew is not any better off than the others (3.9). Remember, he is trying to show that everyone, regardless of his or her excesses, their moralistic self-righteousness or their unique relationship to God—everyone is on a level playing field when it comes to having a relationship with God. God's way is the way of faith, and faith alone. To further drive home this point, Paul then quotes and paraphrases a number of Old Testament passages: "There is none righteous, not even one; there is none who understands, there is none who seeks for God; All have turned aside, together they have become useless; there is none who does good, there is not even one...etc., etc. (3.10-18) It is these verses that some have used to highlight the complete and total depravity of humanity. However, we must realize that Paul was using hyperbole here (exaggeration for emphasis). He is not literally saying that every single person on the planet has absolutely no interest, desire, or hunger for spiritual things. He has already stated that all three of these groups have some revelation of God. Spiritual longings are inherent within the human soul. That is continually seen in the various people groups of the world. "You have made us for yourself, O Lord, and our heart is restless until it rests in you" (Augustine). People in every generation and every culture have been on a spiritual search...each seeking God as best as they know how with the revelation they have received. It is to these individuals that the idea of inclusivism speaks. Teilhard de Chardin said, "We are not human beings having a spiritual experience. We are spiritual beings having a human experience." The quest for spiritual truth is as much a part of the human drama as is our need for water, food, or air.

[10] Adam Hamilton, *Seeing Gray in a World of Black and White,* pp. 109-110. Used with permission. All rights reserved.

13

For the Beauty of the Earth

For the beauty of the earth
For the glory of the skies,
For the love which from our birth
Over and around us lies.

Refrain:
Lord of all, to Thee we raise
This our hymn of grateful praise.[1]

"God blessed them, and God said to them, 'Be fruitful and multiply, and fill the earth and subdue it; and have dominion over the fish of the sea and over the birds of the air and over every living thing that moves upon the earth.'"

–Genesis 1.28

By all accounts, the human race has done a more than adequate job in fulfilling God's command to be fruitful and multiply. Although it's hard to get accurate estimates, it appears that during the first century CE the human population on planet Earth was around 300 million. That's less than currently live in the United States. The United Nations has predicted that global population will reach seven billion this year (2011) and climb to nine billion by 2050, "...with almost all of the growth occurring in poor countries, particularly Africa and South Asia," said John Bongaarts of the non-profit Population Council. To feed all those mouths, "We will need to produce as much food in the next 40 years as we have in the last 8,000," said Jason Clay of the World Wildlife Fund at the annual meeting of the American Association for the Advancement of Science (AAAS). Clay said that if current trends continue "by 2050 we will not have a planet left that is recognizable"[2] Based on a 2003 United Nations study, close to 25,000 children die every day from starvation.

Some view statements like these as nothing more than the radical rantings of environmentalist tree huggers and human population control advocates. It's obvious that the human race has done a very good job of dominating this planet and its resources. I know there are many who say that global warming is a hoax and that we don't have a food shortage problem; rather we have a distribution problem. Indeed, those things may be true and one may choose to believe them, but doesn't common sense tell us we can't continue to misuse the earth and its resources without experiencing some consequences? The individuals and organizations that ring alarm bells for us in regards to the deteriorating condition of our planet may be viewed by some as extremists, but I'm reminded of the words of Mark Twain, "The radical of one century is the conservative of the next. The radical invents the views. When he has worn them out, the conservative adopts them."

Creation Theology is nothing more than the Christian community developing a greater concern for the environment and the nonhuman world. This attention is important not only for the long-term self-interest of the human race but also because of the biblical understanding of creation. "The

Earth is the Lord's and all it contains."[3] The heavens and the Earth are understood to be God's creations. They are subject to God's loving care and intimate attention. God is so intimately involved with the natural order that to behold God's creation is to behold God's very Self. This idea is strongly reflected in the wisdom literature—Proverbs, Ecclesiastes, and Job. Sadly, because of many Christians' preoccupation with their heavenly home, I'm afraid they have been unconcerned about their earthly one. In the new Re•Formation this will change. We are not the owners of this planet, but rather stewards, and a steward manages something (wisely we hope) that belongs to someone else.

> "We have most often treated the Earth as if it does belong to us. We have seen nature primarily as having instrumental value (its use for us) and not as having intrinsic value (its value in itself, that is, its value to God). Our view has been anthropocentric, human-centered, whereas God loves the whole of creation and not simply human beings. And within our anthropocentric view, we think primarily of ourselves and not very much about future generations—our children and our children's children. The earth belongs to God, not simply to us, and not simply to those of us alive today."[4]

In the preface to *The Radical Center*, I mentioned that in many ways the new Re•Formation is about both stepping back into our rich Christian history as well as moving forward into a bold new world.

It is here, in regard to our relation to creation, that I think stepping back becomes helpful. I believe Celtic Christianity has a great deal to offer us.

There is no plant in the ground
But tells of your beauty, O Christ.

There is no creature on the earth
There is no life in the sea
But proclaims your goodness.

There is no bird on the wing
There is no star in the sky
There is nothing beneath the sun
But is full of your blessing.

Lighten my understanding
Of your presence all around, O Christ.
Kindle my will
To be caring for creation.[5]

The early Celtic Christians were models for us as it relates to a healthy understanding of creation. They lived and breathed the cycles of the natural world, highly aware of the rhythms of land and sea, plant and animal. Their lives revolved around creation's cycles: springtime to harvest, darkness to light. To them ocean waves were like hymns of praise, the song of a bird told of God's handiwork, and the sun displayed God's majesty.

St. Columbanus (7th century) taught that in order to know the Creator, one must understand creation. Nature, he taught, reveals glimpses of who God is. Each day that came, each spring that arrived, and each new life that sprang forth showed that God was still present and active in their world. Eriugena, a Celtic theologian of the 9th century, wrote that if God's voice were silent, creation would cease to exist.

Although they heard God's voice in nature, the Celtic Christians still viewed creation through the lens of Scripture.

According to Genesis 1, God saw that creation is good, and human beings were made in God's image. Though sometimes hidden away and covered by sin, that goodness can never be completely removed. Celtic teaching invites us to view Christ, the Word that was in the beginning, as the One who became flesh and entered into the world to uncover the forgotten goodness that is within all of us.[6]

"In our sin we separate ourselves from the natural environment. Greedily we turn upon it, consuming it, destroying it, befouling it. Natural resources continue to dwindle as the possibilities of long-term damage to the atmosphere and seas increase. Our focus is not for the beauty and unity of all God's creation but for our own survival."[7]

Humanity has taken gross advantage of the created world. The earth and the Christian faith may very well be around a lot longer than any of us think. It's best to invest our energy in bringing them into harmony with one another while we still can. Over the next few generations there will be healthy dialogue on how we are to take seriously our role as caretakers of God's creation and what will be the practical implications of that responsibility.

Endnotes

[1]"Christian Hymn" by Folliott S. Pierpoint (1835-1917) The hymn first appeared in 1864 in a book of poems entitled, "The Sacrifice of Praise."

[2] AFP news article, February 20, 2011.

[3] Psalm 24.1 (NASB)

[4] Borg, *The Heart of Christianity,* p.144. Used with permission. All rights reserved.

[5] Excerpt from *Celtic Prayers from Iona,* by J. Philip Newell, ©1997, Paulist Press, Inc.

[6] *Alive Now,* November/December, 2010, Nashville, Tennessee. "A Sacred Golden Thread" by Kiran Young Wimberly.

[7]From United Methodist Member's Handbook pp. 74-75, Discipleship resources, 2006.

14

Jesus Loses His Hands

"For some time now, the hands and feet of the body of Christ have been amputated, and we've been pretty much reduced to a big mouth."

–Rick Warren

"In our era, the road to holiness necessarily passes through the world of action."[1]

"He has told you, O Mortal, what is good; and what does the LORD require of you but to do justice, and to love kindness, and to walk humbly with your God?"[2]

"Christianity is essentially a social religion, and to turn it into a solitary religion is indeed to destroy it."[3]

"The Gospel of Christ know no religion but social; no holiness but social holiness"[4]

I'm sure that most people at one time or another have seen a picture of the great "Christ the Redeemer" statue which stands up on the top of a hill in Rio de Janeiro, Brazil. In case you haven't seen it…here it is:

Here He is looking out over the city.

This Art Deco-style statue of Jesus stands 125 feet tall, weighs in at 1000 tons, and is located at the peak of the 2330-foot Corcovado Mountain overlooking the city. It's a potent symbol of Christianity, made even more powerful by the fact that Rio is one of the most sensuous cities in the world. Just recently the statue was recognized as one of the new Seven Wonders of the World in a worldwide poll.

Although we can't compete with "Christ the Redeemer," Denver, Colorado has a statute of Jesus too. It's called the "Sacred Heart of Jesus" at the Mother Cabrini Shrine in Golden, just outside of Denver. Three hundred and seventy three steps lead to the 22-foot statue of the Sacred Heart of Jesus, which sits on an 11-foot base. Now I know that a 33-foot statue isn't quite as dramatic as a 125-foot one but in case you haven't seen it, here it is:

There's an interesting thing about the statue. If you'll look closely you'll notice that Jesus' left hand is pulling open his cloak to reveal his heart. It's a compelling symbol of Christianity as well—Jesus showing his heart for the city which he overlooks.

Something very sad (and symbolic I might add) happened to the statue on May 19, 2007. Lightning struck the arms, feet and the base of the statue. Jesus' hand and part of his arm were blown off, and his feet were damaged as well. According to the news report, the Catholic sisters who operate the shrine immediately began to research how Jesus could be fixed.

I think Jesus needs to be fixed. Well, that's not exactly right. I think the followers of Jesus need to be fixed. As I said earlier, it's kind of symbolic, Jesus losing his hand and part of his feet. One of the most fundamental ideas in Christianity is that individuals who claim to be Christ followers are charged with being the hands and feet of Jesus in this world. The Christian imperative has always been a two-fold emphasis: loving God and loving others. In the chapter "The Blind Men and the Elephant Church," I mentioned that I believe the church has been held hostage by two extremes over the last hundred years: the liberals and the conservatives—the perception being that the liberals focus on social justice issues and the conservatives concentrate on getting people saved and having a personal relationship with Jesus. Prayerfully, one of the results of the new Re•Formation will be the synergism of those two extremes. The new Re•Formation is a movement that is bringing back into harmony and wholeness, two fundamental ideas that should never have been split asunder in the first place.

A healthy understanding of a Christian's role in this world has both an Old Testament and New Testament aspect. The continual cry of the Old Testament prophets was for a society in which justice and mercy would reign. The New Testament call is for individuals to treat their neighbors with love and compassion. This two-fold emphasis then—a just and fair society and an individual involvement in ministering to the needs of others—becomes the foundation for understanding our Christian responsibility.

In the Old Testament the call of the Prophets to the nation of Israel was for the establishment of a just society:

- Isaiah 1.17 (NASB) "Learn to do good; seek justice, reprove the ruthless, defend the orphan, plead for the widow."
- Isaiah 59.14 (NASB) "Justice is turned back, and righteousness stands far away; for truth has stumbled in the street, and uprightness cannot enter."
- Jeremiah 7.5-7 (NASB) "For if you truly amend your ways and your deeds, if you truly practice justice between a man and his neighbor, if you do not oppress the alien, the orphan, or the widow, and do not shed innocent blood in this place, nor walk after other gods to your own ruin, then I will let you dwell in this place, in the land that I gave to your fathers forever and ever."
- Jeremiah 9.24 (NASB) "'But let him who boasts boast of this, that he understands and knows Me, that I am the LORD who exercises lovingkindness, justice and righteousness on earth; for I delight in these things,' declares the LORD."
- Ezekiel 22.29 (NASB) "The people of the land have practiced oppression and committed robbery, and they have wronged the poor and needy and have oppressed the sojourner without justice."
- Amos 5.15 (NASB) "Hate evil, love good, and establish justice in the gate!"

- Amos 5.24 (NASB) "But let justice roll down like waters, and righteousness like an ever-flowing stream."
- Micah 6.8 (NASB) "He has told you, O man, what is good; and what does the LORD require of you but to do justice, to love kindness, and to walk humbly with your God?"

What is justice? Some have misunderstood this word. Often it is seen as the opposite of God's mercy. Justice then becomes God meting out punishment for human sin. God's mercy is seen as God's loving forgiveness of us in spite of our guilt. Obviously given this choice, we would all prefer God's mercy and hope to escape the justice of God. However,

> "...seeing the opposite of justice as mercy distorts what the Bible means by justice. Most often in the Bible, the opposite of God's justice is not God's mercy, but human injustice. The issue is the shape of our life together as societies, not whether the mercy of God will supersede the justice of God in the final judgment."[5]

As we read through the Old Testament prophets, it becomes very clear that a just society is one in which the inequities of that society seek to be mitigated as much as possible. The poor, the oppressed, the needy, the strangers in the land, the orphan, the widow, and all the disenfranchised, marginalized people of a society are to be the focus when seeking to establish justice in a society. Why? Because every human being is made in God's image and God cares for all people. All people matter to God. Therefore, all people need to matter to us. A society that panders to the rich, the influential, the powerful, and the elite while neglecting the marginalized is an odious thing to a caring, compassionate God.

As an example from history, I turn again to John Wesley. Though part of the educated elite in England, Wesley's heart was for the poor in that society. A contemporary commentator put it this way, "When the poor gathered in huge throngs to hear Wesley preach, the ruling classes said he was threatening the social order. Indeed he was, not because he had a political message, but just because he treated the lower classes as human."[6]

In any society there are social systems that deeply affect people's lives. Social systems would include the political system of a country, economic systems, and systems of convention that would include cultural attitudes and values embraced by the people of that society. Systemic injustice (long held patterns in a society which marginalize various groups, i.e. slavery, segregation, the subordination of women) does not change overnight. It is deeply rooted and often takes decades and generations of people rising up to speak out against the injustice.

Often it is only after the fact that the negative impact of those systems on human lives is fully seen. Slavery is an example. The system of slavery was monstrous, yet up until a few centuries ago it was practiced in many Christian countries and sanctioned by law, convention, and the Bible. The system of segregation was monstrous, yet up until a few decades ago it was a reality in "Christian" America. The system of marginalizing sexual minorities is monstrous, yet it is still deeply embedded in our political and economic structures and in our conventional attitudes. Prayerfully, years from now we will look back in retrospect and be ashamed at how some within our society have been treated. "We will have to repent in this generation not merely for the hateful words and actions of the bad people but for the appalling silence of the good people."[7]

A passion for this kind of justice is one aspect of love. It is one of the ways we fulfill the second part of the great commandment—loving our neighbor as ourselves. To stand up for justice means that we not only speak up, but also reach out and do what we can to help those who are treated unjustly.

When we move into the New Testament the question is asked: what was the message of Jesus? What was the heart and passion of his ministry? We don't have go far into the Gospels to get our answer: "Now after John the Baptizer was arrested, Jesus came to Galilee, proclaiming the good news of God, and saying: 'The time is fulfilled, and the kingdom of God is at hand; repent and believe in the good news.'"[8]

The vast majority of New Testament scholars will agree that the heart of the message of Jesus of Nazareth was centered in this concept of the Kingdom of God. The Gospel of Mark (our earliest gospel) uses the opening scene of Jesus' public ministry—his "inaugural address"—to state the theme of his gospel: the Kingdom of God. Many of Jesus' parables had the Kingdom of God as their subject. The center of the Lord's Prayer is: "Thy kingdom come, thy will be done on earth as it is in heaven."

Jesus used many metaphors and symbols in his teaching. The Kingdom of God is one of those and has more than one meaning in the message of Jesus. It can refer to the power of God working in Jesus as he healed and exorcised demons. Sometimes it has a mystical meaning, referring to the presence of God. It can refer to the kingdom at the end of human history when God wraps things up and ushers in a new age.

It also has a political meaning. Living in a world where there were literal kingdoms, the term was used to refer to the political system under which the first century Jews lived. It was the kingdom of Rome, ruled by the powerful and wealthy. When Jesus spoke of the Kingdom of God, his hearers would wonder—how does the Kingdom of God differ than Herod's kingdom, or the kingdom of Caesar? What then is the kingdom of God? "In a sentence: it is what life would be like on Earth if God were king and the rulers of this world were not."[9]

Significantly, this kingdom is for this Earth, not for heaven. As John Dominic Crossan remarked, "Heaven's in great shape; earth is where the problems are."[10] The vision of Jesus was for an Earth where the poor would be blessed and happy, where the hungry would be filled, where those in sorrow would laugh (see the Beatitudes). It is in this kingdom where Jesus is Lord, "...when you give a banquet, invite the poor, the crippled, the lame, the blind..." (Luke 14.13).

The question for Christians in every generation is: how can we help inaugurate the kingdom of God in our world? To some degree, I believe the answer to that is found in one of the most famous parables Jesus told: the Parable of the Good Samaritan. It is within that parable that we see the practical application of the second part of the great commandment—loving our neighbor as ourselves. Today, we ask the same question that was asked of Jesus 2000 years ago—exactly who is my neighbor?

In Luke 10:25-29, an expert in the law confronts Jesus: "'Teacher,' he asked, 'what must I do to inherit eternal life?' When Jesus asked him what was written in the Law and how this expert understood its interpretation, the man said: 'Love the Lord your God with all your heart and with all your soul and with all your strength and with all your mind and love your neighbor as yourself.' Jesus agreed but the man persisted in trying to trick Jesus by asking: 'And who is my neighbor?'" Jesus answers in the form of a parable (Luke 10.30-37).

This is the story of a traveler who was robbed and left for dead by his attackers. A priest saw the man, but passed by on the other side of the road, presumably in order to maintain ritual purity. A Levite also refused to assist the beaten, half-dead traveler. Finally a passing Samaritan stopped and gave assistance, going beyond even the normal assistance by offering to cover the expenses for the man as he recovered in a local inn.

What modern readers of this story often miss is the deep hatred that Jews felt for Samaritans in those days, and it is worth looking at the cause of that hatred to place the parable in context. Samaritans lived in their own kingdom in central Palestine called Samaria. They were a group of Jews who broke from orthodox Jewry during the 6th century BCE and constructed a temple on the mountain Gerizim. They married non-Jews and were considered "half Jews" or of a "mixed race." Like most breakaway groups throughout history, they were intensely disliked by the group of people they had left.

While the average Jew hated them, it is interesting to note that Jesus and his disciples often travelled through Samaria and interacted with the Samaritans. There is the story about Jesus and the Samaritan woman at the well (John 4.4-42). In fact, that story finishes with the comment that many Samaritans became believers. The tolerance that Jesus showed to Samaritans must have annoyed the orthodox Jews, especially the ruling Priests, and this possibly played a role in their decision to convince the Romans to kill him.

When Jesus spoke of the "Good Samaritan" he was using as an example a group of people hated by those in his audience. If Jesus were to retell that story today, how do you think he might do it? Here are some possible versions:

> *The Parable of the Good Muslim*
> A Jew was going from Jerusalem to the Gaza Strip when he fell into the hands of robbers. They stripped him of his clothes, beat him and went away, leaving him half dead. A rabbi happened to be going down the same road but, when he saw the man, he passed by on the other side. So too, a Levite, when he came to the place and saw him, passed by on the other side. But a Muslim came where the man was and, when he saw him, he took pity on him. He gave the man first aid, dressing his wounds and stopping the bleeding. As soon as the man was able to travel the Muslim took him to a nearby hospital. "Look after him," he said, "and when I return I will pay for any extra expenses."
>
> *The Parable of the Good American*
> A Sunni Muslim was traveling from Damascus to Baghdad when thieves attacked him. They stole his wallet and his watch, beat him and went on their way, leaving him half dead. An Imam happened to be going down the same road but, when he saw the man, passed by on the other side. So too a Shi'a Muslim passed by on the other side of the road, ignoring him. But an American saw the man and took pity on him. He went to him and bandaged his wounds. Then he put the man in the backseat of his SUV and, ignoring the blood that stained the seats, took him to the nearest hospital. The next day he took out money to pay for his hospitalization. "Look after him," he told the hospital staff, "and when I return I will pay for any extra expenses."

> *The Parable of the Good Skater*
> A businessman was going from Manhattan Island to Newark when he was mugged. He was robbed, beaten severely and left in the gutter, half dead. A Baptist preacher happened to be going down the same road but, when he saw the man, passed by on the other side. An Episcopal priest passed by on the other side of the road, ignoring him as well. Then along came a young skater, with greasy unwashed hair, piercings in his nose, tongue and eyebrows, and a tattooed sleeve on both arms. He saw the man and took pity on him. He made him comfortable and called an ambulance. He then followed it to the hospital. "Look after him," he told the hospital staff, "and when I return I will pay for any extra expenses."[11]

Who is our neighbor? Jesus said, "You have heard that it was said, 'Love your neighbor and hate your enemy.' But I tell you: Love your enemies and pray for those who persecute you." (Matthew 5:43) Is our neighbor the couple living next door? Is it friends we hang out with on the weekend? Is it our nice coworkers with whom we get along? Yes. Those are all our neighbors. But there are others. Our neighbors are not just the people we like, but also the people we don't like. They are the people who have a different cultural upbringing than us; a different skin color; a different belief system; a different sexual orientation; a different shape to their eyes; a different language; a different worldview, a different political persuasion. For serious Christ followers, our neighbor is anyone and everyone with whom we come in contact. If we have it within our ability, power, and resources to help another human being in need—that person becomes our neighbor.

There is an old Jewish legend in which God mourns over the way that his people are acting. In tears God says to the angels, "My children remember me but forget my ways. How I wish they would forget about me and keep my ways." The key to understanding this idea lies in the notion that God is affirmed in, and only in, acts of love—not a love that loves only those who love back, but a love that embraces the stranger, the outsider, the enemy.

Love—pervasive, all encompassing love—is the atmosphere of the Kingdom of God. Love means being as concerned about the needs and welfare of others, as we are about our own. Love is not passive, it is active. It is willing to be uncomfortable for the sake of making someone else comfortable. It is intentional, proactive, burdened by a heart of compassion. It is sensitive, crying with those who hurt, angry at those who cause hurt, determined to help and willing to take a risk in order to offer that help. In the Kingdom of God, there will be human completeness and wholeness because everyone will be loved, valued, nurtured, and cared for.

This is the vision for the Kingdom of God on this Earth. A pipe dream? I've often wondered how our nation might change if every one of the tens of millions of men and women who claim to be Christian would simply get involved in one cause that might help alleviate the heartache and suffering of another? What would our own society look like? I wonder if in the new Re•Formation we might be able to get a little closer to the Kingdom of God on Earth. Why do we need wait with baited breath for the Kingdom yet to come? Why not begin working on it now?[12]

> "I have the audacity to believe that people everywhere can have three meals a day for their bodies, education and culture for their minds, and dignity, quality, and freedom for their spirits. I believe that

what self-centered men have torn down, other-centered men can build up."

–Dr. Martin Luther King, Jr.

"Speak up for the people who have no voice, for the rights of all the unfortunate. Speak out for justice. Stand up for the poor and destitute."

–Proverbs 31.8-9

"I am only one, but still I am one. I cannot do everything, but still I can do something; and because I cannot do everything, I will not refuse to do something I can do."

–Edward Everett Hale

"I expect to pass through this world but once; any good thing therefore that I can do, or any kindness that I can show to any fellow creature, let me do it now; let me not defer or neglect it, for I shall not pass this way again."

–Stephen Grellet (Quaker Missionary)

Endnotes

[1] Dag Hammarskjold, *Markings* (New York: Alfred A Knopf, ©1964), p. 122.

[2] Micah 6.8 (NRSV)

[3] Thomas Jackson (ed.), *The Works of John Wesley, A.M.*, Third Edition (London: John Mason, 1829), VIII, 340. Hereafter cited as Works.

[4] John Emory (ed.) *The Works of the Reverend John Wesley, A.M.* (New York: 1831), VII, 593.

[5] Borg, *The Heart of Christianity,* p. 127

[6] George F. Will, "The Subversive Pope," *Newsweek*, October 15, 1979.

[7] Martin Luther King, Jr. "Letter from a Birmingham Jail;" April 16, 1963.

[8] Mark 1.14-15. A comment on the word "repent" in this verse: Borg offers the insight that the word means something quite different from the common meaning of "being sorry for one's sins." It is related to the Hebrew Bible's understanding of "return"—returning to God, returning from exile, and its Greek roots suggest, "to go beyond the mind that you have."

[9] Ibid, p. 132.

[10] Ibid, p. 133. John Dominic Crossan is an Irish-American religious scholar and former Catholic priest best known for co-founding the Jesus Seminar. He is a major figure in the fields of biblical archaeology, anthropology, and New Testament textual and higher criticism.

[11] I know some may be thinking, "Right. Like a skater could ever afford to pay for someone's medical bills—especially considering the outrageous costs of a typical hospital stay in this day and age!" However, I hope you'll stay focused on the point I'm trying to make.

[12] If God is tugging at your heartstrings, there is a multitude of ways you, as an individual can do something. My first

recommendation is to look within yourself and ask the question, "What breaks my heart?" Find the answer to that and you will discover where to put your energy. If you are part of a denomination, check out their website. All denominations (PCUSA, RCA, CRC, Lutheran, Baptist, Methodist, UCC, Episcopal, Catholic, etc.) are involved in various kinds of social action and social justice ministries. These might generate some ideas for where you can direct your efforts. Look locally within your own community for places to serve:

- Salvation Army or charitable donation ministries that gives aid to the poor
- Local food pantry ministries
- Gospel Mission or halfway houses
- Homeless Shelters
- Juvenile homes, jails, or prisons
- Homes for runaways
- Meals on Wheels
- Abuse shelters or YMCA/YWCA
- Social work agencies and caseworkers
- Department of Community Health — these people have the inside track on people who live in your community and what needs are present.
- Hospitals, nursing homes, hospice facilities
- HIV/AIDS patients
- Local schools (adopting a classroom, after school tutoring)
- Police, fire departments
- Crisis pregnancy centers

15

A Rope of Sand

"The neighborhood bar is possibly the best counterfeit there is to the fellowship Christ wants to give His Church. It's an imitation dispensing liquor instead of grace, escape rather than reality. But it is a permissive, accepting, and inclusive fellowship. It is unshockable, it is democratic. You can tell people secrets and they usually don't tell others, or want to. The bar flourishes, not because most people are alcoholics, but because God has put into the human heart the desire to know and be known, to love and be loved, to be accepted, not rejected and so many seek a counterfeit at the price of a few beers."[1]

"Confess your faults one to another and pray one for another that ye may be healed."

–James 5.16 (KJV)

"Carry each other's burdens, and in this way you will fulfill the law of Christ."

–Galatians 6.2 (NIV)

"By yourself you're unprotected.
With a friend you can face the worst.
Can you round up a third?
A three-stranded rope isn't easily snapped."

–Ecclesiastes 4.12 (The Message)

What is Christian fellowship? I'm afraid that for a large majority of the Christian community, fellowship is considered to be nothing more than shaking hands with an official greeter at the door of the church, grabbing a donut and some coffee (could we even have church without donuts and coffee?), asking about your church friends' week and then sitting down, singing some songs, listening to a sermon, getting up, and going home. Truth be told, there's probably more genuine life-sharing and true relationship building that goes on in most bars than what happens in most churches on a Sunday morning.

Although it first aired 20 years ago, *Cheers* still remains a popular television show in reruns. Set in a bar in Boston, the show featured a cast of offbeat people who gathered at the bar every day after work to kibbutz, to trade war stories, to tell a few jokes, to blow off steam, and to commiserate with one another. Each week millions of people tuned in to watch the characters sit around and talk about their joys and sorrows, their victories and defeats, their good times and their bad times, their problems at home, and their dreams for the future. That was the whole show. It doesn't sound very profound, yet *Cheers* touched something deep within the American public. Each week, in their own quirky way, the characters talked about life and we tuned in to listen.

Do you remember the theme song?

> "You wanna be where you can see our troubles are
> all the same.
> You wanna be where everyone knows your name."

There is a deep hunger in the hearts of people today for significant, meaningful, deep, accepting relationships. Mother Teresa said, "The most terrible poverty is loneliness and the feeling of being unloved." God made us to be in relation with others. Yet the hyper-individualism that infects both society and the church makes it extremely hard for these kinds of relationships to develop. Though they could benefit from them, some simply don't want relationships like that. Others yearn for them, yet cannot find them.

A number of years ago we were sitting in a church where the associate pastor was giving the morning announcements. They were beginning a Celebrate Recovery Program. Celebrate Recovery is a Christian version of the 12-Step program made popular by Alcoholics Anonymous. The comments he made regarding this program still resonate with me today. He said, "Celebrate Recovery is a program for those of you with hurts, habits, and hang-ups. You will meet on Friday nights up in room ___, and it will be a great program for you to get involved with." At the time he said this I thought to myself, "Why is it that we separate people with 'hurts, habits, and hang-ups' from the rest of us? Why can't the church acknowledge that all of us have hurts, habits, and hang-ups and we could all benefit from some mutual accountability and confessing our faults to one another and praying for each other?" Although it's a wonderful program, the announcement was framed in such a way to make it seem like the people who attended that Friday evening class were "different" than the rest. Although I know he didn't mean it this way, the pastor's words conveyed an "us" versus "them" mentality. There are first class passengers on the plane to heaven (those who don't have hurts, habits, and hang-ups) and then there are coach passengers sitting in the rear (those unfortunate ones who do).

I believe that one of the great blessings of the new Re•Formation will be a rediscovering of and a renewed commitment to relationships. This is one of the great cries of the emerging generations. They are all about relationships—deep, transparent, honest, heartfelt and committed relationships. For those of us who have cut our spiritual teeth on Christian individualism, this will be a hard, if not impossible transition to make. We fear rejection, judgment, and condemnation. So rather than taking a risk, we choose to exist by skimming the surface with others—exchanging niceties, smiling pleasantly, and firmly shaking hands, but longing inside for someone to know us and accept us as we are—warts and all.

In my previous book I quoted the song from Ken Medema, a Christian composer, singer and songwriter. In his 2006 CD entitled *25 to Life,* there is a song entitled, "If This Is Not the Place." Here are the words:

> "If this is not a place where tears are understood,
> then where shall I go to cry?
> And if this is not a place, where my spirit can take wings,
> then where shall I go to fly?
>
> I don't need another place for trying to impress you,
> with just how good and virtuous I am.
> No, no, no, I don't need another place,
> for always being on top of things.
> Everybody knows that it's a sham, it's a sham.
> I don't need another place, for always wearing smiles,
> even when it's not the way I feel.
> I don't need another place, to mouth the same old platitudes;
> everybody knows that it's not real.
>
> So if this is not a place where my questions can be asked,
> then where shall I go to seek?

> And if this is not a place, where my heart cry can be heard,
> where, tell me where, shall I go to speak?
> So if this is not a place, where tears are understood,
> where shall I go, where shall I go to fly?"

I believe that Celtic Christianity can again be of help to us here. They drew heavily on the biblical model of community, often gathering around a common "rule": live simply, be inclusive, and live in harmony.

They also were strong believers in "soul friends." Life can be a lonely journey unless someone is with you. In Ireland these soul friends were referred to as "anam cara"—individuals who hold us accountable to help us attain wholeness in life. They had a saying: "A person without a soul friend is like a body without a head." According to John O'Donahue, an accomplished Irish poet, philosopher, and Catholic priest,

> "...you are joined in an ancient and eternal union with humanity that cuts across all barriers of time, convention, philosophy and definition. When you are blessed with an anam cara, the Irish believe, you have arrived at that most sacred place: home."

Here again is where I find relevance in Methodism. One of the strengths of early Methodism was its insistence on small group accountability. The way the movement was structured helped connect individuals with one another so that they would not be isolated, trying to live the Christian life alone. In fact Wesley said, "Follow the blow, never encourage the devil by snatching souls from him that you cannot nurture. Converts without nurture are like stillborn babies."

He also felt that the Church of England (the Anglican Church) had not done a very good job of introducing true

Christian fellowship and support to its members. Some priests within the Church of England opposed the Methodist Societies and said that they were divisive. In response Wesley said,

> "But the fellowship you speak of never existed. Therefore it cannot be destroyed. Which of these true Christians had any such fellowship with these? Who watched over them in love? Who marked their growth in grace? Who advised and exhorted them from time to time? Who prayed with them and for them, as they had need? This and this alone, is Christian fellowship: But alas! Where is it to be found? Look east or west, north or south; name what parish you please: Is this Christian fellowship there? Rather, are not the bulk of the parishioners a mere **rope of sand?** [emphasis mine] What Christian connection is there between them? What intercourse in spiritual things? What watching over each other's souls? What bearing of one another's burdens? What a mere jest is it then, to talk so gravely of destroying what never was? The real truth is just the reverse of this: We introduce Christian fellowship where it was utterly destroyed. And the fruits of it have been peace, joy, love, and zeal for every good word and work."[2]

The way early Methodism was structured is fascinating to me. It organized people into smaller and smaller groups so that they could connect to each other and give an account of how they were growing in their faith.

> "This method of organization consisted of three layers of fellowship: the society meeting, the class meeting, and the band meeting. The society meeting was the largest level of organization, where the people gathered to worship God. The society meeting was very similar to today's congregational worship.

At the society meeting, people would gather to sing hymns, pray, and hear a sermon.

The class meeting had seven to twelve people in it. This group met weekly to check in on how each person was doing spiritually. The question, 'How is it with your soul?' or 'How does your soul prosper?' was asked of each person in the group. This was a way of asking each person, 'How are you doing spiritually? How is God working in your life?' This weekly practice helped people develop the habit of listening for God in their lives and expecting God to be at work in their lives. The class meeting was a requirement of early Methodism, and for quite a while, each person had to attend the class meeting in order to get a ticket to go to the society meeting. In other words, if you wanted to attend the fellowship gathering, you had to have a ticket to get in! That is how important Wesley thought the class meeting was. The main advantage of the class meeting was that every single Methodist talked to a trusted, loving group of people…about what was happening in his or her life with God.

The final level of organization was the band meeting. In the band meeting, members would confess any sins they had committed and admit to ways they had fallen short, and they would express to one another the forgiveness that Jesus Christ offers them. These groups consisted of about six people. Due to the intense and intimate subject matter—confessing specific sins—the band meetings were divided by gender. And because of their level of intensity, unlike the class meetings, the band meetings were considered optional.

The ultimate goal of this method was to create a model that would help Methodists practice their faith and guarantee that they would not only be

> Christians in name, but also that they would actually become deeply committed followers of Jesus Christ."[3]

Before proceeding, let me give a couple of observations. First of all, can you imagine a contemporary situation where a ticket would be required to get into a Sunday morning worship service? We have so elevated and exalted that time at 11:00 on Sunday morning as the most important and sacred time of the week for Christians that it's unthinkable for us to envision that a person couldn't attend unless they had proof they had been to a small group meeting the previous week. Plus, our infatuation with bigness and building mega-churches totally negates this concept. That would certainly not be "seeker friendly." Second, while earlier it might have seemed that I was minimizing the importance of Celebrate Recovery groups (which was not at all my intent), isn't it interesting that hundreds of years ago, that's precisely what the band meetings were?

A third observation is this: when you see the questions Methodist Christians were to ask one another in their class and band meetings, you might find yourself quite relieved that you're living in the 21st Century rather than the 18th!

Here is a list of some of the questions:[4]

1. Have you the forgiveness of your sins?
2. Have you peace with God through our Lord Jesus Christ?
3. Have you the witness of God's Spirit with your spirit that you are a child of God?
4. Is the love of God shed abroad in your heart?
5. Has no sin, inward or outward, dominion over you?
6. Do you desire to be told of your faults?
7. Do you desire to be told of all your faults?

8. Do you desire that every one of us should tell you, from time to time, whatsoever is in his heart concerning you?
9. Consider! Do you desire we should tell you whatsoever we think, whatsoever we fear, whatsoever we hear concerning you?
10. Do you desire that, in doing this, we should come as close as possible; that we should cut to the quick, and search your heart to the bottom?
11. Is it your desire and design to be, on this and all other occasions, entirely open, so as to speak everything that is in your heart without exception, without disguise and without reserve?

Any of the above questions could be asked of each other as often as needed. The following five questions were to be asked at every meeting:

1. What known sins have you committed since our last meeting?
2. What temptations have you met with?
3. How were you delivered?
4. What have you thought, said, or done, of which you doubt whether it be sin or not?
5. Have you nothing you desire to keep secret?

These are incredibly personal questions, aren't they? Today, most of us would take great exception to someone getting into our personal space in such an intimate manner. "How is it with your soul?" Or today we would ask, "How are you doing spiritually…really?" With this question the early Methodists made their distinctive mark on the world. By asking this and the other questions above, they lived out their belief that to grow as a disciple of Christ begins with mutual accountability. This was a fundamental premise of the movement. Once a person entered into a relationship with God through Christ, there was the expected intent that they would go on to maturity and aggressively pursue spiritual growth and development. And the primary way this growth was accomplished was through mutual accountability—that was at the heart of discipleship. It recognized that we are weak and sinful people, unable to redeem ourselves. It also recognized that we need each other if we are to be transformed into the likeness of Christ.

At the heart of the class meetings, is John Wesley's admonition to "watch over one another in love." These groups were not about power or control. They were about individuals giving themselves to one another, trusting that together they could become the people that God wanted them to be. Sadly, for Methodism and the Christian church at large, the class meeting has almost entirely disappeared. What we have today in the form of small groups is a far cry from this type of intense, mutual accountability.

Having pastored a church for almost thirty years, my observation has been that current small group ministries are falling woefully short in helping Christians experience transformation. I think one of the primary reasons is because of the wrong focus. Today most small groups focus around the study of the Bible or a Christian book. Go back and review the questions above and notice that they focus on relationship and personal awareness, not information. I've also noticed that after a group has been together for a while, frequently even the study time disappears and people will just sit around and talk (and eat cake). At the end of the meeting there might be a few minutes of sharing prayer requests and folks are on their way. Others may have a different experience, but mine has been that not much transformation is taking place in the lives of Christians who are even serious enough about putting a small group meeting into their regular schedule. Yet, as I said earlier, the heart of the Christian life is about transformation, not information.

For those who are hungering for something different than their current small group experience might be providing, I offer a suggestion. First of all, I highly commend you for even being committed to a small group—you are already involved in something that has the potential to radically change your lives. Second, on a very practical level, find the time that works best for you. Weekly would probably be best, but don't put yourself on a guilt trip. If a weekly meeting just doesn't fit for your schedule, try every other week. Third (and I know this will sound like heresy to some), consider stopping the Bible study and begin focusing on each other with greater intention. Assuming you are in a church where you are receiving some good, practical teaching from your pastor and you are doing your own personal Bible study or devotions, you're probably getting more than enough Bible each week. Of course, focusing on each other and asking hard questions requires honesty and transparency—a big hurdle for many. Finally, regularly (at least once a month or every six weeks) do a service project as a small group. Find places in the community where you can minister to others as a group and go be the hands and heart of Jesus to others—it will help keep you from becoming ingrown and it will also help keep your heart soft and broken for the hurting of the world.

It was Wesley's feeling that every member should feel responsible for every other member in the body of Christ.

That wasn't the unique brainchild of Wesley—the idea is found in the New Testament. I do believe however, this is a practice worth rediscovering. It may be that the recovery of these kinds of honest, open, small groups for sharing, caring, and growing will be a key ingredient in the church once again becoming a real community of God's people in today's world. Prayerfully, it will be a foundational piece of the new Re•Formation.

Endnotes

[1] Bruce Larson & Keith Miller, *The Edge of Adventure,* (Fleming H. Revell Co, Revised edition ©1991) p. 156.

[2] *Works,* Vol. 8. pp. 251-252.

[3] Kevin M. Watson, *A Blueprint for Discipleship,* (Discipleship Resources, Nashville, Tn. ©2009) pp. 43-44. Used with permission. All rights reserved. This is a great resource for church leaders if they want to build quality discipleship in their churches. The material can be ordered at www.upperroom.org/bookstore or by calling their toll free number 800-972-0433.

[4] Lovett H. Weems, Jr. *John Wesley's Message Today,* (Abingdon Press edition ©1991) pp. 49-50.

16

What is the Radical Center?

"A genuine man goes to the roots.
To be a radical is no more than that: to go to the roots."
–Jose Marti

"No Christian can be a pessimist, for Christianity is a system of radical optimism."
–William Ralph Inge

The word "radical" conjures up a wide array of images in the minds of people who hear it being used. In politics, there's the radical left or the radical right, signifying two very extreme positions that would be considered outside the populist center. In the field of medicine there is radical surgery that is performed after all other less invasive options have been exhausted. In popular culture there is radical feminism that opposes patriarchy, the male oppression of women, and calls for a reordering of society. Tom Wolfe coined a new term—radical chic—to describe the pretentious adoption of causes by celebrities and socialites (which they generally know very little about). It's very sad that, in one sense, the word has become associated with things that are considered excessive or fanatical. The root meaning of the word radical (from the Latin, radicalis) simply denotes going to the root or origin of something, getting to the fundamental.

With the Christian church currently being held hostage by what some might term the radical left (liberalism) and the radical right (Fundamentalism, Evangelicalism, and Pentecostalism), just what is the radical center? I appreciate the comment by Jose Marti that to be radical is nothing more than to go to the root of something and that if a person is to be truly genuine, they will seek to go to that root. Simply stated then, the radical center is the new Re•Formation's attempt to excavate the heart and intent of original Christianity out from under centuries of ecclesiastical debris. It is the effort to try and get Christianity back to its roots. I'm reminded of a trite but true saying that, "The main thing is to keep the main thing the main thing." Over the last many centuries we have lost sight of the main thing in our faith. It is now time to dig it up, dust it off, and refocus our energies around it. It is also time to take that historic faith and, with integrity and genuineness, seek to bring it to bear on a post-modern, post-Christian world.

In the previous chapters I've attempted to show that both the left and the right within current Christianity are falling short. From the left, the mainline churches have been in a free-fall for the last many decades,

> "…in part due to their focus on the social gospel without a simultaneous effort to help people grow in a personal relationship with God. They have encouraged people to view their faith through the lens of intellect while neglecting emotion and heart. They have maintained a kind of traditionalism in worship that it is devoid of meaning and relevance for many."[1]

They also missed a huge cultural shift that took place in our society. During the turbulent 1950s, 1960s and early 1970s when our country was going through a time of tremendous social upheaval, people were longing for absolutes and a clarion call from their faith leaders that addressed both the inner angst and outer turmoil that was so prevalent. People desperately needed an anchor in their lives that would provide stability during a confusing and unstable time. At this most crucial juncture, when many were looking to their churches to be that anchor, the left appeared to be as unstable and uncertain as the general culture.

On the right, I've also tried to show that today the three popular expressions of Christianity are where mainline churches were back in the 1960s. "The conservative, Christian right has reached its zenith of growth, power, and influence. Over the last four decades, the movement helped elect politicians, claimed to represent American values, and welcomed millions of Americans into its churches."[2] It provided absolutes for people to believe in, gave comfort and security—a shelter from the storm, so to speak. And whether with intention or through simple ignorance, the movement has fed the individualistic narcissism inherent within all of us—it's always appealing when someone can make me feel better about myself. "These churches will see their growth stalled and then watch as they enter a period of decline similar to the mainline denominations unless they recognize the changes that are currently happening in our society."[3] If they don't they will miss the huge cultural shift presently taking place and that will leave them increasingly disconnected and relegated to the fringes of contemporary culture.

In the midst of all this, there seems to be a significant shift on both sides, moving toward the center. We see this happening in a variety of ways. From the conservative side:

- "The rise of what is called the Emergent Church, which is composed of many former conservative Christians who no longer identify with Fundamentalism or Evangelicalism's approach or interpretations of the gospel."[4]
- Conservative seminaries where both students and professors are questioning the doctrine of inerrancy.
- Frustration over the pettiness and narrowness of those in leadership within conservative denominations and churches. People shake their head in disbelief at comments like the one from Bob Jones III, former president of Bob Jones University: "The Bible itself is intolerant, and true followers of God's word should be as well."
- A growing movement that recognizes the call of Christ to care for those in need in our society rather than just focusing almost exclusively on evangelism and a personal relationship with God. A man I have the utmost respect for was Dr. Vernon Grounds, the former President of the conservative, evangelical Denver Seminary. In writing about his own spiritual pilgrimage shortly before his death he said, "I am concerned that my own discipleship be lived out more and more in keeping with what I take to be the New Testament norm. That's a very difficult balance between personal piety and social involvement. In my earlier years…I suspect that my concept of Christianity was very lopsided. It was world-denial and world-withdrawal. God increasingly has burdened me and God has helped me to discern…that there must be not only love for

Himself, but there must be love for neighbor which is incarnate in some social activity."

- "A growing willingness within a number of traditionally conservative churches to embrace women in leadership positions in the church, including female pastors."[5]
- A growing group speaking out against global warming, despite the fact "...that some leading conservatives dismiss global warming as a hoax."[6]
- A small but determined group of conservative, evangelical churches that welcome Lesbian, Gay, Bisexual and Transgendered individuals as full participants in their church family.

This move to the center is happening from the left as well:

- "Many mainline churches are expressing a renewed passion for evangelism.
- They are embracing forms of worship that speak not only to the intellect but also to the heart.
- There is a renewed emphasis on starting new churches.
- There is a growing recognition in mainline seminaries of the importance of spiritual formation and the spiritual disciplines of the Christian life."[7]
- There is a new commitment to the idea of personal transformation coupled with social engagement.
- There is a desire to have church members know, understand, and embrace the Bible in a renewed way. The Methodist church my wife and I attend has had over 2,000 of its members go through the four year Disciple program which builds a solid foundation of biblical understanding.

- "Pastors and leaders of mainline churches are being energized by an approach to the gospel that brings together the best of both the right and the left."[8]

At the extreme ends you have the far left being represented by Bishop John Shelby Spong, who has developed the reputation of being America's most outspoken liberal Christian. On the far right you have a man like the late Jerry Falwell, who believed that the Bible was to be taken literally and that wherever the modern world conflicted with the Bible, the modern world was wrong. "There will always be Christians on the far right and the far left, but there is an increasing number of believers who are being drawn to the radical center—Christians who are learning to appreciate what the other side brings to the table, who are humbly willing to learn from others, and who are able to say with John Wesley[9], 'Though we cannot think alike, may we not love alike? May we not be of one heart, though we are not of one opinion? Without all doubt, we may. Herein all the children of God may unite, notwithstanding these smaller differences.'"[10]

What then is the Radical Center?

Can the radical center be defined? To some degree, yes. Yet as with anything new, those on the cusp of the movement are only beginning to unpack and wrestle with the issues. However, there are some defining parameters, ideas and directions with which the movement is wrestling. These thoughts will become the vortex of the growing radical center that will be the heart of the new Re•Formation. Having touched on them in various ways and to varying degrees in previous chapters here is a précis of those ideas:

- "It embraces the evangelical gospel that proclaims that human beings are wounded by sin and are in need of saving and that Jesus Christ is God's antidote to the human condition."[11] "Man is born broken. He lives by mending. The grace of God is glue."[12]
- It also recognizes however, that beneath the sin, there is a fundamental goodness within the person, having been created in the image of God, and God having called it very good. This goodness predates and supersedes the wounding caused by sin. It is this inherent goodness that a person is to build upon, pursue, and cultivate as part of their spiritual journey.
- It also recognizes that while we are to walk in the path of Jesus, it does not deny the legitimacy of other paths that God may provide for humanity. It acknowledges that no one faith tradition has all the answers; that God is bigger than all faith traditions combined and that fundamentally humanity is on a search for a lost relationship to be restored—for the creation to once again be in harmony with its Creator.
- It understands that wherever love of God and neighbor are practiced, whether or not it bears the name of Jesus—that path bears the identity of Christ and has the image of the creator God stamped upon it.
- "It embraces the social gospel that seeks to love our neighbor as we love ourselves and recognizes the Christian's responsibility to address the great problems of poverty, racism, the environment, and war. The evangelical gospel without the social gospel is spiritual narcissism. The social gospel without the evangelical gospel remains afflicted by sin and holds,

in the words of the Apostle Paul, 'to the outward form of godliness but denying its power.'" (II Timothy 3.5)[13]

- "It understands that the gospel is incomplete without both its evangelical and social witness."[14] That is such an unassuming sentence, and the concept behind it so simple, it seems like it should be part of every Christian's first grade education. Yet the church has been impotent in being able to effectively and simultaneously emphasize those two powerful themes. How is it that we have managed to so efficiently eclipse the obvious? How is it that those two sides of the same coin (or two different parts of the same elephant) have been split asunder with different groups each claiming they have the ultimate answer to what Christianity is supposed to be all about?
- "It holds a fundamental conviction that God is 'gracious and merciful, slow to anger and abounding in steadfast love.' (Psalm 145.8) God does not act unjustly. At the same time, it holds that God is holy, and calls us to holiness: 'as he who called you is holy, be holy yourselves.' (I Peter 1.15). It recognizes that grace without holiness is what Bonheoffer called 'cheap grace.'[15] But it also recognizes that holiness without grace negates the gospel and reverts to legalism."[16]
- It recognizes (though it may not yet be fully understood) that a loving and gracious God will not allow the vast majority of the human race to spend eternity in hell; such a punishment is disproportionate to the crime—an eternity of suffering for seventy or eighty years of sin? It recognizes that something within our current interpretation of Scripture or our understanding of hell is amiss. However, it also holds that in some

way there will be justice meted out for the most depraved and evil among us.

- "It holds together a progressive spirit that is open-minded, searching for truth, generous, and always reforming, with a conserving spirit that is unwilling to discard historic truths simply because they are historic. It is willing to question anything, but requires a high level of evidence before setting aside what has been treasured and believed as truth by previous generations."[17]
- "It recognizes in the Scriptures both the reflections of human beings as they wrote of their faith and the self-disclosure of God to people."[18] It recognizes that the Scriptures were formed in distinct historical and cultural contexts, yet were informed by God's Spirit that transcends all ages and times.
- It studies the Scriptures critically, analyzing the historical context, the various situations that led the authors to write the biblical texts, and the complex ways in which the biblical text came together. "It is unafraid to admit that the Bible has challenging passages that likely reflect the theological worldview of its authors more than the nature and character of God who came to us in Jesus Christ. Yet it also recognizes that the Bible is our anchor, through which God has been revealed and in which God converses with us."[19]
- "It sees the Bible as the history of a people who have sought to walk with God, and their theological insights and reflections. It also sees the Bible as a form of sacrament through which God's Spirit speaks and God's grace is poured into our lives. It is read, memorized,

meditated upon, but not worshiped or mindlessly followed."[20]

- It affirms that followers of Christ are to engage in prayer and meditation, personal and community study and interpretation of Scripture, and that these disciplines are central ways we discern God's voice in everyday life.
- It does not claim that God's Word is restricted to what may be contained in a written document, or that either the recording of God's Word in Scripture or our interpretation of it is infallible.
- It acknowledges that the canon of Scripture—the body of texts the church as a whole counts as authoritative—was never created by unanimous vote. The New Testament canon is set by human usage, not by divine decree. Throughout history, preachers and theologians have questioned the authority of various books found within the Bible. Even the great Martin Luther called the Epistle of James, the "epistle of straw," he ignored the book of Revelation, and vocally contradicted any writing that he felt did not keep Christ's Gospel of grace and love central and paramount.
- It embraces the expansive idea that, "Every happening, great and small, is a parable whereby God speaks to us, and the art of life is to get the message."[21] In a variety of different ways, God still speaks; the question is, are we listening? "Never place a period where God has placed a comma. God is still speaking."[22]
- "It holds that God gives us both an intellect and a heart and that both are essential to our faith. We can experience and know God with our hearts, and this personal knowledge of God is utterly life transforming

and is the source of our comfort, joy, and hope. At the same time, God gave us the capacity to reason and think and ask questions, and God expects us to engage our minds in our pursuit of truth. We don't check our brains at the door when we enter church."[23]

- "It recognizes that scientists, whether they recognize it or not, are instruments of God's self-disclosure as well. They help us see and understand the Universe. Science is not antithetical to faith but a partner in understanding God and God's creation."[24]
- "It avoids criticizing either the right or the left, though those in the center may be attacked by both extremes. It will just be a fact that those in the radical center will not be conservative enough for the conservatives or liberal enough for the liberals. But two defining characteristics of the radical center will be a willingness to find what is good and true in others, and a commitment to practicing love."[25]
- It will champion the "Rule of Love." This goes back at least as far as the fourth century and probably before then. It is essentially this: if a passage in Scripture appears to contradict the essence of Jesus' command to love God with all our heart, mind, soul, and strength or to love our neighbor as ourselves, then the passage, or our interpretation of it, must be held suspect.
- It is a Re•Formation that is both a step forward as well as a step back. It steps forward to embrace modern scholarship and its commitment to hearing God's new Word revealed in ancient texts. It is also stepping back to a way of viewing Scripture that is not as concerned with historical accuracy as it is with its truth-bearing quality that measures those truths against the

standard of how well they reflect Jesus' command to love God, neighbor, and self. "You shall love the LORD your God with all your heart, and with all your soul and with all your mind and with all your strength. And you shall love your neighbor as yourself. There is no other commandment greater than these." (Mark 12.30-31)

- It reclaims the Rule of Love for discerning scriptural authority. It refuses to recognize any passage or interpretation of Scripture that moves us away from the love commanded by Jesus. If we interpret Scripture in a way that is hurtful to people, we can be sure we are not glorifying God. It seeks to uncover the deep truths of Scripture even while questioning the historicity of certain stories and events. This is what it means to take the Bible seriously and authoritatively, but not literally.
- It recognizes prayer as outranking Scripture in the hierarchy of things spiritual. "As it is the business of tailors to make clothes and of cobblers to mend shoes, so it is the business of Christians to pray."[26] No matter how highly one values Scripture, it is no substitute for direct contact with God. A book—even an inspired book like the Bible—does not outrank a relationship. Our spiritual ancestors would have thought us to not be very interested in spiritual things if they heard us claim that one could have a relationship with God primarily through studying a book. That would be like reading the Facebook bio of your future spouse and then confidently asserting that you are intimately acquainted with her.

- It is characterized by a far more tolerant, joyful, and compassionate presence in society than we currently see. Rather than being separatist, judgmental, condemning, condescending, and unloving, it will be more buoyant and expansive than anything we have seen or imagined in the last half millennium, if not longer.
- It affirms that the followers of Christ are to recognize their role and act as caring stewards of the Earth. It acknowledges that the Spirit of God and the glory of God pervade and are reflected in all of God's Creation—the Earth and its ecosystems, the sacred and secular, the Christian and non-Christian, the human and non-human. "God writes the Gospel not in the Bible alone, but also on trees, and in the flowers and clouds and stars."[27]
- It seeks to engage people with authenticity, as Jesus did, treating everyone as creations made in God's image, regardless of race, gender, sexual orientation, age, physical or mental ability, nationality, or economic class. All individuals are welcome and invited to full participation in the community of faith. It challenges and inspires all people to live according to their high identity (their inherent goodness) rather than view people through the narrow lens of a category or class.
- It does not arrogantly assume that we have "finally arrived." Quite the contrary it is, *Ecclesia reformata simper reformanda* (a reformed church always reforming). This was the cornerstone of the Protestant Reformation. This thought inspires and sometimes torments Christians to extend the circle of God's love and compassion beyond their immediate comfort zone. It recognizes that the guest list for God's great

party is a lot larger than previously imagined. This is especially relevant to the current battle that is raging around the issue of homosexuality.

- It stands as Jesus did, with the outcast and oppressed, the denigrated and afflicted, and seeks peace and justice with or without the support of others. It recognizes the local congregation as the primary context for offering such care, even as it seeks to extend that support beyond a local faith community into the wider world.
- It honors the essential unity of spirit and matter by connecting worship and theology with concrete acts of justice, and righteousness, kindness, and humility. "He has told you, O mortal, what is good; and what does the LORD require of you but to do justice, and to love kindness and to walk humbly with your God." (Micah 6.8, NRSV)

> "...how [is it that] Americans can believe that homosexuality is a major issue in the Bible and at the same time believe that the only relevant thing the Bible says about the poor is Jesus' (misinterpreted) statement that 'the poor you will always have with you' (Matthew 26.11)? There are at most six passages in all of Scripture that could be interpreted to have direct bearing on the subject of homosexuality—and all of them are open to legitimate debate. Compare this with over two thousand passages that have to do with wealth and poverty and our responsibility to the poor."[28]

Christianity is in desperate need of a new Re•Formation. The fundamentalism of the last century is waning and has created an intense revulsion among the un-churched in our society toward the Christian faith. That disgust is reflected in the bumper sticker I saw recently: "Too many Christians, not enough lions." The liberalism of the last hundred years has jettisoned too much of the historic Christian gospel and made it impotent—robbing it of its transforming power. Christianity's next Re•Formation will arise out of the radical center. "It will draw upon what is best in both fundamentalism and liberalism by holding together the evangelical and social gospels; by combining a love of Scripture with a willingness to see both its humanity as well as its divinity; by coupling a passionate desire to follow Jesus Christ with a reclamation of his heart toward those whom religious people have often rejected;"[29] by acknowledging that all people regardless of sexual orientation are invited to service in the family of God; by recognizing that God is greater than any one faith tradition and that all faith traditions have some facet of divine truth; by developing a new creation theology that sees our great need to be caretakers of this planet; and by rediscovering the value of genuine community—of having "anam cara" relationships so that the narcissistic individualism so rampant in current Christianity is assuaged.

For those of you who have felt disenfranchised from a faith you've longed to take seriously, my sincere hope is that some of the thoughts presented here resonate with you. Maybe you are even getting excited, excited to realize that the old ways of being church and doing church aren't the only way anymore. There are new possibilities on the horizon. I don't expect you to agree with everything that's been laid out in this book, but here are some things I hope for:

- I hope you are sensing a stirring in your own heart toward deeper spirituality;

- I hope you are appreciating the fact that you're not alone—there are others like you who are longing for something different, vibrant, real, and intensely radical;
- I hope you are coming to realize that life is not lived on the black and white fringes but rather in the center where there are multiple shades of gray;
- I hope you are becoming willing to live your life within the tension of unanswered questions;
- And I hope that where you are now is not where you are content to stay.

If so, then your mission my friend is to begin to explore, search out, read, study, pray, and be willing to boldly go wherever your new journey of faith leads you—into the exhilarating world of the new Re•Formation. Are you ready to enter the Radical Center?

"Behold, I am about to do something new.
See, I have already begun! Do you not see it?
I will make a pathway through the wilderness.
I will create rivers in the dry wasteland."

(Isaiah 43.19, New Living Translation)

Endnotes

[1] Adam Hamilton, *Seeing Gray in a World of Black and White*, p. 227. Used with permission.

[2] Ibid, p.228. Used with permission.

[3] Ibid, p. 228. Used with permission.

[4] Ibid, p. 228. Used with permission.

[5] Ibid, p. 229. Used with permission.

[6] Ibid, p. 229. Used with permission.

[7] Ibid, p. 230. Used with permission.

[8] Ibid, p. 231. Used with permission.

[9] Wesley, from the sermon "Catholic Spirit," 1755.

[10] Hamilton, *Seeing Gray in a World of Black and White,* p. 231. Used with permission.

[11] Ibid, p. 232. Used with permission.

[12] Anne Lamott, T*raveling Mercies: Some Thoughts on Faith,* (Anchor Books, ©2000).

[13] Hamilton, *Seeing Gray in a World of Black and White,* p. 233. Used with permission.

[14] Ibid, p. 233. Used with permission.

[15] Bonhoeffer's understanding of "cheap grace" was as follows: "Cheap grace is the deadly enemy of our Church. We are fighting for costly grace. Cheap grace means grace as a doctrine, a principle, a system. Cheap grace means the justification of sin without with justification of the sinner. Cheap grace is the preaching of forgiveness without requiring repentance, baptism without church discipline, Communion without confession. Cheap grace is grace without discipleship, grace without the cross, and grace without Jesus Christ." *The Cost of Discipleship,* 1937

[16] Hamilton, *Seeing Gray in a World of Black and White,* p. 233. Used with permission.

[17] Ibid, p. 233. Used with permission.

[18] Ibid, p. 233. Used with permission.

[19] Ibid, p. 233. Used with permission.

[20] Ibid, p. 234. Used with permission.

[21] Malcolm Muggeridge

[22] Gracie Allen

[23] Hamilton, *Seeing Gray in a World of Black and White,* p. 234. Used with permission.

[24] Ibid, p. 234. Used with permission.

[25] Ibid, p. 234. Used with permission.

[26] Martin Luther

[27] Attributed to Martin Luther

[28] Eric Elnes, *The Phoenix Affirmations,* p. 75.

[29] Hamilton, *Seeing Gray in a World of Black and White*, p. 235. Used with permission.

Epilogue

"Man's chief end is to glorify God and enjoy Him forever."[1]

"My little children, with whom I am again in labor until Christ is formed in you…"

–Galatians 4.19

"Would to God that all party names and unscriptural phrases and forms which have divided the Christian world were forgot and that we might all agree to sit down together as humble loving disciples, and at the feet of our common master to hear his word, to abide in his spirit and to transcribe his life into our own."

–John Wesley

For those of us who seek to live our lives in submission to Jesus Christ, our goal is to glorify God in all that we do. The "glory of God" has always been a mysterious concept to me. I think I can grasp it with my mind, but the question I wrestle with is how? Practically, how do I glorify God in my life? For me, part of the answer is found in Galatians 4.19. Like a woman in labor, Paul desperately wanted the Galatians to have Christ formed in them. What does that mean? Simply, I think it means we are to be "little Christs." We are to live our lives in obedience and submission and in that process, as we yield our will to him, we become reflections of the Son of God. His heart becomes our heart. His mind becomes our mind. His attitudes, values, compassion, tenderness, kindness, and love all become ours. Everything Jesus was, we are to become in him. This is to be our lifelong ambition, our aim, and the goal we continually strive to achieve. It is our spiritual journey. It is a tragic indictment on us when a man like Gandhi said, "I like your Christ. I do not like your Christians. They are so unlike your Christ."

I realize that various thoughts presented within *The Radical Center* might be disturbing to some. For readers who have already started the journey into a new form of Christianity, much of what you've read here might be old news. For whatever reason, your own spiritual voyage has already led you into dialogue with others, and you've begun interacting with some of the concepts the new Re•Formation will address. As mentioned early on, there are many dissatisfied, disenfranchised Christians filling the pews of churches these days. You might be one of them. No longer content with Christianity as you've experienced it, yet still serious about following God, you've started down the road into your own Re•Formation. Prayerfully, what you've read here has been affirming and confirming to you that you are on a good path. I pray it's been helpful and if nothing else, an encouragement for you to keep on keeping on.

I also realize that for others, you may feel like the apple cart of your faith has suddenly been turned over and you're now left scrambling trying to pick up all the apples. You might have a multitude of emotions swirling within you: anger, disillusionment, frustration, doubt, anxiety, uncertainty, concern, on and on the list goes. I mean this with all sincerity when I say, I feel your pain. Up until about five years ago, I had spent my entire Christian life (almost 40 years) within the spiritual framework of Evangelicalism. In many ways it was a comfortable place to be. It was a secure place to be, for it provided many convenient (albeit insufficient) answers to many difficult issues. As a Christian seeking to honor God and as a pastor I sought to live my life within those evangelical boundaries. At the same time there were niggling questions that I would not allow myself to think about. Sometimes I would justify that position by rationalizing, "I don't have time to think about those things." Realistically however, I think it was more because of fear, fear of the unknown, fear of where the road might take me, fear that if I opened Pandora's Box, it might unleash a host of evils that would lead me astray. Fear can be a paralyzing and imprisoning emotion.

God had other plans. Like it or not, I was pushed out of the nest, forced to face my fears, and I began to take some steps onto a road with which I was unfamiliar. When everything is said and done, it has been a very liberating experience. Being able to explore new concepts, think through other possibilities, and understand the positions of some of my Christian brothers and sisters with whom I had very little contact (and sadly, some misconceptions) has opened my eyes. Through this process I've been growing and changing. I genuinely feel excited about the future of our faith. I know I won't live long enough to see some of the ideas of the new Re•Formation fully realized, but prayerfully I'll be able to watch a bit of it unfold.

I've been reminded of a truth that I needed to be reminded of: God is a very big God. God is so much bigger than the little box I'd kept God in. And as we go through this season of change with our faith, this Re•Formation process, it is important that we not become judgmental of one another. This way is not the only way. One way is not better than another way. They are just different ways. God is quite capable of providing multiple ways for people to express their devotion, commitment, and love. In fact, to assume otherwise—that God has only one way for people to express that relationship—truly does make God a very small God indeed. The old hymn, "There's a Wideness in God's Mercy" speaks poetically to this point:

There's a wideness in God's mercy,
Like the wideness of the sea;
There's a kindness in His justice,
Which is more than liberty.

There is no place where earth's sorrows,
Are more felt than up in Heaven;
There is no place where Earth's failings,
Have such kindly judgment given.

There is welcome for the sinner,
And more graces for the good;
There is mercy with the Savior,
There is healing in His blood.

For the love of God is broader,
Than the measure of our mind;
And the heart of the Eternal,
Is most wonderfully kind.

It is God: His love looks mighty,
But is mightier than it seems;
'Tis our Father: and His fondness,
Goes far out beyond our dreams.

But we make His love too narrow,
By false limits of our own;
And we magnify His strictness,
With a zeal He will not own.

Was there ever a kinder shepherd,
Half so gentle, half so sweet;
As the Savior who would have us,
Come and gather at His feet?[2]

Regardless of where you have come from—conservative, liberal, or somewhere in between, we all need to keep asking ourselves some basic questions. Is my life reflecting Jesus? Is Christ being formed in me? Is my spiritual journey producing a transformed life? For you see, regardless of all of the continual changes our world experiences (and there are many), and regardless of where we as individuals are on the spectrum of Christian thought, people will always have the same basic needs:

- Love
- Acceptance
- Meaning
- Purpose
- Forgiveness
- Dignity
- Significance

And, people will always have the same basic struggles:

- Selfishness
- Fear
- Guilt
- Resentment
- Worry
- Boredom
- Loneliness

It is the calling of the Christian to be the hands and heart of Christ to those struggling and in need. That is our mission. That should be our desire.

My final thoughts to you are personal. We reflect Jesus best when we love God and others most. The Great Commandment, lived out in our lives, is the living proof of a life transformed. If your current faith system (your personal beliefs, the church you attend, the friends you associate with) are consistently making a difference in your life by helping you grow in love for God and others, then I cannot encourage you strongly enough—stay where you are and keep doing whatever it is that you are doing.

If you are becoming more...

- Loving
- Compassionate
- Humble
- Patient
- Kind
- Tenderhearted
- Faith-filled
- Joyous
- Content
- Dependent on God
- Forgiving of others and yourself
- Welcoming and inclusive of all people
- Generous with your resources
- Involved in helping alleviate problems in your corner of the world
- Concerned about the marginalized in society...

then I'll say it again—stay where you are and keep doing what you're doing. As best as I can see it, you are following the way of Christ. I like to live by the adage, "If it ain't broke, don't fix it." It would seem to me that you are growing in God and becoming the kind of person Jesus wants you to be.

On the other hand, if your current place in life and the particular faith system you embrace is making you more...

- Judgmental
- Condemning
- Narrow-minded
- Self-focused rather than other focused
- Hateful
- Jealous
- Unforgiving
- Condescending
- Envious
- Proud
- Bigoted
- Apathetic
- Guilt ridden
- Stingy with your resources
- Unconcerned about the needs of those around you…

then it might be time for you to consider a change. You may need to embark on your own journey into the unknown by challenging your belief system, by forging some different friendships, by searching for a different church. Why? Because as best as I can see it, you are not following the way of Christ. I'm not sure that the direction you are heading is the path Jesus would want you on.

The church of Jesus Christ has so much to offer the world. Yet I fear we've grieved God by withholding the treasures we steward. The world is poorer because of it. So are we.

> "There was a time when the church was very powerful—in the time when the early Christians rejoiced at being deemed worthy to suffer for what they believed. In those days the church was not merely a thermometer that recorded the ideas and principles of popular opinion; it was a thermostat that transformed the mores of society. Whenever the early Christians entered a town, the people in power

> became disturbed and immediately sought to convict the Christians for being 'disturbers of the peace' and 'outside agitators.' But the Christians pressed on, in the conviction that they were 'a colony of heaven,' called to obey God rather than man. Small in number, they were big in commitment. They were too God-intoxicated to be 'astronomically intimidated.' By their effort and example they brought an end to such ancient evils as infanticide and gladiatorial contests.
>
> Things are different now. So often the contemporary church is a weak, ineffectual voice with an uncertain sound. So often it is an arch-defender of the status quo. Far from being disturbed by the presence of the church, the power structure of the average community is consoled by the church's silent—and often even vocal—sanction of things as they are.
>
> But the judgment of God is upon the church as never before. If today's church does not recapture the sacrificial spirit of the early church, it will lose its authenticity, forfeit the loyalty of millions, and be dismissed as an irrelevant social club with no meaning for the twentieth century. In deep disappointment I have wept over the laxity of the church. Be assured that my tears have been tears of love. There can be no deep disappointment where there is not deep love."[3]

250 years ago, John Wesley taught his preachers to pray the following prayer:

> "I am not my own but thine.
> Put me to what you will, rank me with whom you will.
> Put me to doing, put me to suffering.
> Let me be employed by you or laid aside for you,
> Let me be exalted for you or brought low for you.
> Let me be full or let me be empty.
> Let me have all things or let me have nothing.
> I freely and heartily yield all things

to thy power and disposal.
And now, O glorious and blessed God,
Father, Son and Holy Spirit,
you are mine, and I am yours. So be it.
And this covenant which I have made on Earth,
let it be ratified in heaven. Amen."[4]

It would seem this might be a good prayer for us to pray. For those who think the radical center is a wishy-washy, moderate, middle-of-the-road, offending no one, embracing everyone approach to Christianity, I would strongly beg to differ. Wesley's prayer was not a moderate prayer. It was not reflective of a moderate faith. This is radical faith. It's radical in its pursuit of truth wherever it can be found. It is radical in its commitment to love. It is radical in its desire to follow Jesus no matter what the cost. People who choose to live in the radical center and move into the new Re•Formation will be attuned to praying a prayer like this—for themselves and others.

For those who think this new Re•Formation Christianity is going to be nothing more than old time liberalism wrapped up in a different package, this is not true. Rather, the new Re•Formation is truly progressive—a movement forward—taking our historic, life-changing faith and making it relevant to the world in which we now live. My prayer is that the new Re•Formation will be the next chapter in the plan of God that will reawaken a sleeping giant. That giant, once aroused from its slumber, will bring hope to the hopeless, love to the unloved, acceptance to those rejected. May God use the new Re•Formation to once again bring light to a world walking in darkness.

And I pray for you:

"May God bless you with discomfort at easy answers, half truths, and superficial relationships, so that you may live deep within your heart.
May God bless you with anger at injustice, oppression, and exploitation of people, so that you may work for justice, freedom, and peace.
May God bless you with tears to shed for those who suffer from pain, rejection, starvation and war, so that you may reach out your hand to comfort them and to turn their pain into joy.
May God bless you with enough foolishness to believe that you can make a difference in this world, so that you can do what others claim cannot be done.
And may the blessing of God, who creates, redeems, and sanctifies, be upon you and all you love and pray for, for this day and forever more. Amen"[5]

Endnotes

[1] Westminster Catechism

[2] Fredrick W. Faber (1814-1863), "There's a Wideness in God's Mercy" (Italics mine).

[3] Martin Luther King, Jr. "Letter from a Birmingham Jail;" April 16, 1963.

[4] Methodist Hymnal, p. 607 slightly modified.

[5] Franciscan Blessing

Bibliography

Unless otherwise indicated, all Scripture quotations are taken from the Holy Bible, New International Version, copyright © 1973, 1978, 1981. Used by permission of Zondervan Bible Publishers. All rights reserved.

Scripture quotations marked NRSV are taken from the New Revised Standard Version of the Bible, copyright © 1989 by the Division of Christian Education of the national Council of the Churches of Christ in the United States of America. Used by permission. All rights reserved.

Scripture quotations marked CEV are from Contemporary English Version® Copyright © 1995 American Bible Society. All rights reserved. Used by permission of the American Bible Society, 8065 Broadway, New York, NY 10023

Scripture quotations marked TNIV are taken from the Holy Bible, Today's New International Version® Copyright © 2001, 2005 by Biblica®. Used by permission of Biblica®. All rights reserved worldwide.

Scripture quotations marked NASB are taken from the New American Standard Bible®, Copyright © 1960, 1962, 1963, 1968, 1971, 1972, 1973, 1975, 1977, 1995 by The Lockman Foundation. Used by permission.

Scripture quotations marked KJV are taken from the Holy Bible, King James Version, Public Domain.

Scripture quotations marked NKJV are taken from the New King James Version®, Copyright © 1982, Thomas Nelson, Inc. All rights reserved. Used by permission.

Scripture quotations from the Douay Rheims Bible are from the 1899 edition of the John Murphy Company, Baltimore, Maryland. Public Domain.

Scripture quotations marked NCV are taken from the New Century Version, Copyright © 2005 by Thomas Nelson, Inc. Used by permission. All rights reserved.

The New Testament in Plain English, Copyright © 3rd Edition, 2009, Bauscher/Lulu publishers. All rights reserved. Used by permission.

The Jerusalem Bible, Copyright © 1966, 1967 and 1968 by Darton, Longman & Todd Ltd and Doubleday and Co. Inc., All rights reserved. Used by permission.

The Lamsa Bible, Copyright © 1933, Editor George M. Lamsa, Aramaic Bible Society, All rights reserved. Used by permission.

The New American Bible, Copyright © 2002 by the United States Conference of Catholic Bishops, 3211 4th Street, N.E., Washington, DC 20017, Used by permission. All rights reserved.

John Nelson Darby, *The Gospels, Acts, Epistles, and Book of Revelation: Commonly called the New Testament. A New Translation from a Revised Text of the Greek Original.* London: G. Morrish, 1867, 1872, and 1884. Public Domain.

Robert Young's Literal Translation of the Bible, 1862, 1887, 1898. Public Domain.

Noah Webster, ed., The Holy Bible, Containing the Old and New Testaments, in the Common Version. With Amendments of the Language. New Haven: Durrie and Peck, 1833. Public Domain.

Scripture quotations marked NLT are taken from the Holy Bible, New Living Translation, copyright © 1996, 2004. Used by permission of Tyndale House Publishers, Inc., Wheaton, Illinois 60189. All rights reserved.

A personal note...

It would be an honor to hear from you and I would enjoy receiving your thoughts on *The Radical Center*. If there are others in your circle of friends and contacts you think might find the book helpful, I would appreciate you letting them know about it.

Thank you.
Paul

Contact Paul at:
Paul@PhoenixRisingCoach.com

You can order additional copies of *The Radical Center* at:
www.PhoenixRisingCoach.com